EARTHQUAKES

EARTHQUAKES

Bruce A. Bolt

University of California, Berkeley

W. H. FREEMAN AND COMPANY
New York

Earthquakes is a revision of *Earthquakes: A Primer* (1978).

Library of Congress Cataloging-in-Publication Data

Bolt, Bruce A., 1930–
 Earthquakes.

 Bibliography: p.
 Includes index.
 1. Earthquakes. I. Title.
QE534.2.B64 1987   551.2′2   86-31982
ISBN 0-7167-1909-6
ISBN 0-7167-1874-X (pbk.)

Printed in the United States of America

2 3 4 5 6 7 8 9 0 VB 6 5 4 3 2 1 0 8 9 8

To
GILLIAN, ROBERT, HELEN, and MARGARET
who were raised in earthquake country

Contents

Preface

Earthquakes continue to wreak havoc around the world. Inevitably, the fight against damage, destruction, and death must continue.

The first step toward a major victory over the disastrous effects of earthquakes is the recognition that earthquakes are natural phenomena, like droughts and floods, and that practical steps can be taken to ensure that the damage and loss of life they cause is minimal. Scientific insight into the way that seismic waves are generated is increasing, giving promise of reliable calculations of the intensity of ground shaking in future earthquakes. The rate of occurrence of earthquakes and the reasons for them are now generally well understood in most seismic areas of the world. From experience and through experiment, engineers have been able to design and construct disparate structures that resist earthquake shaking even in the largest earthquakes. Emergency-services organizations have developed ways to improve their earthquake-preparedness as well as their ability to alleviate suffering after earthquakes occur.

All these trends are encouraging. We can begin to look forward to a time when the danger from earthquakes is reduced. Reducing this danger depends on a better understanding of all aspects of earthquakes—a goal foremost in my mind when writing this revision.

Earthquakes: A Primer has been well received in the 10 years since it was first published. It is used as a textbook in high schools and colleges. Reviews by professionals have generally been favorable. Some reviewers' suggestions involved inclusion of greatly expanded material, but I did not want to produce a much lengthier and more expensive book. Instead, I have clarified the text where needed and in a number of sections have replaced the original material with new and especially topical case histories and discussions. The result is only a moderate expansion overall.

It is particularly pleasing that *Earthquakes: A Primer* has been distributed internationally through the publication of adaptations in six languages: Russian, Spanish, Italian, German, Chinese, and French. I would like to thank the editors and translators of these foreign-language editions for their attention to the spirit of the English text and for the helpful special appendixes that have been added. Some of the changes have been incorporated in *Earthquakes*.

The international nature of seismology has been emphasized in the last few years by cooperative studies of several major damaging earthquakes that attracted worldwide attention: in particular, the great Chile earthquake of March 3, 1985, and the great Mexico earthquake of September 19, 1985. In the Chile disaster, significant damage occurred in the central part of the country, including the capital, Santiago. About a hundred people were killed and 3000 persons injured. I went to Chile as part of a U.S. team of seismologists and engineers to study the earthquake. Some of the results of this trip and subsequent studies are described in Chapter 2. Chapter 12 discusses the catastrophic Mexico earthquake, which centered along the Pacific coast with strong shaking in Mexico City, 350 kilometers inland, where about 10,000 deaths and enormous economic losses occurred.

Seismologists study not only the effects of earthquakes on human society but also their causes, occurrence, physical properties, and scientific use. Seismic waves spread from the earthquake source and carry with them the imprint of the interior architecture of the Earth. Subsequent deciphering of the seismograms recorded at stations around the world provide information about the structure of the inside of the Earth and its physical properties. In particular, seismic waves produced by artificial means, such as explosions, are the key tool in oil and mineral exploration. Seismic waves also provide the crucial clues to distinguish between underground nuclear explosions and natural earthquakes occurring in remote places.

This first revision includes additional material on the topics mentioned above, especially in Chapter 8. I have also chosen new illustrations from worldwide sources, although naturally I have emphasized my work at the Seismographic Stations of the University of California at Berkeley. In 1987, this earthquake observatory, which includes the first permanent seismographic stations in the western hemisphere, celebrated its centennial anniversary. It was originally established by E. S. Holden, the president of the university and an astronomer, who said his reason for the installation of seismographs was "to keep track of the effect of earthquakes on the telescope." As time passed, the observatory established the importance of providing continuous details on the seismicity of tectonically active regions such as California and the western United States.

In summary, the reader will find much new material in *Earthquakes*. Chapter 1 provides a more substantial description of plate tectonics.

Chapter 3 discusses important recent studies of the 1979 Imperial Valley earthquake in California, which was recorded on many instruments near the source of the waves. In Chapter 5, some recent case histories reinforce the fascinating story of the relation between volcanoes and earthquakes. Chapters 6 and 7 explain more up-to-date ways of measuring earthquakes, and Chapter 8 provides a brief account of the fundamental way that seismology has "x-rayed" the interior structure of the Earth. Additional case histories of the stimulation of earthquakes by large water reservoirs are outlined in Chapter 9, and Chapter 10 recounts the extraordinary discovery of clues to great earthquakes in the distant past. Chapter 10 also discusses earthquake prediction, including the current Parkfield, California, experiment. The sections on emergency preparedness and earthquake engineering in Chapters 11 and 12 have additional material on mitigating the effects of earthquakes and suggestions about ways that readers can participate. Finally, the original appendix on world earthquakes has been brought up to date, and an additional appendix on important earthquakes in Central and South America has been included.

I would like to repeat my personal thanks to colleagues and friends who provided criticism of *Earthquakes: A Primer*. In particular I would like to thank Dr. N. Abrahamson, Dr. R. D. Adams, Mr. R. Darragh, Dr. P. Dehlinger, Dr. R. Eisner, and Dr. R. Sherbourne.

I did the final work on this revision while I was a guest at Churchill College, Cambridge, England, and the Institute for Theoretical Physics, Trieste, Italy. Once again, I am much indebted to my wife, Dr. Beverley Bolt, for reading the manuscript, helping with the index, and assisting in other ways.

Seismographic Stations   BRUCE A. BOLT
University of California, Berkeley

Preface to
Earthquakes: A Primer

Oddly enough, I felt my first earthquake in 1959 in the Sydney suburb of Coogee, Australia while I was sitting quietly in my study. It was the place of occurrence that was so unlikely because Australia is not very active seismically, although earthquakes do occur in various areas in that great continent. On that day in September, 1959, a sudden movement had occurred in the Earth's crust some 350 kilometers away from Sydney, near the Snowy Mountains in southern New South Wales.

In the years since, I have felt many earthquakes: quite a few at my home in Berkeley, California; aftershocks of the main earthquake in 1971 in San Fernando, California; and many earthquakes of the famous swarm of hundreds of thousands of them that occurred in Matsushiro, Japan in 1967. I have felt earthquake jolts in Tokyo, in the Venezuelan Andes, in Seattle, in Romania, and elsewhere. So far, I have not experienced a major earthquake.

Seismology is truly an international science. As I was putting the finishing touches to this manuscript, a tragic earthquake struck Romania. At about 9:30 P.M. on March 4, 1977, a magnitude 7.2 earthquake spread out from a center under the Carpathian Mountains and heavily damaged part of Bucharest, Ploesti, and other Romanian towns. It was probably the strongest earthquake to occur in Central Europe in modern times: its shaking was felt as far away as Rome and Moscow, and damage occurred in Yugoslavia and Bulgaria. About 2,000 persons were killed. In an effort to learn from the disaster, in order to reduce the hazards in future earthquakes, a group of seismologists and engineers, of which I was a member, left the United States for Romania within a few days. Some of the lessons we learned will be incorporated in seismological knowledge and applied as the years go by.

It is the task of the seismologist to study all aspects of earthquakes, their causes, their occurrence, and their properties. The seismologist also makes use of seismic waves to study the interior of the Earth, to assist in oil and mineral exploration, and to detect secret underground nuclear explosions in distant places. Of course, earthquakes are also of strong interest to other professional people, particularly engineers, architects, city and regional planners, and even politicians. There is an abiding fascination with earthquakes among the public, not only in earthquake country such as California, New Zealand and Japan, but in areas where earthquakes are never experienced as well.

But in spite of the continuing demand from colleges, schools, professional people, and nonspecialists for popular books on earthquakes, very few are available that make easy reading for the person who is curious but has little or no background in earth science. The aim of this book is to provide a short, simple, and up-to-date account of our present knowledge of earthquakes that will be of general interest to people from various countries. I have used some of the more interesting studies of earthquakes as illustrations; they do not require any special mathematical or technical knowledge. Naturally, I have drawn on my fifteen years' experience as Director of the Seismographic Stations at the University of California at Berkeley. Although this earthquake observatory is in great part concerned with advanced research on earthquakes, it also has the important responsibility of providing details on the seismicity of California. Numerous requests for earthquake information come in every week. Some are letters, and others are made in person by visitors. In particular, children write in for help with school projects.

After finishing this book, readers will be able to answer questions about the causes of earthquakes—where and when to expect them—and to specify what protective measures can be taken against them. As a challenge, a list of questions is given at the back of the book. The answers to the questions can be obtained from the pages of the book. Important terms are defined in the glossary, and a list of suggested further readings is given in the bibliography. The appendixes provide useful but more specialized details in certain aspects of seismology.

A number of colleagues and friends have furnished me with photographs, references, examples, and criticism. I would like to extend to all of them my personal thanks. I am particularly indebted to Dr. P. Byerly, Dr. D. Boore, Dr. L. Weiss, Dr. L. Drake, S. J., Dr. F. Wu, Dr. D. Tocher, and Mr. T. R. Monteath either for material or for reading parts of the manuscript and making valuable suggestions for its improvement.

The basic draft was written while I was a guest of the Departamento de Fisica de la Tierra y del Cosmos, University of Barcelona. I am most grateful to Professor A. Udias, S. J., for his hospitality and comments. The task of preparing figures and tables was greatly lightened by the assistance of Mr. R. Miller and Mr. R. McKenzie. Mrs. A. McClure and Mrs. L. Martin ably typed and proofread the manuscript. My wife, Dr. Beverley Bolt and my daughter Gillian helped construct the index.

Berkeley, California   Bruce A. Bolt
January 1978

EARTHQUAKES

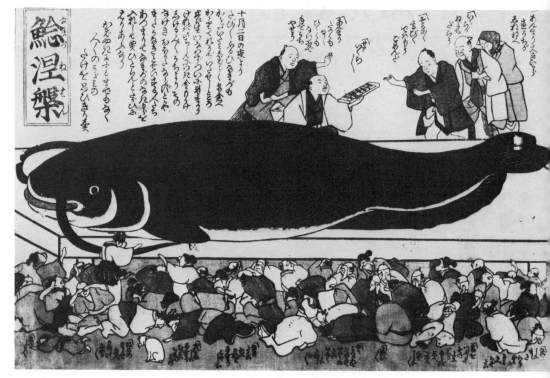

Fishmongers selling flesh from a *namazu* (catfish) whose excessive movement in a large Edo (Tokyo) earthquake has killed it. The people complain of profiteering from their tragedy.

Some say the Earth was fevrous and did shake.

—SHAKESPEARE, *Macbeth*, II, 3

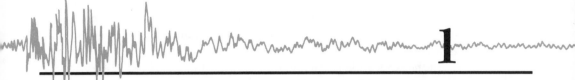

1

Where Earthquakes Occur

Earthquakes in Past Times

Earthquakes can be violent, and they have been unpredictable. Their convulsions have so often produced helplessness and injury that people have always feared them. In many countries, popular legend attributed earthquakes to grotesque monsters that supported the Earth. In ancient Japanese folklore, for example, a great catfish (*namazu*) lay beneath the ground and caused earthquakes by thrashing its body (see the print on the facing page). The namazu's activity was restrained by a god (*daimyojin*) who wielded a large stone mallet. But when the attention of the daimyojin wandered, the namazu moved and the ground shook.

The first systematic and nonmystical treatment of earthquakes occurred in Greece, where its people experienced Aegean volcanoes and earthquakes along the Mediterranean Sea, sometimes accompanied by "tidal" waves (*tsunamis*). A number of the Greek philosophers offered mechanical explanations for these natural events. Strabo, for example, noted that earthquakes occurred more frequently along the coast than inland. He, like Aristotle, suggested that earthquakes were caused by rushing subterranean winds, igniting combustible materials underground.

1

As the practice of writing spread, descriptions of severe earthquakes were recorded. The oldest of these are the Chinese records dating back 3000 years. This amazing catalog is thought to document every moderate to large earthquake in central China from 780 B.C. to the present. In Japan, the catalog of damaging earthquakes is not as long but is essentially without gaps from about 1600 A.D.; less reliable lists are available back to about 416 A.D. Such historical catalogs are crucial to our understanding of the relation of earthquakes to the geological features of our planet and to our assessment of seismic hazards to large engineering structures such as dams and nuclear reactors.

In the western hemisphere, there is a well-documented history for the eastern part of the Alpine belt, from Greece to Afghanistan, for about 17 centuries. Even earlier than this, sporadic allusions to large earthquakes in the Mediterranean region are found in the Bible and in Arabic writings. It has been claimed that the first biblical mention of an earthquake is the experience of Moses on Mount Sinai. More definite references are probably the accounts of the collapse of the walls of Jericho about 1100 B.C. and perhaps of the destruction of Sodom and Gomorrah. Palestinian earthquakes are associated with geological faults of the rift valley that runs north from the Gulf of Eilat through the Dead Sea. Although in this century the Jordan Valley rift has been the site of only a few small to moderate earthquakes, historical studies indicate that the whole area suffers, on the average, two or three damaging earthquakes each century.°

In the more recently settled parts of the world, such as the United States and Canada, the historical earthquake chronicles are, of course, quite short. One of the first accounts describes an earthquake that struck Massachusetts in 1638, toppling stone chimneys to the ground. Somewhat more extensive reports describe a large Canadian earthquake in the Three Rivers area of the lower St. Lawrence River on February 5, 1663. For California, there are descriptions dating back to 1800 by the Franciscan fathers who documented the development of the Spanish missions. Thus we know that a series of earthquakes in 1800 damaged Mission San Juan Bautista, and that 1812 was called "the Year of Earthquakes" because of the great amount of seismic activity felt at that time.

Investigating earthquakes that happened long ago is frustrating work. There is a story of Professor George Louderback, a geologist at the University of California at Berkeley, who had a keen interest in disentangling the history of California earthquakes. The historical reports spoke of an earthquake on the morning of December 8, 1812 (a Tuesday), that de-

---

° Historical seismic activity has often occurred near the monastery of Saint John the Baptist, where Jesus was baptized. A large local shock occurred on May 23, 1834.

stroyed Mission San Juan Capistrano, killing 40 American Indians attending Mass. Louderback asked: Why were they worshiping on Tuesday? He determined that that day was a holy day, so attendance in church was understandable. Further enquiry showed, however, that that particular holy day was currently not being celebrated in Rome. Why then were the American Indians in church on a Tuesday? Thus, historical enquiries sometimes lead to further puzzles.

By the mid-nineteenth century, documentation in California was fairly detailed. In the description of the great earthquake of January 9, 1857, for example, several independent references were made to extensive cracking of the Earth in central California near the settlement of Fort Tejon. This earthquake was one of the first indications of rupture on what is now called the San Andreas fault. The Fort Tejon shock is the most recent great earthquake to occur along the southern portion of the San Andreas.

Observatories to Study Earthquakes

Early in this century seismographic stations were established at many points throughout the world. At these stations, sensitive seismographs operate continuously and record even tiny earthquake waves that have been generated at distant places. For example, the 1906 San Francisco earthquake was well recorded at dozens of seismographic stations in a number of foreign countries, including Japan, Italy, and Germany.°

The significance of this worldwide network was that earthquake documentation no longer rested solely on subjective reports of felt and visual effects. There developed a cooperative international program in which earthquake readings could be exchanged to help pinpoint earthquake locations. For the first time, the temporal statistics of earthquake occurrence and the geological distribution of earthquakes, even in unpopulated regions, became known. This information is called the *seismicity* of a region.

By 1960, about 700 earthquake observatories were operating in numerous countries, with a hodgepodge of seismographs. The ability to locate accurately earthquakes of moderate size at any place on the Earth's surface was subsequently greatly improved when the United States established the Worldwide Standardized Network of seismographs. By 1969,

---

° In 1968, I used these records to compute the location of the point of initiation of the 1906 earthquake, using modern methods. It was only a few kilometers from the Golden Gate Bridge!

about 120 of these special stations were distributed in 60 countries. A comparable step forward was also made in the technology of earthquake observation in nonparticipating countries. Recently, a new global network of latest-technology seismographs was begun; these seismographs record earthquake ground motions on magnetic tapes in a discrete or digital format that can be used directly in computers.

The Global Mosaic of Earthquakes

The position of the center of an earthquake can be calculated from the earthquake wave readings at different seismographic observatories. In this way, a uniform picture of earthquake distribution around the world has been obtained (see Figure 1). Clear belts of seismic activity separate large oceanic and continental regions, themselves almost devoid of earthquake centers. Other concentrations of earthquake sources can be seen in the oceanic areas; these are the sites of gigantic submarine mountain ranges called midoceanic ridges. The seismically active ridges of the Atlantic and Indian oceans meet south of Africa, and the mid-Indian ridge circles below Australia to connect with the East Pacific ridge, which extends eastward toward Central America and into the Gulf of California. The geological unrest that prevails throughout this global ridge system is evidenced by great mountain peaks and deep rift valleys. Volcanic eruptions are frequent, and earthquakes originating along these ridges often occur in "swarms," so that many hundreds of shocks are concentrated in a small area in a short time.

Dense concentrations of earthquake centers also coincide with beautifully symmetrical island arcs, such as those of the Pacific and the eastern Caribbean (see Figure 4). One of the finest examples of these island chains is the crescent-shaped Aleutian arc, swinging westward from Alaska toward the Kamchatka arc. Southward from the eastern Soviet Union, the islands of Japan form an arc that extends southward to the island arc of the Marianas. From Indonesia to the south Pacific, a number of seismically active arcs drape around Australia like a garland, with the Tonga-Kermadec trench as its eastern border.

On the other side of the Pacific, the whole western coast of Central and South America is agitated by many earthquakes, great and small. High death tolls have ensued from the major ones, such as the 1976 Guatemala earthquake (see Chapter 3). In marked contrast, the eastern part of South America is almost free from earthquakes and can be cited as a good example of aseismic country. Other seismically quiet continental areas

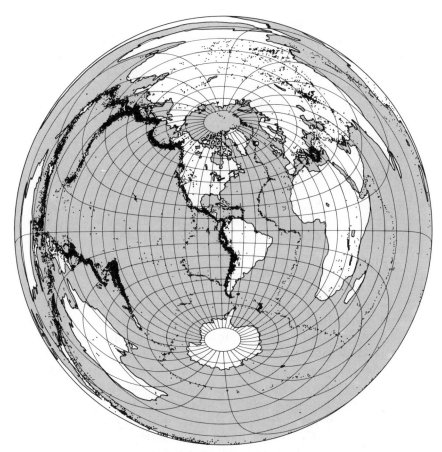

Figure 1 A view of global seismicity. Epicenters for earthquakes of magnitude 4.5 or greater are plotted from 1963 through 1973. [Courtesy of National Geophysical Data Center, NOAA.]

can also be seen in Figure 4; earthquakes seldom occur in the large central and northern areas of Canada, much of Siberia, west Africa, or great parts of Australia. But note the long *trans-Asiatic* zone of high seismicity running approximately east-west from Burma° through the Himalaya Mountains and central Asia to the Caucasus Mountains and the Mediterranean Sea.

In Europe, earthquake activity is quite widespread. To the south, in

---

°On July 8, 1975, a violent earthquake seriously damaged many temples and pagodas at Pagan in Burma. Ancient inscriptions there refer to restorations after former earthquakes.

Turkey, Greece, Yugoslavia, Italy, Spain, and Portugal, large numbers of people have died in disasters throughout the years. An earthquake off southwest Iberia on November 1, 1755, produced a great ocean wave, which alone caused many of the 50,000 to 70,000 deaths occurring in Lisbon, Portugal, and surrounding areas; the shaking was felt in Germany and the Low Countries. In Alicante, Spain, on March 21, 1829, an earthquake killed about 840 persons and injured many hundred more; total or partial destruction of more than 5000 houses was reported in and near Torrevieja and Murcia. A devastating earthquake hit Messina, Italy, on December 28, 1908, causing 120,000 deaths and widespread damage. On December 27, 1939, in Erzincan, Turkey, 23,000 lives were lost from a major earthquake. Similar killer earthquakes have occurred in Turkey in recent years. Another earthquake struck Italy on May 6, 1976, in the Friuli region near Gemona; about 965 persons were killed and 2280 injured (see Figure 2). A similar tragedy occurred in southern Italy on November 23, 1980, when the Campania earthquake caused over 3000 deaths and left 250,000 homeless.

North of the Mediterranean margin, Europe is much more stable. However, destructive earthquakes do occur occasionally in Germany, Austria, and Switzerland, and even in the North Sea region and Scandinavia. For example, on October 8, 1927, an earthquake near Schwadorf in Austria caused damage in an area southeast of Vienna. This earthquake was felt in Hungary, Germany, and Czechoslovakia at distances of 250 kilometers from the center of the disturbance.

Damaging earthquakes have also occurred in Great Britain in historical times. On December 17, 1896, an earthquake series caused some damage in Hereford, a city of 4565 inhabited houses. About 200 chimneys had to be repaired or rebuilt, and the cathedral was slightly damaged. The area affected was just over 1000 square kilometers. A notable recent case was the earthquake in north Wales on July 19, 1984, which was felt over a wide area. Offices were evacuated as far away as Bristol, but damage was minor.

Seismicity maps such as that in Figure 1 are drawn up from data taken over a fairly short-term period. Consequently, if conclusions or predictions about the likelihood of earthquake occurrence in a given area are founded only on such maps, they can be discredited by the abnormal occurrence of an earthquake in an area that is not usually regarded as seismically active.

An example of infrequent and dispersed seismicity is the occurrence of earthquakes in Australia. There are sound geological reasons why this is so: much of the western part consists of ancient rocks of the Australian Precambrian shield, and the continent as a whole is remote from the active ocean ridges and island arcs that surround it. Nevertheless, this country does have some areas of significant present-day seismicity. Of particular interest is a damaging earthquake of moderate size that was centered near Meckering, western Australia, on October 14, 1968, and was associated with fresh surface faulting about 30 kilometers long.

Seismicity maps—carefully worked out by the cooperative efforts of hundreds of seismologists—have contributed in essential ways to our knowledge of the Earth. For example, global patterns of earthquake occurrence have helped us to understand the evolution of mountain ranges, continents, and oceans. As well, seismicity maps are consulted by planners, geologists, and engineers whenever the mitigation of earthquake hazard is a consideration in the construction of large structures.

Figure 2   Damage to weak masonry structures in northern Italy in the Friuli earthquake of May 6, 1976. [Courtesy of I. Finetti.]

Depths of Earthquakes

Earthquakes are merely the shaking of the ground. The waves that make up the earthquake are called *seismic waves*. Like sound waves radiating through the air from a gong that has been struck, seismic waves radiate through the rocks from a source of energy somewhere in the outer part of

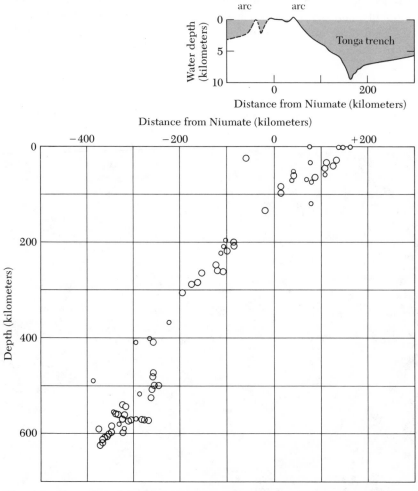

Figure 3   Foci of earthquakes in 1965 occurring under the Tonga arc in the southwest Pacific. The vertical section shows that most earthquake centers cluster along a narrow zone starting under the trench and dipping under it at an angle of about 45° to depths of more than 600 kilometers. [Courtesy of B. Isacks, J. Oliver, L. R. Sykes, and *J. Geophys. Res.*]

the Earth. Although in natural earthquakes this source is spread out through a volume of rock, it is often convenient to specify an earthquake source as a point from which the waves first emanate. This point is called the earthquake *focus*. The focus of natural earthquakes is at some depth below the ground surface. For artificial earthquakes, such as underground nuclear explosions, the focus is essentially a point near the Earth's surface. The point on the ground surface directly above the focus is called the earthquake *epicenter*.

How far down in the Earth are the foci? One of the early intriguing discoveries by seismologists was that, although many foci are situated at shallow depths, in some regions they are hundreds of kilometers deep. Such regions include the South American Andes, the Tonga Islands, Samoa, the New Hebrides chain, the Japan Sea, Indonesia, and the Caribbean Antilles (see Figure 4); each of these regions is associated with a deep ocean trench. On the average, the frequency of earthquake occurrence in these regions declines rapidly below a depth of 200 kilometers, but some foci are as deep as 680 kilometers. Earthquakes with foci from 70 to 300 kilometers deep are arbitrarily called *intermediate focus*, and those below this depth are termed *deep focus*. Some intermediate- and deep-focus earthquakes are located away from the Pacific region, in the Hindu Kush, in Romania, in the Aegean Sea, and under Spain.

When the foci of earthquakes near island arcs and ocean trenches are compared with their depths, an extraordinary pattern emerges. Consider the vertical section of the Earth at the top of Figure 3, which is drawn at right angles to the Tonga arc in the South Pacific. To the east of these volcanic islands lies the Tonga trench, as deep as 10 kilometers in places. In the bottom part of the figure, the depths of the foci are plotted against their distance from Niumate, a point on Tonga Island. Notice that the foci lie in a narrow but well-defined zone, which dips from near the trench beneath the island arc at an angle of about 45°. In some dipping zones, the foci actually lie along two parallel planes about 20 kilometers apart. Below depths of 400 kilometers, the active zone steepens, with some foci occurring below 600 kilometers. In other regions of deep earthquakes, some variation in the angle of dip and distribution of foci is found, but the general feature of a dipping seismic zone° is common to island arcs and deep ocean trenches. This universal but simple pattern is discussed later in this chapter.

This book concerns mainly shallow-focus events, whose foci are just below the Earth's surface. Shallow earthquakes wreak the most devastation, and they contribute about three-quarters of the total energy released

---

°Called the *Benioff zone* after a famous California seismologist, Professor Hugo Benioff (1899–1968).

in earthquakes throughout the world. In California, for example, all the known large earthquakes to date have been shallow-focus. In fact, in the coast ranges of central California the great majority of earthquakes originate from foci in the upper 10 kilometers of the Earth, and only a few are as deep as 15 kilometers. Unfortunately, for various reasons, the determination of the depth of an earthquake focus is not as precise as the location of its epicenter on the surface. Yet depth can be of vital practical concern, because stronger ground shaking may affect a site (such as that of a large dam) when the focus is at a depth of 10 rather than 40 kilometers.

Most moderate-to-large shallow earthquakes are followed, in the ensuing hours and even during the next several months, by numerous smaller earthquakes in the same vicinity. These earthquakes are called *aftershocks*. The great Rat Island earthquake in the Aleutian Islands on February 4, 1965, was followed, within the next 24 days, by more than 750 aftershocks large enough to be recorded by distant seismographs. A few earthquakes are preceded by smaller foreshocks from the source area, and it has been suggested that these can be used to predict the main shock (see Chapter 9).

Sometimes, if foci can be precisely located, they indicate the shape and size of the region beneath the ground surface that is the source of the earthquakes. This seismological mapping of the deeper rock structures is an extension of normal field methods used by geologists to map surface features. One successful demarcation of such a zone for shallow local earthquakes near Oroville, California, is given in Chapter 9, Figure 3. Another mapping was made after the 1984 Wales earthquake sequence, referred to earlier, which had focal depths of a surprising 19 to 23 kilometers.

Tectonic Patterns and Quiet Gaps in Earthquake Zones

One recent and broadly satisfying explanation of the majority of earthquakes is in terms of what is called *plate tectonics*. The basic idea is that the Earth's outermost part (called the *lithosphere*) consists of several large and fairly stable slabs of solid and relatively rigid rock called *plates*. The ten largest plates are mapped in Figure 4.

Each plate extends to a depth of about 80 kilometers; the plate moves horizontally, relative to neighboring plates, on softer rock immediately below. At the edge of a plate, where there is contact with adjoining plates, large deforming (or *tectonic*) forces operate on the rocks, causing physical

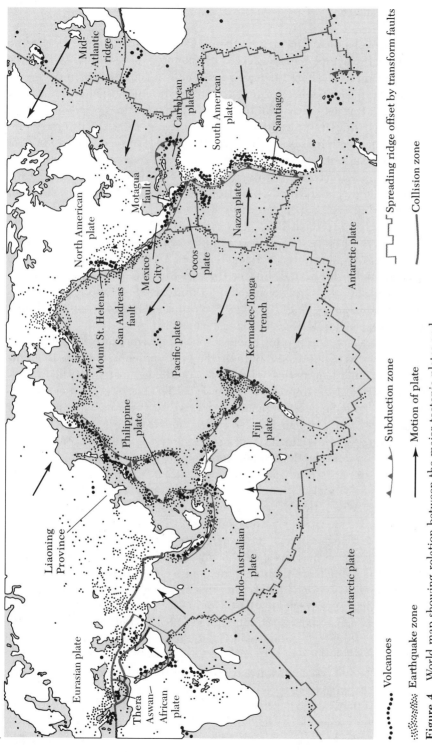

Figure 4 World map showing relation between the major tectonic plates and recent earthquakes and volcanoes. Earthquake epicenters are denoted by the small dots, and the volcanoes by large dots.

Volcanoes

Earthquake zone

Subduction zone

Motion of plate

Spreading ridge offset by transform faults

Collision zone

Mid-Atlantic ridge

Caribbean plate

North American plate

Motagua fault

South American plate

Santiago

Nazca plate

Mexico City

Cocos plate

Mount St. Helens

San Andreas fault

Pacific plate

Kermadec-Tonga trench

Antarctic plate

Philippine plate

Fiji plate

Liaoning Province

Indo-Australian plate

Antarctic plate

Eurasian plate

Thera Aswan—African plate

and even chemical changes in them. At these plate edges the Earth's geological structure is most affected by the forces of reaction between the plates, and this is where the massive and radical geological changes occur.

Geophysical evidence suggests that plate structure (such as that shown in Figure 4) is not permanent but is undergoing constant, gradual change. Lava is continually upwelling at the midoceanic ridges. This newly emplaced rock then moves slowly across the Earth's surface as new sea floor on either side of the ridge. In this way, plates spread and move at a uniform speed across the surface, like great conveyor belts, cooling and aging as they get farther away from the ridges. For this reason, midoceanic ridges are called *spreading zones*.

The spreading zones have been plotted in Figure 4. Notice that none of the lines of epicenters appear as unbroken linear trends, but they are disrupted by intermittent horizontal offsets. These offsets coincide with a special kind of horizontal slip (see Chapter 3) between two crustal blocks. At either end, the slip is changed or "transformed" by the emergence of new oceanic floor along the ridge. Such slips are called transform faults, and many earthquakes occur along them.

If new plates, constituting the lithosphere, are constantly being created, what happens to old plates? Because the Earth probably remains the same size over quite long periods of geological time, large areas of the moving plates must also be absorbed at some place. The burial ground of plates is believed to be the ocean trenches associated with advancing continents or island arcs. At these places, called *subduction zones*, the surface layers of rock plunge into the Earth's interior (see Figure 4, and Chapter 5, Figure 3). At the greater depths, temperature and pressure increase, and the sinking lithosphere is gradually reworked until it becomes mixed and absorbed into the rocks of the deeper interior. At present, the plates containing Africa, Antarctica, North America, and South America are growing, while the Pacific plate is getting smaller.

From this perspective of a changing, mobile Earth, earthquakes occurring along the ocean ridges are thought to be produced by the growth of the plates. Along these submarine mountain chains are many surface ruptures and downdropped blocks, and this breaking of the rocks releases the energy for the earthquakes. "Head on" plate collisions result in massive mountain chains (such as the Himalayas and the Alpine belt of the Mediterranean) and are accompanied by almost continuous earthquake activity.

As a plate bends downward at the ocean troughs, fractures generating shallow earthquakes occur within it. In the process of its downward movement, additional force is generated, causing further deformation and fracturing, thus giving rise to deep-focus earthquakes. The deep earthquakes occurring along this descending plate (called the downgoing slab) define the remarkably regular dipping seismic zone—the Benioff zone—that we discussed earlier (see Figure 3). Finally, at depths of 650 to 680 kilometers, either the plate has been altogether absorbed into the rocks of the interior or its properties have been altered enough that it can no longer release earthquake energy.

This general geological theory has a number of implications for our understanding of earthquakes. First, many more earthquakes will occur along the edges of the interacting plates (*interplate earthquakes*) than within the plate boundaries. However, as the map in Figure 4 shows, earthquakes also take place within plates, and the theory does not explain these in an obvious way. Such *intraplate earthquakes* must arise from more localized systems of forces, perhaps associated with structural complexities from very ancient geological conditions or with variations in temperature and strength of the lithosphere. A number of intraplate earthquakes have occurred in the United States, the most important of which was a succession of great earthquakes that struck the New Madrid area of Missouri in 1811 to 1812 (see Chapter 7, Figure 1). They caused considerable damage in the area and were felt as far away as Washington, D.C. They may have been produced when rocks fractured because of the enormous weight of alluvial deposits extending along the Mississippi River system from the Gulf of Mexico to the vicinity of New Madrid, perhaps in conjunction with intrusions of dense rock thrust upward in this region.

Second, because the directions of forces on plates (Figure 4) vary across them, the mechanism of the sources of earthquakes and their size differ in different parts of a plate (see Chapter 4). Only about 10 percent of the world's earthquakes occur along the ocean-ridge system, and these contribute only about 5 percent of the total seismic energy of earthquakes around the world.

In contrast, the earthquakes of the trenches contribute more than 90 percent of the world's release of seismic energy for shallow earthquakes, as well as most of the energy for intermediate- and deep-focus earthquakes. Most of the largest earthquakes, such as the 1960 and 1985 Chile earthquakes, the 1964 Alaska earthquake, and the 1985 Mexico earthquake, have originated in the subduction regions as a result of the thrusting of one plate under another.

Third, the grand scale of the plate pattern (shown in Figure 4) and the steady rate of plate spreading imply that along a plate edge the slip should, on average, be a constant value over many years. Thus, if two slips some distance apart along a trench produce earthquakes, we might expect that a similar slip will occur between them in due course. This idea suggests that the historical patterns of distance and time intervals between major earthquakes along major plate boundaries provide at least a crude indication of places at which large earthquakes might soon occur.

The scheme described above is illustrated in Figure 5 for the plate boundary of the Alaska-Aleutian arc. The sites of the inferred seismic-energy release areas of some recent large earthquakes are indicated in the figure by the contours. If all such earthquake locations for the last 50 years are plotted, many sections of the arc are covered. There remain, however, some "seismic gaps" (indicated by the heavy lines), which could be likely areas for plate slip and thus for major earthquakes in the future.

At the center of Figure 5 is the Shumagin gap, for which there is evidence of rupture in 1788, 1847, and perhaps 1903. The Yakataga section, at the north of the arc, was the source of an earthquake in 1899. Surveys indicate that the American plate converges into the subduction zone at a rate of about 16 millimeters per year in a N15°W direction, roughly perpendicular to the Alaska arc. Strain accumulation has been measured from distances between ground markers in both these seismic regions since about 1980. With this evidence, the two regions may be the most likely sites for the next great thrust earthquakes along the Alaska-Aleutian arc. Yet the surveys have not detected any significant crustal deformation in the Shumagin gap, raising the speculation that subduction is sometimes episodic, with long intervals of strain accumulation occasionally interspersed by episodes of rapid accumulation. In the Yakataga gap, the surveys indicate that the rocks are being strained at an appropriate rate for the eventual occurrence of another great earthquake.

In California there is a seismic gap along the San Andreas fault between the northern site of the 1906 earthquake and the southern site of the 1857 Fort Tejon earthquake (see Chapter 10). Another example of a

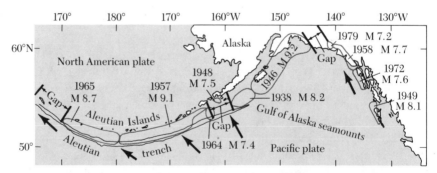

Figure 5   Rupture areas of large, shallow earthquakes (with approximate magnitudes) from 1930 to 1979 and seismic gaps along the Alaska-Aleutian arc. The Yakataga gap is at longitude 143°W, and the Shumagin gap is at 160°W. The dark arrows show the direction of the motion of the Pacific plate relative to the American plate. [After J. C. Savage, M. Lisowski, and W. H. Prescott, *Science*, 231, 585, 1986.]

seismic gap is given in Chapter 12 in the discussion of the tragic 1985 Mexico earthquake, which occurred when the subduction zone under the Pacific margin of Mexico slipped. We must be cautious, however, about simple applications of a seismic-gap theory, because there are known exceptions. For example, in 1979, a moderate earthquake in the Imperial Valley of California was produced by energy release along the Imperial fault in the same section that was observed to slip in an earthquake of similar size in 1940 (see Chapter 3). Thus quick repetition of earthquakes from the same fault section cannot be ruled out.

Devastation of ground in the Turnagain Heights slide in the
March 27, 1964, Alaska earthquake. [Courtesy of U.S. Coast
and Geodetic Survey.]

*A bad earthquake at once destroys the oldest associations; the
world, the very emblem of all that is solid, had moved beneath
our feet like a crust over a fluid; one second of time has created
in the mind a strong idea of insecurity, which hours of reflection
would not have produced.*

—CHARLES DARWIN (reflecting on the devastating February 20, 1835,
earthquake in Concepción, Chile)

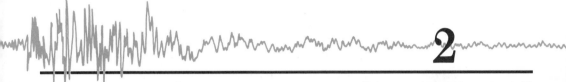

2

What We Feel
in an Earthquake

The 1906 San Francisco Earthquake

April 18, 1906, early morning in California. By the Golden Gate slum-
bered San Francisco, a city of 400,000 people. Built in a series of economic booms during the previous century, it was a mixture of old and
new buildings, all constructed with little heed to natural hazards. Already
the downtown area was dotted with steel-frame high rises,° but it was still
dominated by older buildings of wood and unreinforced brick that lined
the narrow streets and unprotected openings. Around the wharves were
more structures, erected on former marsh land that had been used for so
long as a garbage dump that it was completely dry. Farther away from
the bay were two- and three-story wooden Victorian homes, more elegant
but equally combustible.

°Such as the Spreckels building of 19 stories and the Chronicle building of 16 stories. These
high-rise buildings were not so heavily damaged as to be unsafe.

At 5:12 A.M., a few kilometers from the Golden Gate, a section of rock snapped along the San Andreas fault. The break spread quickly along the fault southward and northward. As this rupture in the rocks grew, seismic waves radiated out through the Earth, shaking the ground surface across a wide area of California and Nevada.

Professor Alexander McAdie, head of the San Francisco Weather Bureau, wrote soon after,

> My custom is to sleep with my watch open, notebook open at the date, and pencil ready—also a hand torch. They are laid out in regular order, torch, watch, book, and pencil. I entered in the book, "Severe shaking lasting forty seconds." I remember getting the minute-hand position after waking, previous to the most violent portion of the shock.

Cool accounts like this one, by reliable eyewitnesses, are as important as they are rare. How many people living in earthquake country make the kind of preparation described by McAdie? But, as McAdie demonstrated, it is possible to think clearly even during strong earthquake shaking. He was calm enough to carry out a simple scientific experiment, which yielded a useful measure of the duration of strong shaking in this great earthquake.

The long rupture of the San Andreas fault (see Figures 1 and 2) occurring on that day was later mapped by field geologists, who concluded that it extended 430 kilometers, from near Cape Mendocino in Humboldt County to San Juan Bautista, near Hollister, in San Benito County.° The offset along the fault was mainly horizontal and reached 6 meters in Marin County, just north of San Francisco, with the west side moving northwest of the east side. The observed maximum vertical displacement across the fault was less than a meter. Near San Juan Bautista to the south, the fault displacement declined gradually to a few centimeters and then disappeared.

The total area significantly affected by an earthquake of this magnitude was surprisingly small. When the strength of the shaking was mapped, it was seen that the zone of intense ground motion was long, narrow, and parallel to the San Andreas fault. The places of most severe damage (called *meizoseismal* areas) were generally restricted to within a few tens of kilometers of the fault rupture. The earthquake was felt as far north as Oregon and south to Los Angeles, a total distance of 1170 kilometers. In general the intensity died off markedly toward the east; Winnemucca in Nevada, 540 kilometers from the San Andreas fault, was

---

°Recent oceanographic evidence of offset submarine canyons and other features on the sea floor has delineated the San Andreas under the ocean from Point Delgado to Point Arena (see Figure 2).

Figure 1 Aerial panorama of part of Marin County, California, showing the majestic San Andreas rift zone from Bolinas Lagoon (foreground) to Bodega Head. In the 1906 San Francisco earthquake, fault offset in this section ranged from 3 to 6 meters. (An interesting place for a field visit is along Highway 1 to Olema, where there is an "earthquake trail" near the Point Reyes National Seashore Park Headquarters.) [Sutherland photograph.]

the easternmost point at which the earthquake was reported. In sum, perceptible shaking occurred across an area of about 1 million square kilometers, which is much less, for example, than the felt area of over 5 million square kilometers in the February 7, 1812, New Madrid earthquake in Missouri, or the 4 million square kilometers reported for the great earthquake centered off the coast of Portugal on November 1, 1755 (see Chapter 7, Figure 1). In the ensuing months of 1906, strong aftershocks were reported in California.°

°Those who would like to judge for themselves the intensity of the 1906 earthquake can do so by reading the *Report of the State Earthquake Investigation Commission*. This fascinating and very readable account was reprinted recently at a bargain price by the Carnegie Institution.

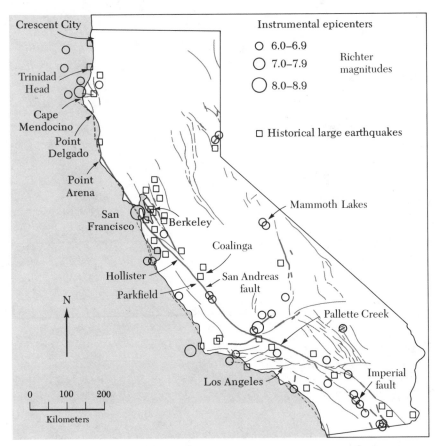

Figure 2 Epicenters of the major earthquakes of California in historical times from 1800 to 1980. The "large" earthquakes (open squares) were so designated on the basis of felt effects. Trends of major mapped faults are shown as continuous lines or (if the location is uncertain) as dashed lines on land and as dotted lines under the ocean.

The restricted meizoseismal area resulting from such a large fault rupture is somewhat reassuring for those Californians who do not live in close proximity to the active San Andreas fault zone. It is probably due to a shallow rupture depth along the fault (believed to be about 10 kilometers) and the high rate of damping of seismic waves in California. There were, however, some exceptional pockets of high intensity that should be considered in the planning and engineering of any construction projects. For example, there was heavy damage at Los Baños, 30 kilometers east of the San Andreas fault, and at the southern end of San Francisco Bay (including the present city of San Jose), where the surficial material is alluvium or recent fluvial deposits. But towns along the east side of San Francisco

Bay, such as Berkeley, 25 kilometers east of the San Andreas fault, suffered little damage. Similarly, Sacramento, 120 kilometers east of the rupture, showed no notable destruction, even to the capital dome.° (A resident, Mr. J. A. Marshall, reminisced later that, "I was awakened by my wife's remark that she believed we were having an earthquake. We arose and observed and verified the phenomena.")

A total of about 700 lives were lost; in San Francisco there were 315 known deaths. The degree of destruction due to the earthquake itself, however, is difficult to estimate because of the fire that broke out almost immediately afterward and raged for 3 days (see Figure 3). The fire produced perhaps 10 times more damage than did earthquake shaking.

Sudden massive rupture of rocks like that of 1906 cannot be reliably predicted at present. Nevertheless, because the San Andreas fault is in a tectonically active region (at the boundary of the North American and Pacific plates) and because direct geodetic observations show strain is now building up along it, we *can* predict with confidence that another great earthquake will occur along it someday (see Chapter 10). The question often asked by the public is, "What will happen when it does?"

To begin with, let us compare the conditions of today with those of 1906. In the years since 1906, California's population has grown and spread: in the San Francisco Bay area alone it has increased from approximately 800,000 to more than 2 million. Structures of new and different architectural types have been introduced into the area. In 1906, there were no large facilities or essential "life lines," such as the Golden Gate and other bay bridges and the bay area rapid transit system, BART, with its tube under the bay. Many deaths and injuries will surely occur. Fortunately, most Californians live in the types of wooden-framed houses that can withstand earthquakes. So if a great earthquake should strike when families are at home, casualties may be *proportionately* fewer than in 1906—perhaps 1000 persons. If it occurred at a busy time when traffic on the freeways and downtown areas was heavy, the toll would be substantially higher—perhaps more than 5000 people. (Some studies have projected an even higher figure, but such estimates are uncertain, and it is hard not to bias the values.)

In a highly industrialized society, the economic impact of a major earthquake that damages structures and their contents over a wide area is great indeed (see Appendix B). Even if there is little serious structural damage to buildings, often the interior walls and fittings, work areas, electrical and mechanical equipment, and plumbing are broken and out of use for many days, causing high loss of investment and production.

°Engineering studies in the 1960s indicated that the capitol, built in 1904, constituted an earthquake risk; strengthening measures were begun in 1976.

Figure 3 Damage in San Francisco in the 1906 earthquake. This is a view of O'Farrell Street before the fire swept the area. [Copyright 1906 by W. E. Worden.]

Yet there is reason for optimism in California: although much remains to be done, building codes have been gradually strengthened over the years, especially in response to the 1933 Long Beach earthquake and the 1971 San Fernando earthquake, both in southern California. Building practices and earthquake-resistant design have improved, particularly for schools, hospitals, freeway overpasses, and most major construction projects. This progress—in stark contrast to conditions in many other parts of the world—is important, because studies of earthquake damage have clearly demonstrated that catastrophic numbers of deaths and injuries are caused, not by the trembling itself, but by the collapse of buildings that cannot withstand even small amounts of ground shaking.

The 1964 Good Friday Earthquake in Alaska

The Aleutian Islands and trench stretch in a sweeping arc across the northernmost Pacific Ocean between Kamchatka in Siberia and south central Alaska. Into this trench the Pacific plate plunges downward and northward. Abundant volcanic and seismic activity occurs along the entire arc and extends eastward into the active and dormant volcanoes of the Rango Mountains (see Chapter 1, Figure 4). Intermittent thrusting of the plate under Alaska occurs frequently, producing earthquakes over a wide region. The underthrusting plate may stick at any one place for centuries, while adjacent parts of it continue to progress onward. Finally, a break occurs (see Chapter 1, Figure 5).

Such an event occurred on Good Friday, March 27, 1964, at 5:36 P.M. The first slip occurred at a depth of about 30 kilometers under northern Prince William Sound, and the rupture in the rocks extended horizontally for 800 kilometers, roughly parallel to the Aleutian trench.

Hundreds of measurements along the shoreline later showed that beds of barnacles and other sea life had been raised above sea level about 10 meters. From such observations and the uplift of tidal bench marks relative to sea level and from geodetic level lines surveyed carefully from the coast into Alaska, it was estimated that about 200,000 square kilometers of the crust were deformed in the Good Friday earthquake. It was the greatest area of vertical displacement ever measured in earthquake history. The subduction-zone slip occurred mainly beneath the ocean; only in a few places, such as on Montague Island in Prince William Sound, were fresh fault scraps visible. The vertical fault displacements on Montague Island amounted to 6 meters in places. Such great slips are not the record for Alaska, however; 14.3 meters of uplift occurred in the Yakutat Bay earthquake of 1899, centered about 320 kilometers to the east.

The sudden upward movement of the Alaskan seafloor along the rupturing fault generated large water waves, acting on the water of the ocean like a gigantic paddle. Such gigantic "tidal" waves, produced in an earthquake, are called *tsunami* (see Chapter 5). The crests of the first waves struck the shores of Kenai Peninsula within 19 minutes and Kodiak Island within 34 minutes after the start of the earthquake. As the tsunami rushed onshore, it devastated waterfront developments along the Alaskan coast, particularly at Valdez and Seward. About 120 persons drowned.

In Anchorage, 100 kilometers from the fault slip in Prince William Sound, strong ground shaking commenced about 15 seconds after the rocks first broke. The heavy shaking continued for more than half a minute. After shaking began, the announcer at radio station KHAR, R. Pate, recorded his thoughts on a tape recorder:

Hey, boy—Oh-wee, that's a good one! Hey—boy oh boy oh boy! Man, that's an earthquake! Hey, that's an earthquake for sure!—Wheeeee! Boy oh boy—this is something you'd read—doesn't come up very often up here, but I'm going through it right now! Man—everything's moving— you know, all that stuff in all the cabinets have come up loose. . . . Whooeee! Scared the hell out of me, man! Oh boy, I wish this house would quit shaking! That damn bird cage—oooo—oh man! I've never lived through anything like this before in my life! And it hasn't even shown signs of stopping yet, either—ooooeeee—the whole place is shaking—like someone was holding—Hold it, I'd better put the television on the floor. Just a minute—Boy! Let me tell you that sure scared the hell out of me, and it's still shaking, I'm telling you! I wonder if I should get outside? Oh boy! Man, I'm telling you that's the worst thing I've ever lived through! I wonder if that's the last one of 'em? Oh man! Oh—Oh boy, I'm telling you that's something I hope I don't go through very often. Maa-uhn!—I'm not fakin' a bit of this—I'm telling you, the whole place just moved like somebody had taken it by the nape of the neck and was shaking it. Everything's moving around here!—I wonder if the HAR radio tower is still standing up. Man! You sure can't hear it, but I wonder what they have to say on the air about it? The radio fell back here—but I don't think it killed it—Oh! I'm shaking like a leaf—I don't think it hurt it. Man, that could very easily have knocked the tower down—I don't get anything on the air—from any of the stations—I can't even think! I wonder what it did to the tower. We may have lost the tower. I'll see if any of the stations come on—No, none of them do. I assume the radio is okay—Boy! The place is still moving! You couldn't even stand up when that thing was going like that—I was falling all over the place here. I turned this thing on and started talking just after the thing started, and man! I'm tell-

Figure 4   Aerial view of the coastline of the Turnagain Heights area after the 1964 Alaska earthquake. Approximately 2.5 kilometers of the bluffs slid toward the ocean after liquefaction of the sand and silt in the clay formations. [Courtesy of G. Housner.]

ing you, this house was shaking like a leaf! The picture frames—all the doors were opened—the dishes were falling out of the cabinets—and it's still swaying back and forth—I've got to go through and make a check to make sure that none of the water lines are ruptured or anything. Man, I hope I don't live through one of those things again. . . .

Building damage in southern Alaska from the 1964 earthquake varied considerably, depending on the foundation conditions and the type of structure. In Anchorage, higher buildings suffered most, whereas frame homes were reasonably unscathed, although their occupants were disturbed and furniture was thrown down. Because of the distance from the rupturing fault, ground shaking consisted mainly of long waves that do not affect small buildings (see the description of the Mexico earthquake in Chapter 12).

In all, Alaska sustained 300 million dollars in property damage from the earthquake; about 130 persons died, only 9 from the effects of shaking. One serious secondary result of the shaking was the temporary change of soil and sand in many areas from a solid to a liquid state. The most spectacular example of such *liquefaction* was at Turnagain Heights in Anchorage, where soft clay bluffs about 22 meters high collapsed during the strong ground motion, carrying away many modern frame homes in a slide that regressed inland 300 meters along 2800 meters of coastline (see Figure 4). Throughout southern Alaska, rock slides, land slides, and snow avalanches were common, damaging roads, bridges, railroad tracks, power facilities, and harbor and dock structures.

The Great 1985 Chile Earthquake

During the last 130 years, Chile has experienced 25 major damaging earthquakes, some of which are listed in Appendix C. At 7:47 P.M., March 3, 1985, another in this tragic series occurred. There were 176 persons killed, 2483 injured, and 372,532 homeless. The relatively light casualties were partly due to the timing: it was a summer Sunday evening when commercial buildings were closed and many people were outdoors. The epicenter was located off the coast, west of the capital city of Santiago (see Figure 5). The source of the earthquake was a sudden slip along the subduction zone that dips from the ocean trench along the Chilean coast under the country toward the Andes Mountains. (This thrust uplifted the coastline a few tens of centimeters, producing a small ocean wave.)

The earthquake shook the most densely populated region of the country, and it was felt as far away as Buenos Aires, Argentina. Because of close acquaintance with several Chilean seismologists and engineers, I spent several days immediately following the disaster examining the seismic effects. The intensity of the seismic effects varied widely. Surprisingly, most of the modern reinforced structures were not seriously damaged. In Santiago (population of 2.5 million), there was only slight damage except to unreinforced masonry buildings, particularly in the old part of the city. Several serious fires broke out but did not spread.

In the modern cities of Valparaíso and Viña del Mar on the coast, near the northern portion of the energy-release zone (see Figure 5), the intensity was about the same as or a little greater than in Santiago. Generally, reinforced-concrete high-rise buildings and other specially designed structures suffered little or no damage, and heavy damage to ordinary structures was not widespread. However, throughout these coastal cities, examples could be found of adobe and panel walls thrown out of frame structures, slipping of tiles on roofs, and cracking of chimneys, columns, and walls. In high-rise buildings, brick or plaster partition walls were often seriously cracked and furniture tossed around.

South of Valparaíso toward the old port city of San Antonio through Algarrobo, another coastal town, little general damage was observed even though the locations were closer to the epicenter than Valparaíso. These observations reinforced the idea that the location of the epicenter is not of great importance when considering the release of energy from an extended seismic source, such as the slipped section of the subduction slab in this case.

In San Antonio, many unreinforced structures collapsed because of foundation-soil movement and landslides. Examples of sand liquefaction could be seen along the harbor margins and in low-lying areas of San Antonio.

Damage to schools was widespread (in contrast, say, with the success of the Field Act in fostering safer schools in California; see Chapter 12.) Although over 20 hospitals and clinics of the 80 in the most affected area were damaged, the health care system treated over 1600 injuries attributed to the earthquake. However, several hospitals were forced to relocate services after the earthquake. The lesson is that essential facilities must remain operational.

Generally, although in many places the intensity of shaking was very high and of long duration, most modern buildings were able to withstand the vibrations. This favorable result was partly due to building codes based on experience with past earthquakes in Chile. Of special note was the successful retrofitting of a church damaged in an earlier earthquake (see page 106).

The Chilean earthquake is of lasting importance in the history of earthquake science: not only were there visual observations of the effect of the shaking on structures of various designs, but also many instruments recorded the shaking of the ground (see Chapter 6 for a description of such

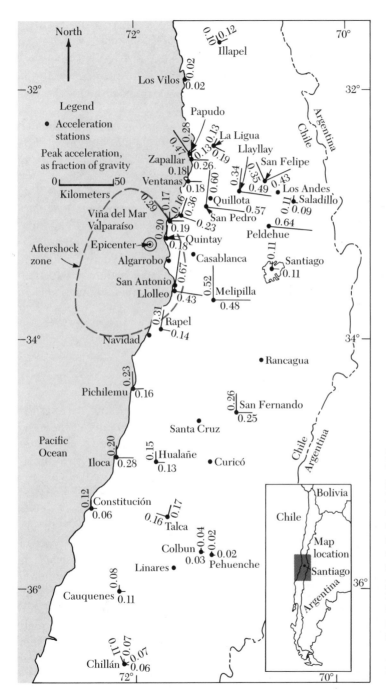

Figure 5
The epicenter of the initial event of the March 3, 1985, Chile earthquake (University of Chile) and the aftershock zone during the first 10 days of the sequence. The recorded peak accelerations (as fractions of gravity) of the two horizontal components of ground motion are also shown. [Courtesy of R. Saragoni and M. Pardo.]

instruments). Before the earthquake, a modern network of stations with sensitive seismographs had recorded many foreshocks. These records and those obtained with portable seismographs provided detailed locations of thousands of aftershocks and enabled seismologists to precisely map the extent of the seismic source of the principal earthquake along the subduction slab.

In addition, instruments responsive only to strong motion provided about 30 clear recordings of the ground shaking. Some ground shaking lasted 40 seconds or more, indicating that the waves were produced from an extended zone of slip along the slab, rather than from a single spot. Some features of the earthquake were puzzling. At Valparaíso and Viña del Mar, along the coast, there were relatively small ground motions compared to the south and the east. For example, the intensity of the ground motion over 700 kilometers to the northeast of Valparaíso was three times its value near the coast. Subsequent studies of these recorded motions will be useful in anticipating strong ground motions from shallow subduction-zone earthquakes along the Peru-Chile trench and other subduction zone regions such as Alaska and Japan.

Types of Seismic Waves in Earthquake Shaking

A hand clap in the air sends sound waves outward to distant places as the air compresses and rarifies; the mechanical energy originally in the moving hands is transformed into air vibrations. A stone thrown into water sends waves spreading across its surface in the form of ripples. In a similar way, a sudden blow to gelatin and other elastic materials produces a quivering as waves spread from the impulse throughout the elastic body. So too, the rocks of the Earth have elastic properties that cause them to deform and vibrate when pushed and pulled by forces applied to them.

Earthquake shaking and damage is the result of three basic types of elastic waves. Two of the three propagate *within* a body of rock. The faster of these *body waves* is called the *primary* or P *wave*. Its motion is the same as that of a sound wave in that, as it spreads out, it alternately pushes (compresses) and pulls (dilates) the rock (see Figure 6a). These P waves, just like sound waves, are able to travel through both solid rock, such as granite mountains, and liquid material, such as volcanic magma or the water of the oceans. It is worth mentioning also that, because of their soundlike nature, when P waves emerge at the surface from deep in the Earth, a fraction of them may be transmitted into the atmosphere as sound waves, audible to animals and humans at certain frequencies.°

_____

°Greater than about 15 cycles per second.

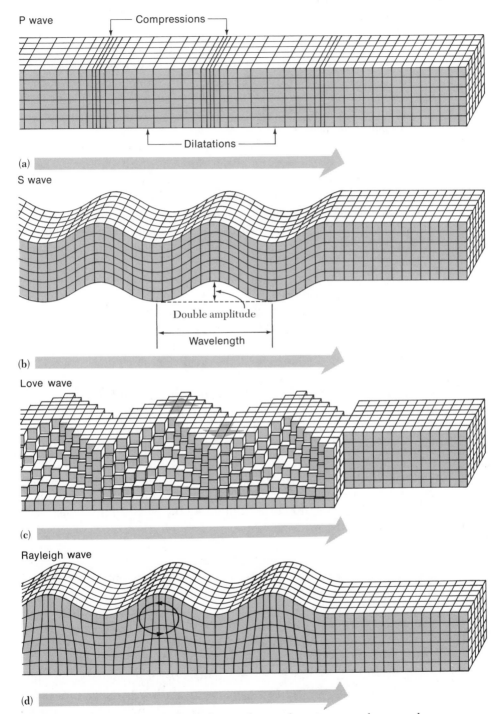

Figure 6 Diagram illustrating the forms of ground motion near the ground surface in four types of earthquake waves. [From Bruce A. Bolt, *Nuclear Explosions and Earthquakes: The Parted Veil* (San Francisco: W. H. Freeman and Company. Copyright © 1976).]

The slower wave through the body of rock is called the *secondary* or S *wave*. As an S wave propagates, it *shears* the rock sideways at right angles to the direction of travel (see Figure 6b). Observation readily confirms that if a liquid is sheared sideways or twisted, it will not spring back. It thus follows that S waves cannot propagate in the liquid parts of the Earth, such as the oceans.

The actual speed of P and S seismic waves depends on the density and elastic properties of the rocks and soil through which they pass. (Some typical velocity values and a list of physical relations are given in the box on page 31.) In most earthquakes, the P waves are felt first. The effect is similar to a sonic boom that bumps and rattles windows. Some seconds later, the S waves arrive with their up-and-down and side-to-side motion, shaking the ground surface vertically and horizontally. This is the wave motion that is so damaging to structures.

The third general type of earthquake wave is called a *surface wave*, because its motion is restricted to near the ground surface. Such waves correspond to ripples of water that travel across a lake. Most of the wave motion is located at the outside surface itself, and as the depth below this surface increases, wave displacements decrease.

Surface waves in earthquakes can be divided into two types. The first is called a *Love wave*. Its motion is essentially the same as that of S waves that have no vertical displacement; it moves the ground from side to side in a horizontal plane but at right angles to the direction of propagation (see Figure 6c). The horizontal shaking of Love waves is particularly damaging to the foundations of structures. The second type of surface wave is known as a *Rayleigh wave*. Like rolling ocean waves, the pieces of material disturbed by a Rayleigh wave move both vertically and horizontally in a vertical plane pointed in the direction in which the waves are traveling. The arrows in Figure 6d illustrate the elliptical movement of a piece of rock as the wave passes.

Surface waves travel more slowly than body waves; and of the two surface waves, Love waves generally travel faster than Rayleigh waves (see the box on page 31). Thus, as the waves radiate outward from the earthquake source into the rocks of the Earth's crust, the different types of waves separate out from one another in a predictable pattern. (An illustration of the pattern occurring at a distant place is shown in Appendix H. In this example the seismograph recorded only the vertical motion of the ground, and so the seismogram contains only P, S, and Rayleigh waves, because Love waves do not possess vertical motion.) Rayleigh waves, because of the vertical component of their motion, can affect bodies of water such as lakes, whereas Love waves (which do not propagate through water) can affect surface water only insofar as the sides of

Propagation of Elastic Waves

The elasticity of a homogeneous, isotropic solid can be defined by two constants, k and μ.

k is the modulus of incompressibility, or bulk modulus

for granite, k is about 27×10^{10} dynes per square centimeter;
for water, k is about 2.0×10^{10} dynes per square centimeter.

μ is the modulus of rigidity

for granite, μ is about 1.6×10^{11} dynes per square centimeter;
for water, $\mu = 0$.

Within the body of an elastic solid with density ρ, two elastic waves can propagate:

P waves   Velocity $\alpha = \sqrt{\left(k + \dfrac{4}{3}\mu\right)/\rho}$

for granite, $\alpha = 5.5$ kilometers per second;
for water, $\alpha = 1.5$ kilometers per second.

S waves   Velocity $\beta = \sqrt{\mu/\rho}$

for granite, $\beta = 3.0$ kilometers per second;
for water, $\beta = 0$ kilometers per second.

Along the free surface of an elastic solid, two surface elastic waves can propagate:

Rayleigh waves   Velocity $c_R < 0.92\beta$

where β is the S-wave velocity in the rock.

Love waves (for a layered solid)   Velocity $\beta_1 < c_L < \beta_2$

where β_1 and β_2 are S-wave velocities in the surface and deeper layers, respectively.

The dimensions of a harmonic wave are measured in terms of period T and wavelength λ.

Wave velocity $v = \lambda/T$.
Wave frequency $f = 1/T$.

lakes and ocean bays move backward and forward, pushing the water sideways like the sides of a vibrating tank.

The body waves (the P and S waves) have another characteristic that affects shaking: when they move through the layers of rock in the crust, they are reflected or refracted at the interfaces between rock types, as illustrated in Figure 7a. Also, whenever either one is reflected or refracted, some of the energy of one type is converted to waves of the other type (see Figure 7b). To take a common example, as a P wave travels upward and strikes the bottom of a layer of alluvium, part of its energy will pass upward through the alluvium as a P wave and part will pass upward as the converted S-wave motion. (Part of the energy will also be reflected back downward as P and S waves.)

Thus, after the first few shakes on land, a combination of the two kinds of waves is usually felt in strong ground shaking. But if you are at sea during an earthquake, the only motion felt on ship is from the P waves, because the S waves cannot travel through the water beneath the vessel. A similar effect occurs as sand layers liquefy in earthquake shaking. There is a progressive decrease in the amount of S-wave energy that is able to propagate in the liquefied layers, and ultimately only P waves can pass through.

When P and S waves reach the surface of the ground, most of their energy is reflected back into the crust, so that the surface is affected almost simultaneously by upward- and downward-moving waves. For this reason, considerable amplification of shaking typically occurs near the surface—sometimes double the amplitude of the upcoming waves. This surface amplification enhances the shaking damage produced at the surface of the Earth. Indeed, in many earthquakes, mineworkers below ground report less shaking than people on the surface.

The above description, however, does not adequately explain the heavy shaking near the center of a large earthquake. Near a fault that is suddenly rupturing, like the San Andreas in 1906, the strong ground shaking in the associated earthquake consists of various kinds of seismic waves that are not distinctly separate. To complicate the matter, because the source of radiating seismic energy is itself spread out across an area, the types of ground motion may be further muddled together. (In Chapters 4, 7, and 8, instrumental records of strong ground motion obtained near the source of an earthquake are analyzed to try to unravel these complicated motions.)

A final point about seismic waves is worth noting. There is considerable evidence, observational and theoretical, that earthquake waves are affected by both soil conditions and topography. For example, in weathered surface rocks, in alluvium and in water-saturated soil, the size of seismic waves may be either increased or decreased as they pass to the surface

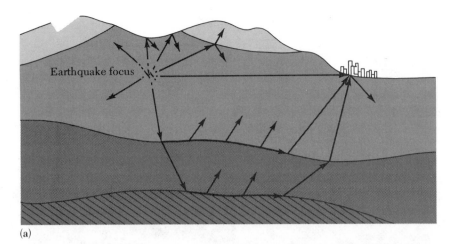

(a)

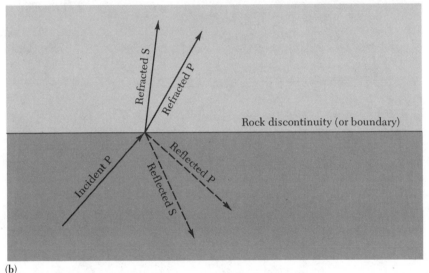

(b)

Figure 7 (a) A simplified picture of the paths of seismic P or S waves being reflected and refracted in rock structures of the Earth's crust. (b) The reflection and refraction of a longitudinal (P) wave in an earthquake after it hits a boundary between two types of rock. [From Bruce A. Bolt, *Nuclear Explosions and Earthquakes: The Parted Veil* (San Francisco: W. H. Freeman and Company. Copyright © 1976).]

from the more rigid basement rock (see Chapter 12). This means that— although the details of these wave effects are complex and there are limits on the amplification of strong ground motion—it is still prudent to build on rock, not on sand; at least foundation conditions are then more stable. Also at the top or bottom of a ridge, shaking may intensify, depending on the direction from which the waves are coming and whether the wavelengths are long or short.

San Andreas fault gash cutting across the Carrizo Plains in California. [Courtesy of Robert E. Wallace, USGS.]

*The Mount of Olives shall cleave in the midst thereof toward the
east and toward the west, and there shall be a very great valley;
and half of the mountain shall remove toward the north and half
of it toward the south.*

—ZECHARIAH 14:4

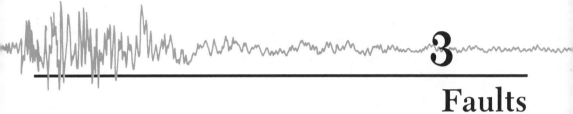

3

Faults
in the Earth

How to Recognize a Geological Fault

Most people—even in casual examination of rock quarries, road cuttings
and sea cliffs—have observed abrupt changes in structure of the rocks. In
some places one type of rock can be seen butting up against rock of quite
another type along a narrow line of contact. In other places, displacements in strata of the same rock have clearly taken place, either vertically
or horizontally. Such offsets of geological structure are called *faults*. Clear
vertical offsets of layers of rock along an exposed fault in the wall of the
Corinth Canal, Greece, can be seen in Figure 1.

Faults may range in length from a few meters to many kilometers. In
the field, geologists commonly find many discontinuities in rock structures which they interpret as faults, and these are drawn on a geological
map as continuous or broken lines. The presence of such faults indicates
that, at some time in the past, movement took place along them. We now
know that such movement can be either slow slip, which produces no

Figure 1   Normal fault that has displaced the almost horizontal beds in young sedimentary rocks on the north side of the Corinth Canal, Greece. Height of the exposure is about 70 meters, and the total offset along the fault amounts to more than 10 meters. [Courtesy of L. Weiss.] Major earthquakes, often with tsunamis, occurred in the Corinth region in 227 B.C., 551 A.D., and 1858, 1928, and on February 24, 1981. In the most recent earthquake, surface fault rupture was observed for a length of about 5 kilometers with vertical slip of up to 0.7 meters.

ground shaking, or sudden rupture, which results in perceptible vibrations—an earthquake. In the preceding chapter we discussed one of the
most famous examples of sudden fault rupture—the San Andreas fault in
April 1906. However, the observed surface faulting of most shallow-focus
earthquakes is much shorter in length and shows much less offset. In fact,
in the majority of earthquakes, fault rupture does not reach the surface
and is thus not directly visible.

The faults seen at the surface sometimes extend to considerable depths
in the outermost shell of the Earth, called the *crust*. This rocky skin, from
5 to 70 kilometers thick (see Chapter 8), forms the outer part of the
lithosphere.

It must be emphasized that slip no longer occurs at most faults plotted
on geological maps.° The last displacement to occur along a typical fault
may have taken place tens of thousands or even millions of years ago. The
local disruptive forces in the Earth nearby may have subsided long ago,
and chemical processes involving water movement may have cemented
the ruptures, particularly at depth. Such an *inactive fault* is not now the
site of earthquakes and may never be again.

Our primary interest is of course in *active faults*, along which crustal
displacements can be expected to occur. Many of these faults are in rather
well-defined tectonically active regions of the Earth, such as the midoceanic ridges and young mountain ranges. However, sudden fault displacements can also occur away from regions of clear present tectonic
activity (see the footnote).

It is possible to determine, by geological detective work, a number of
properties of faults. For example, intermittent fault slip that has occurred
in the past few thousand years usually leaves such clues in the topography
as sag ponds, lines of springs, and fresh fault scarps. Many topographic
clues to the San Andreas fault zone can be seen in Figure 1 of Chapter 2.
But pinpointing the sequence and times of such displacements may be
much more difficult. Such features as offsets of overlying soils and recent
sedimentary deposits may provide this kind of chronological information.
The digging of trenches a few meters deep across faults has also proved an
effective means of studying displacements. Even subtle offsets in layers in
the sides of the trenches can be mapped and the time intervals between
fault offsets determined by fixing the ages of the various soil layers that
have been displaced (see Figure 2 and Chapter 10). Sometimes the actual
dates of movement can also be estimated from the known ages of buried

---

°But sometimes faults not plotted on geological maps are discovered from fresh ground
breakage during an earthquake. Thus, a fault was delineated by a line of cracks in open
fields south of Oroville after the Oroville earthquake of August 1, 1975 (see Chapter 9).

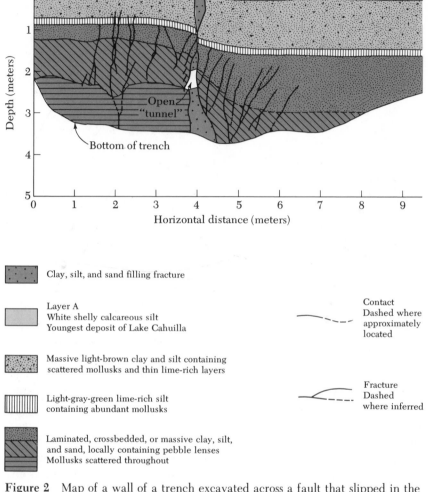

Figure 2   Map of a wall of a trench excavated across a fault that slipped in the 1968 Borrego Mountain earthquake in California. Each time a fracture occurs, there is more displacement between once continuous soil layers. [After M. M. Clark, H. Grantz, and M. Robin, USGS Professional Paper 787, 1972.]

organic material, such as leaves and twigs. Even along the seafloor, modern geophysical methods allow fairly accurate mapping of faults. From research vessels at sea it is possible to detect the passage of sound waves that have been reflected from the mud layers, and offsets in the layers indicated by these seismic records may be identified as faults.

Whether on land or beneath the oceans, fault displacements can be classified into three types (Figure 3). The plane of the fault cuts the horizontal surface of the ground along a line whose direction from the north is called the *strike* of the fault. The fault plane itself is usually not vertical but dips at an angle down into the Earth. When the rock on that side of the fault hanging over the fracture slips downward, below the other side, we have a *normal* fault. The dip of a normal fault may vary from 0 to 90°. When, however, the hanging wall of the fault moves upward in relation to the bottom or footwall, the fault is called a *reverse* fault. A special type of reverse fault is a *thrust* fault in which the dip of the fault is small. The faulting in oceanic ridge earthquakes is predominantly normal, whereas subduction zones are the sites of many thrust-type earthquakes.

Both normal and reverse faults produce vertical displacements—seen at the surface as fault scarps—called *dip-slip* faults. By contrast, faulting that causes only horizontal displacements along the strike of the fault are called transcurrent, or *strike-slip*. It is useful to have a simple term that tells the direction of slip. In Figure 3, for example, the arrows on the

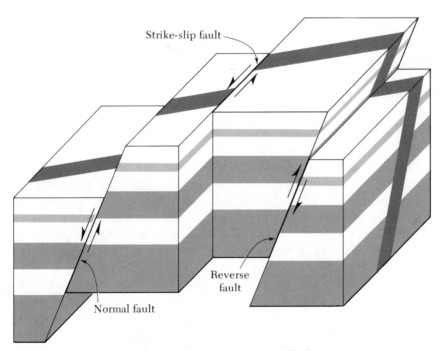

Strike-slip fault

Normal fault

Reverse fault

Figure 3   Diagram showing the three main types of fault motion.

strike-slip fault show a motion that is called left-lateral faulting. It is easy to determine if the horizontal faulting is left-lateral or right-lateral. Imagine that you are standing on one side of the fault and looking across it. If the offset of the other side is from right to left, the faulting is left-lateral, whereas if it is from left to right, the faulting is right-lateral. Of course, sometimes faulting can be a mixture of dip-slip and strike-slip motion.

In an earthquake, serious damage can arise, not only from the ground shaking but from the fault displacement itself, although this particular earthquake hazard is very limited in area. It can usually be avoided by the simple expedient of obtaining geological advice on the location of active faults before construction is undertaken. Areas astride active faults can often be set aside for open areas—for public recreation, golf courses, parking lots, roads, and so on.

In land-use planning, one also needs to know that damage adjacent to fault ruptures—caused by the sliding and slumping of the ground—varies according to the fault type. In dip-slip faulting the scarp produced may spread the damage (by local ground sliding, cracking, and slumping) over a relatively wide zone along the fault itself. But in strike-slip faulting, the zone of ground disturbance is usually much less extended, and buildings just a few meters away from the rupture may not be damaged by it.

The 1891 Mino-Owari Earthquake, Japan

The Mino-Owari earthquake of October 28, 1891, was the greatest inland earthquake experienced in the Japanese islands in recorded history. Tremendous devastation occurred throughout central Honshu, particularly in the provinces of Mino and Owari (see Chapter 10, Figure 1). The number of deaths was 7270, and more than 17,000 persons were injured. More than 142,000 houses collapsed altogether, and many others were damaged. Some 10,000 landslides are known to have occurred throughout the area. Extraordinary surface breaks appeared that could be clearly traced for about 80 kilometers across the countryside. They exhibited maximum horizontal offsets of 8 meters and vertical offsets of 2 to 3 meters in numerous places.

At the time it was widely believed that great shallow earthquakes were caused by underground explosions or magma movements. But Professor B. Koto of the University of Tokyo was so impressed by the extent of faulting in the Mino-Owari earthquake that he departed from established opinion to assert that sudden fault slip had been the cause—a revolutionary idea then.

Figure 4 Fault scarp near Niodami village, Honshu, Japan, as it appeared in August 1966. The faulting occurred in association with the Mino-Owari earthquake of October 28, 1891. Sliding and erosion have altered the original nature of the fault displacement, which was normal with the right (north) side up. [Photograph by Bruce A. Bolt.]

This earthquake has been restudied many times in an effort to assess confidently the likelihood of future earthquake occurrence in the heavily populated and generally highly seismic islands of Japan. The most recent evidence shows that the faulting was quite complicated, with left-lateral displacement on three major preexisting faults. The ruptures, however, were not visible at the surface over the entire length of each of them. Except in a few places, the fault dip was almost vertical, and a few minor fault breaks, shorter than a kilometer in length, occurred.

Among the minor breaks was the Midori fault near Niodami village (see Figure 4), which had a spectacular fault scarp more than 400 meters long with a vertical displacement of 6 meters (northeast side up) and a left-lateral horizontal displacement of 4 meters.° The direction of the ver-

---

°In 1967 I visited Niodami and rephotographed the fault scarp, now somewhat smoothed by weathering. More recently, railroad construction through the valley threatened to obliterate this famous seismological landmark.

tical motion at Midori, however, is somewhat exceptional because most vertical motion is in the opposite direction at other places along the fault rupture.

During the 14 months following the Mino-Owari earthquake, more than 3000 aftershocks were felt at Gifu, the capital of Mino province. Recent seismographic recordings have indicated that small earthquakes are still common along the 1891 fault breaks. The focal depths of the recent earthquakes are confined mainly to the top 15 kilometers of the crust, suggesting that perhaps the 1891 faulting extended only to this depth.

Japanese surveyors made some detailed geodetic measurements around the Mino-Owari fault zone in the years 1894 to 1898 and compared them with similar measurements that had been made prior to the earthquake. Along certain level lines, there had been a widespread crustal uplift of about 70 centimeters, whereas elsewhere in the source region there had been appreciable subsidence, of 30 to 40 centimeters. Such crustal movements indicate the large extent of deformation of crustal rocks that is associated with the production of great earthquakes.

The 1979 Imperial Valley Earthquake, California

Some earthquakes have been instantly elevated to special status because they provide hitherto unavailable measurements. The moderate-size earthquake that occurred at 4:16 P.M. on October 15, 1979, in the southern Imperial Valley of California was one such earthquake. It was produced by right-lateral slip on the northwest-trending Imperial fault (see Figure 5). Fault slip was seen at the surface for approximately 30 kilometers south of the town of Brawley, and possibly for 37 kilometers to the international border. No one was killed.

The unrivaled instrumental measurements of this earthquake near its source shed light on four important questions regarding, first, the repetition of earthquakes along the same fault system and its implications for earthquake prediction; second, the vexed question of sympathetic slip on adjacent faults in earthquake sequences; third, the variation of strong ground shaking as measured by specially arranged groups of seismographs (called "strong motion arrays"); and finally, the seismic resistance of structures built under modern seismic codes.

An almost twin earthquake occurred when the same fault ruptured 39 years earlier, on May 18, 1940. At that time, geologists realized that a

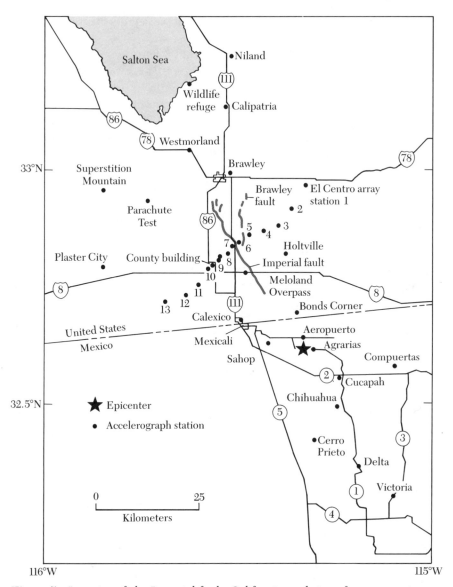

Figure 5 Location of the Imperial fault, California, and sites of strong-motion seismographs that provided measurements of the ground shaking.

previously unknown fault, designated the Imperial fault, had produced the earthquake through right-lateral strike-slip rupture. (This fault is actually a section of the San Andreas fault system; see Chapter 2, Figure 2.)

The fault slip was traced for at least 70 kilometers across the international boundary into northern Baja, Mexico.

There were both striking differences and similarities between the 1940 and the 1979 earthquakes. The fault offsets in 1940 were up to 5.8 meters horizontally and 1.2 meters vertically. The 1940 earthquake was also about the same size. Nine people were killed, and structural and agricultural losses amounted to 6 million dollars. In 1979, the maximum right-lateral fault displacement (see Figure 6) was only about 55 centimeters, and the maximum vertical displacement was measured at 19 centimeters, down to the east. After both the 1940 and the 1979 principal shocks, the locations of aftershocks shifted progressively northward along the Imperial fault, and each had damaging aftershocks near Brawley.

What are we to make of the repetition, after 39 years, of a similar-size earthquake caused by rupture of the same fault? It is not what might be expected from a simple application of the seismic gap theory (see Chapter 1). According to the gap theory, because the 1940 earthquake would have relieved most of the strain on the Imperial fault from Brawley to south of the Mexican border, the next earthquake of comparable size might have been expected to occur either from fault rupture north or south of this section of the San Andreas fault system. Evidently the strain energy that persisted in the rocks, together with an additional amount built up over the ensuing years, was sufficient for the fault to rupture again. The episode indicates the difficulties and hazards of earthquake forecasting.

What is the likelihood of several faults rupturing in great earthquakes? In this case, fault rupture was also observed following the October 15, 1979, earthquake along the Brawley fault which bifurcates from the main Imperial Valley fault. Measurements on this subsidiary fault indicated maximum slip of 15 centimeters dip-slip down to the west and at least 3 centimeters of right-lateral slip. As well, other smaller branch faults were recognized for the first time by geologists following the 1979 event. It is unfortunate that we cannot be certain that slip along the Brawley and other subsidiary faults occurred simultaneously with the main rupture on the Imperial fault. Nevertheless, the evidence is that slip must have taken place within a few hours, and sympathetic rupture at the time of the main rupture is not ruled out.

Regarding the question of variation of shaking, many strong-motion seismographs recorded the strong ground vibrations during the 1979 mainshock (Figure 5), making a valuable contribution to earthquake engineering and seismology. Of particular interest are the records from stations at the southern end (Bond's Corner) and the northern end of the fault (Brawley). The timing of the wave onsets indicated that the rupture

Figure 6 Photograph of the Imperial fault trace crossing a field in the 1979 earthquake. Motion is right-lateral strike-slip. [Photograph by Bruce A. Bolt.]

began toward the southern end of the fault section and then progressed northward. In addition, there was a unique set of ground motions measured by an array of strong-motion instruments set out in a line at right angles to the fault through the town of El Centro. In the 1940 earthquake a seismograph in El Centro recorded a maximum horizontal acceleration of the ground shaking of about one-third that of gravity. For many years, it was the only record available for engineering purposes that showed clearly the ground shaking in a large earthquake near the source of the waves. For this reason "the El Centro record" became a centerpiece for earthquake-resistant design in many countries around the world. In the 1979 earthquake, the same instrument at El Centro recorded the new motion, and key comparisons could be made.

The other 12 stations of the linear array clearly indicated the attenuation of shaking with distance away from the fault rupture and also the differences between stations depending on the soil condition and other factors. Ground motions recorded over 10 kilometers from the Imperial fault resembled those obtained from other earthquakes of the same magnitude. Near the fault, however, the ground motion showed some rather unusual features, including high-frequency vertical ground accelerations about 1 kilometer from the fault as much as 1.7 times the acceleration of gravity. Overall, the vertical ground shaking was stronger than the horizontal shaking by a factor greater than expected from earlier earthquakes in California. It is believed that this was due to the effect that the soil and alluvial rock layers in the Imperial Valley had on the seismic waves.

Finally, the distribution of types of damage is of interest. The cost of damage was estimated to be 30 million dollars, and it was most evident in residential areas of Southern Imperial County and across the Mexican border. In Mexico, notable damage occurred to mobile homes. This is a serious effect also in areas like California, where this type of housing has become common. Householders typically remove the wheels from the structure and support it on unstable concrete blocks. The remedies are to keep the wheels on or to tie the homes down securely.

The most notable damage, however, occurred to the relatively new Imperial County Services Building in El Centro. The east portion of this six-story reinforced concrete structure partially collapsed. Fortunately, no one suffered serious injury. In response to the 1940 earthquake, a system of strong-motion accelerometers had been placed at various levels within the services building. The system functioned properly during the 1979 shaking, thus providing the first multipoint recordings of structural vibrations in a building extensively damaged by an earthquake in California. These measurements even showed, at a particular stage in the shaking, a sudden lurch, which was interpreted as the main failure of the structural columns of the building. The building was subsequently demolished.

Fault Rupture in Guatemala

In the early morning (about 3:02 A.M.) on February 4, 1976, a great earthquake struck the Central American republic of Guatemala, causing more than 22,000 deaths, 70,000 injuries, and widespread devastation. The main source of the seismic waves was a massive rupture of the long Motagua fault (see Figure 7), which is the boundary between the Caribbean and North American plates. The focus of the earthquake was located, from seismic waves recorded on seismographs, toward the eastern end of the ruptured fault at a shallow depth of about 10 kilometers under the Earth's surface.

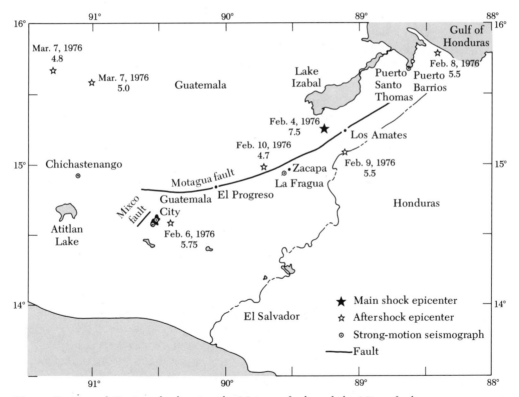

Figure 7 Map of Guatemala showing the Motagua fault and the Mixco fault, both of which ruptured in the 1976 earthquake sequence. The numbers at each epicenter indicate the magnitude of the shock. The epicenter of the main shock is plotted as a full star. [Courtesy of C. F. Knudson, USGS.]

Ground breakage was seen for a distance of about 250 kilometers. The offset was left-lateral with an average slip of 1 meter, but a maximum slip of $3\frac{1}{4}$ meters was measured 25 kilometers north of Guatemala City, along the portion west of El Progreso. The rupture ran roughly east-west from a point about 25 kilometers north of Guatemala City, eastward as far as the Gulf of Honduras, south of Puerto Barrios. Ground rupture along the Motagua fault generally appeared as a series of parallel cracks connected by mounds of soil or "mole tracks" that are characteristic of strike-slip faulting. The crack zone typically varied in width from 1 to 3 meters, but sometimes it was as wide as 9 meters. The fault rupture offset roads, fence lines, and railroad tracks.

Just 5 kilometers to the west of Guatemala City, fresh ground breakage was also found some days after the main earthquake[*] along the short Mixco fault, which trends to the north. It is not known whether this faulting also produced seismic waves or not. Surface displacements were quite different from those along the Motagua fault. Vertical slip was conspicuous at several road crossings, curbs, and house foundations. Maximum slip was 10 to 16 centimeters of downward vertical displacement on the east side and about 4 centimeters of right-lateral offset. Examining the positions of the Motagua and Mixco faults in Figure 7, it is possible to speculate that extensional motion of the rocks on the south of the Motagua fault might have caused the crust to drop down along the Mixco fault; in fact, dropped block structures, called *grabens*, are found in the vicinity of Guatemala City.

Why was the Guatemala earthquake such a tragic one? Undoubtedly the weak adobe construction and the timing of the earthquake were responsible for so much death, injury, and suffering. Families were in bed and, particularly in the towns of the Motagua River Valley and to the west of Guatemala City, adobe-mud brick walls—unable to withstand even small amounts of horizontal motion—cracked and broke, so that wood beams and tile roofs collapsed onto the sleeping occupants. The most common injuries were broken backs and smashed pelvises. Collapse of houses occurred over an area of about 9000 square kilometers, from the vicinity of the faulting to south of Guatemala City, leaving over a million people homeless. Bajareque (mud plaster over wood and lath frames) and wood construction withstood the shaking better than adobe. Nevertheless, within a few weeks, inhabitants of the outlying villages were breaking up the fallen adobe bricks, releveling their lots, and erecting new adobe walls for new houses before the May rains.

---

[*]The magnitude (see Chapter 7) of the earthquake was great, between 7.5 and 8.

The region has long been known to be a seismic one. Historical accounts say that the original capital, Antigua (slightly damaged in this earthquake), was destroyed by earthquakes in 1586, 1717, 1773, and 1874. Before 1976, Guatemala City had experienced intense shaking, and about 40 percent of its houses had been destroyed on December 25, 1917. Yet even in 1976, no building code requiring earthquake-resistant design had been enacted.

Although no complete instrumental record of the seismic waves in the heavily shaken area was obtained, we can learn much that is useful for other places from the intensity of ground shaking in the Guatemala earthquake. In particular, the length of the Motagua fault rupture and the amount of horizontal fault displacement are comparable to those of the 1906 rupture on the San Andreas fault. In the 1906 earthquake, the main damage to structures was also generally restricted to places on weak soil within 20 kilometers of the San Andreas fault.

Guatemala City is located on an elevated plain, approximately 1500 meters above sea level. Generally, the foundation soils remained intact because the water table is many meters below the ground level. But because the terrain is deeply cut by ravines (*barrancas*) and many of the more modern residences were built near to their edges, many foundations failed as a consequence of landsliding. Elsewhere in the city even poorly built brick buildings remained upright, though again the adobe dwellings did not fare well. The only two steel multistory buildings in the city showed no significant damage, and most reinforced concrete buildings survived. However, several large buildings—some of the hospitals, the cathedral, and a large hotel, for example—were severely damaged. There were no fires in the city.

Nearer the Motagua fault, resistance of structures to the shaking varied considerably. Overall, the picture of the effects produced by the seismic intensity of this earthquake agrees well with similar field observations made after the 1906 earthquake. In both earthquakes, timber-frame dwellings, even just adjacent to the fault from which the shaking radiated, suffered little damage. In the towns and cities generally, buildings constructed with care performed well in the seismic shaking. A lot of interior masonry, partition walls, and working equipment inside buildings were heavily damaged, however, leading to great economic loss. Large landslides were common along rivers, sometimes damming them. In the alluvial fans along lakeshores, such as those of Lake Atitlan, were spectacular examples of subsidence of the waterlogged sandy soil, with sand "boils" and lurching of the soil. These caused damage to hotels and other structures along the beaches.

Fault Slippage and Fault Gouge

The huge concrete-lined water tunnel carrying water from the Sierra Nevada, California, to the cities on the east of San Francisco Bay seems protected and durable as it passes through the Berkeley Hills. The Memorial Football Stadium at the University of California, Berkeley, seems indestructible in its reinforced concrete frame. The modern Cienega winery building along Cienega Road near Hollister in the beautiful coastal range of central California looks serenely permanent. Yet all these structures are unobtrusively and almost uneventfully being torn in two.

Earthquakes are not the cause. The tunnel and the stadium straddle the active Hayward fault (see Chapter 4, Figure 2), along which slow right-lateral slip is steadily occurring. When the water tunnel was emptied in 1966, cracks several centimeters across encircled the concrete lining just where the tunnel and fault zone intersect. Under the Memorial Stadium, a concrete drainage culvert now shows considerable cracking where it crosses the Hayward fault trace, and instruments that were placed across the cracks in 1966 show that the right-lateral slip inexorably continues about 2 to 5 millimeters a year.

The present Cienega winery near Hollister is, surprisingly, the third to be built on its site—one located squarely across the San Andreas fault trace. The fault trace is detectable from the slight change in elevation running parallel to Cienega Road on the western side, through the rows of grape vines (see Figure 8). Small springs abound along this trace, and in places the rows of grape vines are offset in a right-lateral sense. From the road the walls of the winery buildings can be seen to be bent by the slow slip occurring under the building. Just to the south an open concrete culvert has been broken and offset by the slip along the fault (see Figure 9).° Measurements of the alignments of the culvert and floor slabs, taken for a decade, yield a relative offset rate across the San Andreas fault at this point of 1.5 centimeters per year. Not far away, in the town of Hollister, the subsidiary Calaveras fault is slowly slipping, producing noticeable offsets and damage to curbs, sidewalks, fences, and even houses.

Horizontal fault slippage has now also been detected on other faults around the world, including the north Anatolian fault at Ismetpasa in Turkey and along the Jordan Valley rift in Israel. Usually, such episodes of fault slip are *aseismic*—that is, they are not accompanied by local earthquakes. When earthquakes do occur associated with the slipping faults, the rate of slip may increase for a short time after the earthquake.

°Here the visitor can stand astride the crack in the culvert and imagine one foot on the Pacific plate and one on the North American plate (see Chapter 1, Figure 4).

Typically, a slip displacement has an amplitude of a few millimeters, and the episodic slip lasts from a few minutes to a few days. Measurements in California indicate that after weeks of immobility, slip will commence and then progress along the fault for tens of kilometers at a speed of about 10 kilometers per day.

What is the nature of aseismic slip on faults? Let us look more closely at the types of rocks in a fault zone. Crushed and highly deformed rock occurs in the zone in a band many meters wide in some places. In the course of millions of years, intermittent yet frequent differential movement along the fault has broken and sheared the rock into fine granular and powdery forms. These have in turn been altered by percolating ground water to produce clays and sandy silts. The resultant material is "*fault gouge*." When a fault section is penetrated by a tunnel or trench,

Figure 8   Aerial photograph of the Cienega winery built across the San Andreas fault near Hollister, California. The fault (indicated by the horizontal arrows) can be seen extending from left to right, through the culvert on the left (south) side of the winery building and through the building itself. [Courtesy of D. Tocher.]

Culvert

Figure 9 Offset of the concrete drainage culvert by slow fault slip along the San Andreas fault at the Cienega winery. This amount of offset has taken place in the course of 20 years. [Courtesy of W. Marion.]

the gouge zone is often found to form a barrier that is fairly impervious to water; the water table sometimes stands at different levels on either side of the fault gouge, and this is why soaks and springs are found along faults.

Wet fault gouge feels like a soft deformable plastic and behaves more like a viscous solid than a brittle elastic one. It is thus hard to conceive that it would resist slip very strongly. The depth of the gouge zones varies considerably, but on major faults it may be several kilometers. Old faults exposed in deep mines sometimes exhibit gougelike material that must have once been at a depth of several kilometers below the Earth's surface.

Because active faults do suddenly slip to produce an earthquake, there must be, below the weaker surface materials, stronger and more elastic rocks that are in bonded contact across the fault planes. Only in this way will the slow straining of the rock store enough elastic energy to produce earthquakes. It is therefore reasonable to surmise that major fault zones, such as the San Andreas, consist of a sequence of rock layers; at the surface, weak, plastic gouge would extend down for several kilometers but progressively give way to stronger crystalline rock in welded contact across the fault surface, down to a depth of 15 or 20 kilometers. Below that depth the increased temperature in the Earth may again soften the rock so that elastic straining is not mechanically feasible. Some support for this model comes from the discovery in the early 1960s that, in central California, earthquakes do not occur at depths below about 15 kilometers. At these profound depths, the rock has perhaps become plastic again and is no longer capable of storing strain energy.

It is sometimes argued that a large damaging earthquake will not be generated along a fault that is undergoing slow fault slip, because the slippage allows the strain in the crustal rocks to be relieved periodically without sudden rupture. However, an alternative view is also plausible. It may be that, as the crystalline rocks of the deeper crust strain elastically and accumulate the energy to be released in a nearby earthquake, the weak gouge material at the top of the fault zone is carried along by the adjacent stronger rock to the side and underneath. This would mean that the slow slip in the gouge seen at the surface is merely an indication that strain is being stored in the basement rocks. The implication of this view is that, on portions of the fault where slippage occurs, an earthquake at depth could result from sudden rupture, but surface offset would be reduced. On the portion where slippage is small or nonexistent, offsets would be maximum. A prediction of this kind can be checked after earthquakes occur near places where slippage is known to be taking place.

Sometimes aseismic slip is observed at the ground surface along a ruptured fault that has produced a substantial earthquake. For example, along the San Andreas fault break in the 1966 earthquake on June 27 near Parkfield, California, offsets of road pavement increased by a few centimeters in the days following the main earthquake. Such continued adjustment of the crustal rock after the initial major offset is probably caused partly by the minor slips that produce aftershocks and partly by the yielding of the weaker surface rocks and gouge in the fault zone as they accommodate to the new tectonic pressures in the region.

It is clear that slow slippage, when it occurs in built-up areas, may have unfortunate consequences. This is another reason why certain types of structures should not be built across faults if at all possible. When utility lines, roads, and railroads must be laid across active faults, they should have jointed or flexible sections in the fault zone.

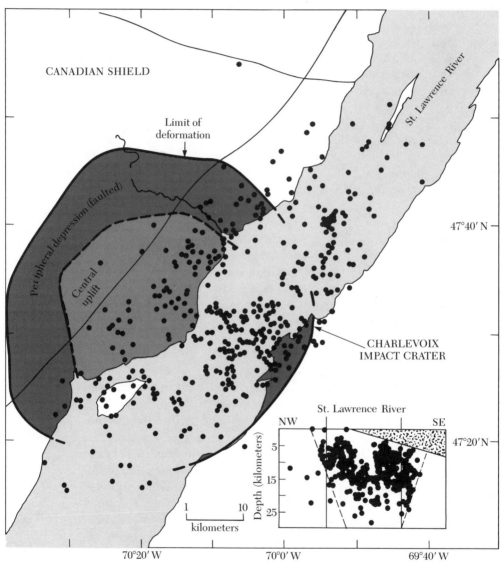

CANADIAN SHIELD

Limit of
deformation

Peripheral depression (faulted)

Central
uplift

St. Lawrence River

47°40′ N

CHARLEVOIX
IMPACT CRATER

St. Lawrence River

NW   SE

47°20′ N

5

Depth (kilometers)

15

25

1   10

kilometers

70°20′ W   70°0′ W   69°40′ W

Epicenters and foci (insert) of recent earthquakes plotted on a
map showing the site of the Charlevoix impact crater, along
the St. Lawrence River, Canada. The meteor, radius 1
kilometer, fell 360 million years ago. The energy of impact
reactivated (restrained) pre-existing faults. [Courtesy H. S.
Hasegawa, Geological Survey of Canada.]

It is probable that the whole movement at any place (along the rupturing fault) did not take place at once, but that it proceeded by very irregular steps.

—H. F. REID, *Report of the State Earthquake Investigation Commission* (The California Earthquake of April 18, 1906)

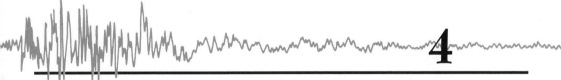

4

The Causes of Earthquakes

Types of Earthquakes

Not so long ago people generally believed that the causes of earthquakes would always remain hidden in obscurity, since they originated at depths far below the realm of human observation. For a long time the prevailing view was that earthquakes came as a punishment for human failings. "The Earthquake," a verse written in about 1750, summarizes this view:

> What pow'rful hand with force unknown,
> Can these repeated tremblings make?
> Or do the imprison'd vapours groan?
> Or do the shores with fabled Tridents shake?
> Ah no! the tread of impious feet,
> The conscious earth impatient bears;
> And shudd'ring with the guilty weight,
> One common grave for her bad race prepares.
> —Anon.

Today earthquakes and most of their observed properties are explained in terms of physical theory. This modern view holds that earthquakes are to be expected because of the constant geological reshaping of our planet. With this in mind, let us examine the current theory of earthquake genesis and the way in which it furthers our understanding of earthquakes and even helps us to predict them.

The first step toward grasping the modern view is the appreciation of the close relation between those parts of the world that are most earthquake prone (shown in Chapter 1, Figure 1) and the geologically new and active areas of the world (Chapter 1, Figure 4). Most earthquakes occur near plate margins; thus, geologists conclude that these global geologic, or tectonic, forces that produce mountains, rift valleys, midoceanic ridges, and ocean trenches are also the underlying causes of great earthquakes. These global forces, though not understood in detail at the present time, are consequences of temperature differences in the Earth—differences due to loss of heat by radiation into space and gain of heat from decay of radioactive elements in the rocks. Fresh faulting at the surface is also often associated with earthquakes (Chapter 3). The majority of the most widely damaging earthquakes—such as the 1906 San Francisco earthquake, the 1891 Mino-Owari earthquake in Japan, and the 1976 Guatemala earthquake—were produced by huge surface fault ruptures.

It is helpful to classify earthquakes by their mode of generation. By far the most common are *tectonic earthquakes*. These are produced when rocks break suddenly in response to the various geological forces. Tectonic earthquakes are scientifically important to the study of the Earth's interior and of tremendous social significance because they pose the greatest hazard. Consequently, in most of the book, we are concerned with this type of earthquake.

A second well-known type of earthquake accompanies volcanic eruptions. In fact, the idea that earthquakes are linked primarily to volcanic activity goes back to the Greek philosophers, who were impressed by the common occurrence of earthquakes and volcanoes in many parts of the Mediterranean. Today, a *volcanic earthquake* is still defined as one that occurs in conjunction with volcanic activity, but it is believed that eruptions and earthquakes both result from tectonic forces in the rocks and need not occur together. The actual mechanism of wave production in volcanic earthquakes is probably the same as that in tectonic earthquakes. (Volcanic earthquakes are discussed in more detail in the next chapter.)

Collapse earthquakes are small earthquakes occurring in regions of underground caverns and mines. The immediate cause of ground shaking is the collapse of the roof of the mine or cavern. An often-observed variation of this phenomenon is the so-called "mine burst." This happens when the induced stress around the mine workings causes large masses of

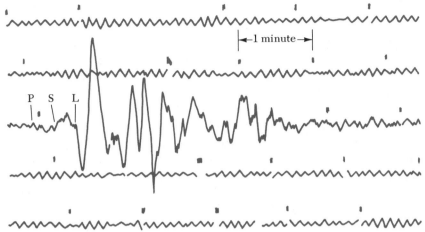

Figure 1 Seismogram showing east-west ground motion at Nana seismographic station, Peru, caused by the Rio Mantaro landslide, 240 kilometers away. The station reader has marked the arrival of the P, S, and surface (L) waves. Time increases from left to right on each trace.

rock to fly off the mine face explosively, producing seismic waves. Mine bursts have been observed in Canada, for example, and are especially common in South Africa.

Collapse earthquakes are also sometimes produced by massive landsliding. For example, a spectacular landslide on April 25, 1974, along the Mantaro River, Peru, produced seismic waves equivalent to a small-to-moderate earthquake.° The slide had a volume of 1.6×10^9 cubic meters and killed about 450 people. As far as we know, this landslide was not triggered by a nearby tectonic earthquake, as often happens. Part of the gravitational energy lost in the rapid downward movement of the soil and rock was converted to seismic waves, which were clearly recorded by seismographs hundreds of kilometers away. Duration of shaking measured on a seismograph 80 kilometers away was 3 minutes; this is compatible with the speed of the slide, which was about 140 kilometers per hour over the observed slippage of 7 kilometers. (Figure 1 shows a seismogram of this event from the Nana seismographic station in Peru.)

A similar collapse earthquake resulted from the greatest landslide to occur in recent history—at Usoy in the Pamir Mountains of Russia in 1911. Prince B. B. Galitzin, a founder of modern seismology, recorded earthquake waves on his seismographs near St. Petersburg (now Leningrad) that must have radiated from the landslide area. He compared the

---

° A Richter magnitude of 4.5 was recorded.

energy in the earthquake waves with that in the landslide and concluded that an earthquake may have triggered the landslide. More recent work—which makes Galitzin's conclusion doubtful—eventually led to techniques for calculating from seismograms the energy released in an earthquake. It was not until 1915 that an expedition, sent to investigate the Usoy landslide, found that the material involved was 2.5 cubic kilometers!

Humans cause *explosion earthquakes*, which are produced by the detonation of chemicals or nuclear devices. Underground nuclear explosions fired during the past several decades at a number of test sites around the world have produced substantial earthquakes. When a nuclear device is detonated in a borehole underground, enormous nuclear energy is released. In millionths of a second, the pressure jumps to thousands of times the pressure of the Earth's atmosphere and the temperature locally increases by millions of degrees. The surrounding rock is vaporized, creating a spherical cavity many meters in diameter. The cavity grows outward as boiling rock vaporizes from its surface, and the rock around it is minutely fractured by the shock of the explosion.

The compression of the rock in the fractured region (an area of perhaps hundreds of meters) produces seismic waves that travel outward in all directions. When the first compressive seismic wave reaches the surface, the ground arches upward, and if the wave energy is sufficient, it will blast the soil and rock away, throwing fragments of rock into the air and producing a crater. If the borehole is deeper, the surface may be only cracked and the rock will lift upward for an instant and then "slap down" on the underlying layers.

Some underground nuclear explosions have been large enough to send seismic waves throughout the Earth's interior; waves with amplitudes equivalent to moderate-size earthquakes have been recorded at distant seismographic stations. Some explosions have produced waves that have shaken buildings in distant cities. On April 26, 1968, a nuclear device called Boxcar was tested at the Nevada Nuclear Test Site.° Before the test, Las Vegas citizens—notably the multimillionaire resident and property owner, the late Howard Hughes—expressed misgivings that such an energetic device might cause structural damage and even deaths. Nevertheless the event took place, and people in the surrounding towns felt the shaking, which in Las Vegas, 50 kilometers away, lasted for 10 to 12 seconds. Fortunately, no significant damage resulted.

Of course, people and animals sometimes produce earthquakes (usually small) in other ways. An illustration in a lighter vein is given in the "Earthquake Quiz" at the end of the book.

°This explosion had an energy equivalent to that produced by 1200 thousand tons of TNT!

Slow Buildup of Energy

As centuries pass in earthquake country, deep-seated forces beneath our feet deform the rocks steadily and unobtrusively. What are the surface manifestations of this crustal warping? What is the evidence for the tectonic forces?

The most obvious manifestations are the great mountain ranges, produced by massive vertical uplift of the Earth's surface above sea level—a process that has taken millions of years. But even crustal movement that has taken place within much shorter periods can be easily detected by careful surveys. In many countries of the world, geodetic surveys now go back at least to the last century.

There are three major types of geodetic surveys. In two, the degree of horizontal movement is determined. In the first survey type, small telescopes are used to measure angles between markers on the ground surface; this is called *triangulation*. In the second, called *trilateration*, distance between markers on the surface is measured along extensive profiles. In a modern trilateration technique, light (sometimes a laser beam) is reflected from a mirror on a distant mountaintop, and the time it takes for the light to travel the two-way path is measured. Because the speed of light varies with atmospheric conditions, in precise surveys, small airplanes or helicopters fly along the lines of sight and measure the temperatures and pressures so that corrections can be made. These surveys are found to be precise to about 1.0 centimeter over a distance of 20 kilometers.

The third type of survey determines the degree of vertical movement by repeated measurements of the difference in level across the countryside. Such leveling surveys simply measure differences in the elevation between vertical wooden rods placed at fixed bench marks. Repetition of these surveys reveals any variations in these differences that occur between measurements. Wherever possible, national level lines are extended to the continental edge, so that the mean sea level can be used as the reference point.

All three survey methods of observing crustal movements show that, in tectonically active areas, such as California and Japan, the Earth's crust moves horizontally and vertically in quite measurable amounts. They also show that, in the stable areas of continents such as the ancient rock masses of the Canadian and Australian shields, little change has taken place, at least in the past century.

Geodetic measurements of crustal deformation in a seismically active region began as early as 1850 in California. In 1959, special observations along the San Andreas fault that could be useful in earthquake prediction were initiated as an offshoot of the study of crustal displacements that might affect the California aqueducts. Optical and laser-beam instruments called geodimeters are used to measure the distance between monuments on the tops of mountains on each side of the San Andreas fault system. Some results of these measurements—along five lines in central California from 1959 through 1970—are sketched in Figure 2. Trends in the strain are spectacularly clear. If we examine line 17 in Figure 2, which crosses the San Andreas fault near Gilroy, we will see a decrease in length at the rate of about 2 centimeters a year. This is in agreement with right-lateral deformation along the San Andreas fault. Survey lines, such as 21, which do not lie across the major faults, show very little change in length.

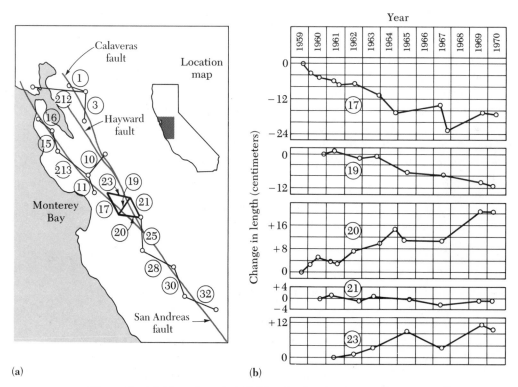

Figure 2 (a) Map of central California showing survey lines across the San Andreas fault system as established by the State Department of Water Resources and Division of Mines and Geology. The location of the entire area surveyed is shown in the location map at the right. (b) The temporal changes in lengths of lines 17, 19, 20, 21, and 23 are plotted. [After Bruce A. Bolt and F. Moffitt.]

The displacement occurring between the Pacific and North American plate along the San Andreas fault enables geologists to make a graphic—if long-range—forecast. The city of Los Angeles, which sits on the Pacific side of the San Andreas fault, is grinding northward relative to San Francisco at the rate of 5 centimeters or so per year. This means that in 30 million years it will become a new suburb of San Francisco; in yet another 30 million years Los Angeles will have moved an additional 600 kilometers northward to rainy northernmost California!

Geodetic studies conducted after the 1906 San Francisco earthquake led to our basic understanding of earthquake generation. Three sets of triangulation measurements that had been taken across the region traversed by the 1906 fault break along the San Andreas fault were compared by H. F. Reid (one set for 1851–1865, another for 1874–1892, and the third taken just after the earthquake). These indicated that significant horizontal displacements parallel to the ruptured San Andreas fault had occurred both before and after the earthquake. Reid noticed that distant points on opposite sides of the fault had moved 3.2 meters over the 50-year period prior to 1906, with the western side moving north.°

Elastic Rebound

The forces that produced the 1906 earthquake are drawn diagrammatically in Figure 3. Imagine this illustration to be a bird's-eye view of a road running at right angles across the San Andreas fault. A white line along the center of the road runs straight for many kilometers on each side of the fault. As the tectonic forces slowly work, the line bends, the left side shifting in relation to the right. The deformation amounts to a few meters in the course of 50 years or so. This straining cannot continue indefinitely; sooner or later the weakest rocks, or those at the point of greatest strain, break. This fracture is followed by a springing back, or rebounding, on each side of the fracture. Thus, in Figure 3 the rocks on both sides of the fault at D rebound to the points D_1 and D_2. Figure 4 shows the effect after the 1906 earthquake.

This *elastic rebound* was believed by Reid to be the immediate cause of earthquakes, and his explanation has been confirmed over the years. Like a watch spring that is wound tighter and tighter, the more that crustal rocks are elastically strained, the more energy they store. When a

---

°From his work, Reid made an approximate prediction of when the next great San Francisco earthquake could be expected. Earthquake prediction is discussed in Chapter 10.

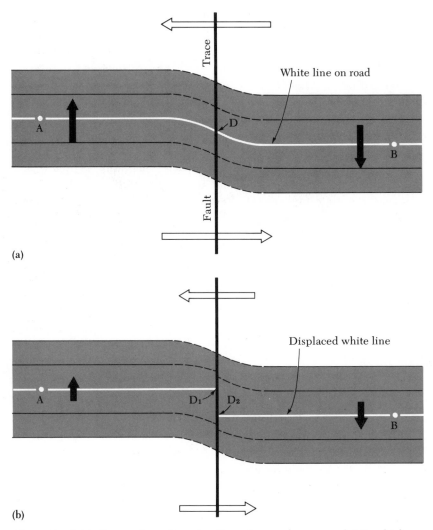

(a)

(b)

Figure 3   A bird's-eye view of marker lines drawn along a road AB, which crosses a fault trace at the ground surface. (a) In response to the action of tectonic forces, points A and B move in opposite directions, bending the lines across the fault. (b) Rupture occurs at D, and strained rocks on each side of the fault spring back to D_1 and D_2. [From Bruce A. Bolt, *Nuclear Explosions and Earthquakes: The Parted Veil* (San Francisco: W. H. Freeman and Company, Copyright © 1976).]

fault ruptures, the elastic energy stored in the rocks is released, partly as heat and partly as elastic waves. These waves are the earthquake.

   Straining of rocks in the vertical direction is also common. The elastic rebound occurs along dipping fault surfaces, causing vertical disruption in

Figure 4 Right-lateral horizontal movement of the San Andreas fault in the 1906 earthquake across the old Sir Francis Drake Highway north of San Francisco, at the southern end of Tomales Bay, California. The offset was 6.5 meters (20 feet). [Photo by G. K. Gilbert; courtesy of USGS.]

level lines at the surface and sometimes fault scarps (see Figure 5). Vertical ground movement—produced by earthquakes or other phenomena—can amount to tens of centimeters across wide areas.

In two Japanese earthquakes, such vertical movement was quite striking. In the catastrophic Kwanto earthquake of September 1, 1923—in which over 100,000 persons lost their lives (about 68,000 in fire-ravaged Tokyo)—extraordinary changes in water depths in Sagami Bay, south of Tokyo, occurred. In places the water depth changed by 250 meters. (It is not known how much of this change was due to submarine slides.) The Boso peninsula exhibited a number of fault ruptures and an uplift of up to 1.9 meters.

In the Niigata shock of June 16, 1964, vertical ground motion was also particularly noteworthy—not as the result of a *major* earthquake but as a precursor. Along the west coast of Honshu, bench marks were used to

Figure 5 A fault scarp in Ixl Canyon, Fairview Mountain, Nevada. [Courtesy of Karl V. Steinbrugge.]

measure the height of the land in relation to the mean sea level in 1898, 1930, 1955, 1958, 1961, and just prior to the earthquake in 1964. From 1898 to 1958, these measurements showed that the coast line of Honshu opposite Awashima Island was rising steadily at a rate of about 2 millimeters a year. The uplift then accelerated through 1961, after which little change occurred until 1964, when the level of the coastline suddenly dropped 15 to 20 centimeters at the time of the earthquake, near Awashima (see Chapter 10, Figure 2).

A controversial case of note, not yet (at the time of this writing) accompanied by a major earthquake, was reported from California in the 1970s. Since the end of the last century, leveling surveys seemed to indicate that discernible elevation changes had taken place in the mountainous regions to the north and east of Los Angeles. During the early 1960s, an extraordinary uplift (35 centimeters maximum) of an area of about 12,000 square kilometers was inferred near Palmdale, 70 kilometers north of Los Angeles.° The area of crustal swelling, sometimes called "The Palmdale Bulge," attracted much public and scientific attention as a possible precursor of an imminent major earthquake. Many related studies of old and new measurements were undertaken with an indication that the original elevation changes may have been overestimated.

°By 1977 further surveys hinted that a portion of the uplift had already subsided, and some analyses indicated that a significant part of the "uplift" could have been statistical error.

Changes in the Rocks

Almost everywhere, not many meters below the Earth's surface, the rocks are permeated by ground water. This water saturates the rocks and fills up the cracks and pores within them. Scientists have now examined what happens to saturated rock samples when, in the laboratory, they are squeezed to high pressures by powerful jacks (similar to those used for lifting automobiles). It has been found that, under some circumstances, wet rocks under shear strain *increase* their volume rather than decrease it. This increase in volume during deformation is called *dilatancy*. There is evidence that the volume increase from pressure arises from opening and extending the many microcracks in the rocks. The ground water that then moves into the microcracks is much less compressible than air, so the cracks no longer close easily under pressure.

Suppose that we could look into the crust of the Earth with a lens while it was being strained. What sequence of events would we see? First, the slow straining of the crust under the local tectonic forces produces many microcracks throughout the rock. As time passes, water diffuses into the cracks and fills them. During this period, the volume of the region dilates; this process might be detectable at the surface by an upward swelling of the ground, discernible by leveling or tide gauges. Particularly in fault zones, these changes to the rocks first weakens them; then the presence of water in the cracks reduces the restraining forces so that a major crack extends along the fault. In this way the elastic rebound of the strained crustal rocks begins and spreads.

As yet this sequence of events has never been directly observed before an earthquake, but there is at least circumstantial evidence that something like it occurs (see Chapter 10). In any event, some speculation on the processes that lead up to earthquakes is helpful when looking for plausible harbingers of earthquakes, such as rapid changes in ground level, ground tilting, and fluctuations of water levels in wells.

The cracks produced by crustal strain provide a reasonable explanation of both foreshocks and aftershocks. A foreshock is caused by an incipient rupture in the strained and cracked material along the fault that did not progress because the physical conditions were not yet ripe. Foreshocks, however, slightly alter the pattern of forces and, perhaps, the movement of water and the distribution of microcracks. Eventually, longer rupture commences, producing the principal earthquake. The flinging of the rocks along the major rupture, together with the heavy shaking produced and the local generation of heat, leads to a physical situation very different from that before the main shock; additional small ruptures occur, producing aftershocks. Gradually, the strain energy in the region decreases, like a clock running down, until, perhaps after many months, stable conditions return.

What Produces Seismic Waves?

Rupture has commenced; the ground begins to shake. The rupture begins at the earthquake focus within the crustal rocks and then spreads outward in all directions in the fault plane (see Figure 6). Notice that the edge of the rupture does not spread out uniformly. Its progress is jerky and irregular because crustal rocks vary in their physical properties from place to place, and the overburden pressure at a particular point in the crust decreases toward the surface. On the fault surface there are rough patches (often called *asperities*) and changes in fault direction and structural complexities that act as *barriers* to the fault slip. Thus the rupture front may come almost to a stop; then, because of the rearrangement of elastic forces, it may suddenly break free and swiftly move out to catch up with the rupture on either side of it. If this rupture reaches the surface (as happens in only a minority of shallow earthquakes), it produces a visible fault trace.

The extent of the fault rupture depends on the variation in strain of the rock throughout the region. The rupture continues until it reaches the places at which the rock is not sufficiently strained to permit it to extend further. Then the rupture episode stops.°

After rupturing stops, the adjacent sides of the fault spring back to a less strained position (Figure 3). During the rupture, the rough sides of the fault rub against one another so that some energy is used up by frictional forces and in the crushing of the rock. The surfaces are locally heated. Earthquake waves are generated at the same time by the rebounding of adjacent sides of the fault at the rupture surface as well as by the rubbing and crushing.

This whole process can be demonstrated in a school laboratory or in the kitchen. To do so, make a model of the elastic crust out of stiff jelly in a shallow mold. Pull the sides of the jelly in opposite directions and then make a small slit in the surface of the jelly. The rupture will spread throughout a plane in the jelly, and the two sides of the jelly will spring back until rupture ceases. While the rupture is tearing through the jelly, the jelly will quiver as elastic waves spread throughout it. Similarly, earthquake waves radiate out from numerous places on the fault plane.

Can this explanation of earthquake genesis be supported by the properties of seismic waves recorded on seismographs around the world? Yes,

---

° A scientific "first" was witnessed in conjunction with the Borah Peak, Idaho, earthquake of October 28, 1983. Two elk hunters, D. Hendriksen and J. Turner, saw a prominent fault scarp nearly 2 meters high form about 20 meters in front of their road vehicle. They described, first, dizziness (P waves from the distant focus?) and then, in 2 to 3 seconds, the more-or-less simultaneous perception of the new scarp and violent rocking.

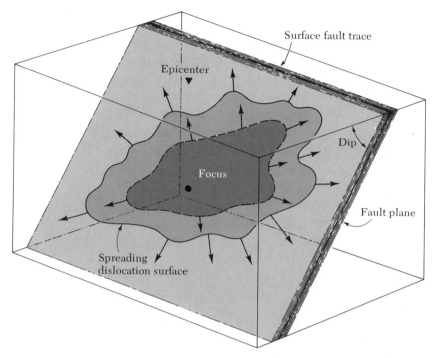

Figure 6 Side view into the Earth's crust showing rupture of the rocks spreading out from the focus of the earthquake along the dipping fault plane. Two stages of the rupture are shown. The arrows indicate the direction of the spreading rupture. (The epicenter is the point on the Earth's surface directly above the focus.) [From Bruce A. Bolt, *Nuclear Explosions and Earthquakes: The Parted Veil* (San Francisco: W. H. Freeman and Company, Copyright © 1976).]

and furthermore, the recorded waves give information on fault motions that may be completely below the surface of the Earth.

For simplicity, let us consider only the first seismic waves to arrive—that is, the P waves, which are simply pushes and pulls of the rocks in the Earth (see Chapter 2). It thus follows that a P wave will be detected at the surface as either a push or a pull.

Suppose, first, that the source of the recorded P waves is a small explosion at a point in the Earth some distance from the seismograph. Then the first P wave to be generated would, like the air blown into a balloon, push outward on a spherical surface. Seismographs would detect this P wave as a push upward from the ground. This upward movement is referred to as a *compression*.

If the P wave arises from rupture on a fault (such as in Figure 6), a quite different pattern of first P-wave motions must be expected. Now the first P motions, if plotted on a sphere, are not all compressions; nor will

Method of Obtaining Direction of Faulting from P-Wave Directions on Seismograms

In the upper diagram on page 69, F is the focus and E is the epicenter of an earthquake generated at some depth under the Earth's surface by the sudden (right-lateral) slip along a vertical fault plane (bFb'Z). Displacements due to the slip are shown as arrows. The large circle on the surface (A'B'AB) is a projection of the equator (a'b'ab) of a small sphere drawn around the focus. The projection is formed by drawing a cone from below Z through points on the equator.

Consider four paths of travel of P waves from the focus F to four stations on the ground surface S_1, S_2, S_3, and S_4. The arrows on these paths FS_1, FS_2, FS_3, and FS_4 show how the compressions (pushes) and dilatations (pulls) along the fault plane (bFb'Z) are transferred from depth to the surface by the first motion of the P wave.

The lower diagram is a plan view looking down on the circle A'B'AB. For this earthquake, a quadrantal pattern of compressions and dilatations would be observed at the surface. One of the lines A'EA' or BEB' that separate the different motions will indicate the strike and dip of the fault plane. (In this case, BEB' corresponds to the direction of the fault.)

they occur on a jumbled way. Rather, the P waves will be recorded in a simple pattern on the Earth's surface, depending on the direction in which they left the fault. Seismographs located at points from which the fault is moving away will record pulls or *dilatations* for the first P motion. Only those seismographs located at points toward which the fault is moving will record pushes or compressions. The resulting pattern will be four quadrants of alternating compressions and dilatations (see Figure 6).

The top figure in the box is a diagram of the pattern of first motions of P waves at the Earth's surface that radiated—along a simple vertical strike-slip fault—from a shallow earthquake focus a few kilometers below the surface. (Appropriate diagrams can also be drawn for P waves that travel from other types of faults.) The lines separating areas of different first motions of P waves correspond to places on the ground surface at which no P motion occurs. Thus one line corresponds to the surface trace of the fault plane itself.

The reader can appreciate the great elation of seismologists in the 1930s when fault rupture directions, predicted in this way at distant observatories, were found to check with field reports from the epicentral region. An early form of remote sensing!

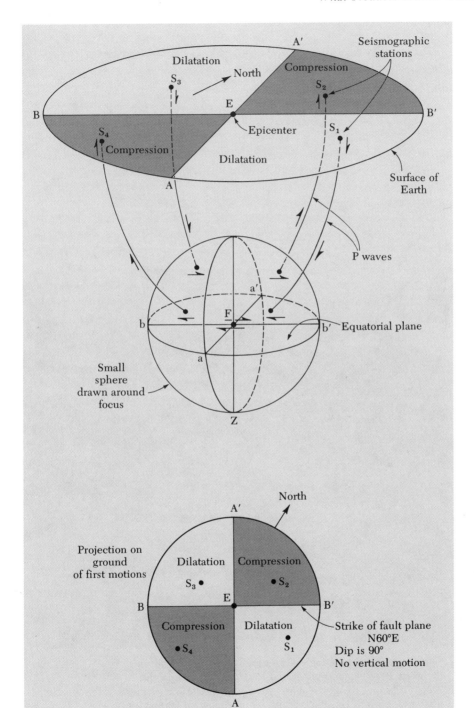

Dilatation

North

S_3

Compression

A'

Seismographic stations

S_2

E

B

B'

Epicenter

S_1

S_4

Compression

Dilatation

A

Surface of Earth

P waves

a'

b

F

b' Equatorial plane

a

Small sphere drawn around focus

Z

North

A'

Projection on ground of first motions

Dilatation

S_3

Compression

S_2

B

E

B'

Compression

S_4

Dilatation

S_1

Strike of fault plane
N60°E
Dip is 90°
No vertical motion

A

Seismic sea wave crashing over the pier at Hilo, Hawaii, in the great 1946 tsunami generated by an earthquake in the Aleutian Islands. Note the man in the path of the waves. He was never seen again. Photograph by an unknown seaman on the S.S. *Brigham Victory*. [Courtesy of R. L. Wiegel.]

*For nearly forty million years the first island struggled in the
bosom of the sea, endeavoring to be born as observable land. For
nearly forty million submerged years its subterranean volcano
hissed and . . . spewed forth rock, but it remained nevertheless
hidden beneath the dark waters of the restless sea . . . a small
climbing pretentious thing of no consequence.*

—JAMES A. MICHENER, *Hawaii*

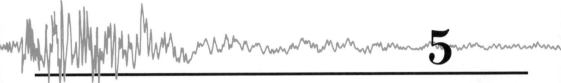

5

Earthquakes, Volcanoes, and Tsunamis

Eruptions in Hawaii

The most severe earthquake to strike the Hawaiian Islands since 1868
occurred in the early morning (4:48 Hawaiian Standard Time) of November 29, 1975. The focus was about 5 kilometers below the surface, and
the epicenter was approximately 45 kilometers south of Hilo, on the big
island of Hawaii's southeastern coast (see Figure 1). About 1 hour earlier a
smaller, precursor earthquake, with nearly the same focus, had shaken the
vicinity.

Two companion events occurred. The fault movement under the ocean
that had caused the earthquake also generated a tidal wave, or tsunami.
The sea waves crested at heights of 12 meters at isolated localities on
Hawaii, but generally the water height did not exceed 6 meters. The tsu-

71

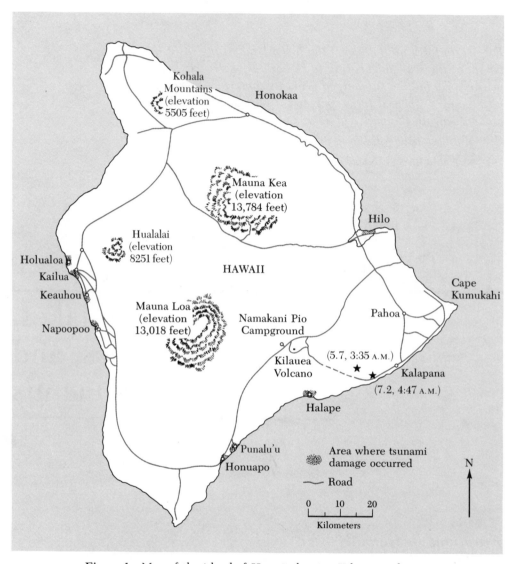

Figure 1 Map of the island of Hawaii showing Kilauea and Mauna Loa volcanoes. The stars denote the epicenters of the earthquakes of November 29, 1975. The magnitude and time of occurrence for each are given in parentheses. [Courtesy of USGS.]

nami waves inundated camp sites at Halape Beach where 36 people were spending Thanksgiving holiday weekend. At least one man was killed and others were hospitalized with minor injuries. As shown in Figure 2, homes and other light structures were destroyed at Punalu'u, where the tsunami traveled inland about 150 meters. Docks and boats sustained damage at places along the coast such as Hilo, where the wave height in the Wailoa

River reached about 4 meters. (The tsunami should not have come as a surprise. An earthquake in the same region on April 2, 1868, was followed by a tsunami that ran up almost 3 meters high at Hilo.)

The second striking event, the same day, was an eruption of Kilauea volcano. Lava erupted on the floor of Kilauea's caldera less than an hour after the main earthquake. Lava issued from fissures, and lava fountains rose as high as 50 meters into the air. New fissures also opened on the east wall of Halemaumau crater within the caldera. By the following morning, November 30, the volcanic activity had ceased, less than 18 hours after it began.

The earthquake itself produced significant damage on Hawaii amounting to more than 4 million dollars. Roads were cracked, and some were rendered impassable as a result of rock slides and slumping. Electrical power was cut off in some areas. In Hilo, the urban center closest to the earthquake source, light to moderate damage from shaking was prevalent. Plate-glass windows were broken in some old wood-frame shops, furniture was shifted or overturned, and a few older homes partially collapsed. Fortunately, strong-motion seismographs were available to record for posterity the actual ground shaking during the earthquake; these showed that strong seismic waves lasted about 14 seconds.

Figure 2   Damage at the Punalu'u area of the Big Island, resulting from the tsunami generated by the earthquake centered off Kalapana, Hawaii, on November 29, 1975. [Courtesy of Christopher Rojahn and B. J. Morrill, USGS.]

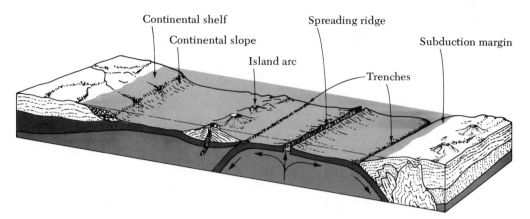

Figure 3 Generalized cross section through the ocean crust showing the uppermost layers of rocks under the ocean spreading out from the midoceanic ridge and sliding down under the volcanic island arc and active continental margin along the deep trench. Earthquake foci are concentrated at the tops of the descending layers and along the ridge. Magma rises upward above the subduction zones, and the erupting lava builds spectacular volcanic cones.

This conjunction of three types of energy release—earthquake, tsunami, volcanic eruption—on Hawaii in 1975 provides us with a context for exploring the links between them. In the preceding chapter, we noted that earthquakes and volcanoes often, but by no means always, accompany each other in certain tectonic regions, particularly midoceanic ridges and near deep ocean trenches. At the *subduction* zones, that is, along the trenches, the mechanical link is the downward movement of the lithospheric plates into the Earth. This movement is schematically illustrated in Figure 3. As the surface rocks bend and plunge downward at a deep trench, they become strained and fracture, thus producing earthquakes. At the same time, the temperature rises and local melting of the dipping plate occurs; the chemical composition of the rocks changes, and a molten fraction of the rocks makes its way to the surface, where it may be stored for a time in *magma chambers*—huge reservoirs underneath volcanic vents. From these pressure chambers, magma moves upward from time to time to issue forth as lava. In contrast, at places where two tectonic plates are moving together along a transform fault (such as the San Andreas fault) or collision zone (such as at the Himalayas), volcanoes are usually absent (see Chapter 1, Figure 4).

Now let us look more closely at volcanoes of the Hawaiian archipelago type, where there is no present evidence for a downgoing slab. A current speculation—for which there is much evidence—is that such places mark regions of the deeper interior of the Earth that are at especially high temperature. Slender, isolated columns of molten rock rise slowly to the surface under continents and oceans. As the tectonic plate moves sideways over such a major *hot spot*, the rocks are locally melted and magma erupts onto the surface of the plate. Thus the chain of Hawaiian volcanoes is a series of eruptions above the mid-Pacific hot spot; the volcanoes are progressively younger toward the southeast.

Volcanic activity and local earthquakes occur together in two ways. First, often before an eruption, minor seismic activity—called *volcanic earthquakes*—increases in the vicinity of the volcano. Some kilometers below the volcanic vent, very hot viscous magma moves sluggishly under great steam pressure through a network of tubes and pipes from one storage chamber to another. As this motion takes place, various parts of the surrounding rock become hotter and more strained as the magma pushes through them. These forces fracture the neighboring rocks, and strain is relieved by the elastic rebound mechanism discussed in Chapter 4.

Sometimes, fault rupture precedes the motion of magma and eruption of lava. As in the episode of November 1975 in Hawaii, earthquake waves from a nearby rupturing fault may shake up the molten material in the storage reservoirs beneath the volcano. In a way similar to the violent shaking of a bottle of soda pop, steam and gas—which previously dissolved in the magma—may then begin to boil off, forming bubbles of superheated steam that accelerate the escape of the lava from surface tubes and then escape as gaseous material. In turn, this release of superheated steam and gas disturbs the unstable equilibrium of the magma below the vent, thereby producing further flow in the subterranean tubes and the stimulation of local volcanic earthquakes.

Near active volcanoes, the population is subject to the definite danger of lava flow onto fields and property or, in some areas, of cataclysmic ejection of gas and superheated water, mud, and other materials. As with any geological hazard, each individual must decide whether the risks posed by a nearby volcano are reasonable ones. On Hawaii, most people believe that the risks are not excessive and are no worse than the natural hazards of other areas—such as tornadoes. Although volcano insurance is available in some parts of the world, it is usually expensive.

Volcanic hazards have two mitigating features: First, even though lava may cover the land surface, the land can be used again, at least for certain types of agriculture, after a few decades. Also, when a volcano begins to erupt, warning signs often occur soon enough to allow evacuation from the threatened area. To be sure, specific prediction of a damaging eruption is not yet often possible and may never be in a practical sense. Nevertheless, certain clues are indications of an impending eruption: rising water temperature in fumaroles and the changing composition of erupting gases; also, deformation of the ground surface around volcanoes sometimes precedes eruptions. One possible explanation is that the swelling occurs when the magma reservoirs beneath the vents are filling, indicating that a lava flow is likely to occur. Seismographs have also been tried as a predictive tool, because networks of these instruments around active volcanoes sometimes detect significant changes in background seismicity. For example, sometimes the foci of earthquake swarms migrate from one place to another, perhaps indicating the movement of magma upward.

This predictive idea is not without verification: one example is a recent eruption of Mauna Loa on Hawaii. Workers at the Hawaiian Volcano Observatory had detected signs of increased restlessness beginning in April 1974, when there was a marked increase in the number of small earthquakes near the summit of the big volcano. Subsequently, little change in the earthquake frequency occurred until July 1975. Then, the recorded seismicity noticeably increased and became shallower. A glow was reported from the erupting lava before midnight on July 5, and by the early morning, observers in aircraft saw a line of fountains extending along the summit caldera. Mauna Loa had ended a 25-year period of dormancy, since its last great eruption of June 1950. The eruption lasted 2 days and covered approximately 13.5 square kilometers of land with new lava. Although a warning was issued to residents that might be threatened, the lava flows did not reach developed areas.

Explosion of Mount Saint Helens, 1980

A violent volcanic eruption occurred in the United States at Mount Saint Helens, Washington, on May 18, 1980 (see Chapter 1, Figure 4). It was one of the largest natural releases of energy since the great volcanic eruption at Krakatoa in 1883.

Mount Saint Helens is one of a row of towering volcanic peaks that extends along the Cascade range from northern California to southern Canada. These volcanic cones consist of alternating layers of tephra and lava flows, producing what are called *composite volcanoes*. At their summits is a *caldera*—a crater produced by rock collapse after a great eruption.

In their mature stages, composite volcanoes erupt explosively, throwing out many cubic kilometers of glassy ash and pumice. Such cataclysms are like the one at Vesuvius in 79 A.D. in which the Roman scholar, Pliny the elder, died; thus they are called Plinian eruptions. They are potentially a great hazard.

For some time, the hazards from the Cascade volcanoes had been discussed; predictions based on geological volcanic deposits along the range indicated that there might be a large eruption before the twenty-first century. In March 1980, an earthquake swarm near Mount Saint Helens began a sequence that led to the Plinian eruption 2 months later. By the end of March, seismographs in the vicinity recorded swarms of hundreds of earthquakes each day. By mid-April, a bulge was observed developing on the snow-covered summit, and it continued to enlarge through early May 1980. These events were interpreted as the emplacement of a large volume of magma near the top of the volcano. As a result, the forest and resort regions on the north flank of the volcano were evacuated.

The sequence of events leading to the most violent phase of the eruption then becomes uncertain, but the best evidence indicates that it started just after 1530 Universal Time° on May 18, 1980, with a small earthquake at a focal depth of about 3 kilometers beneath the mountain. The ground shaking triggered a massive landslide on the north slope of Mount Saint Helens, releasing about half a minute later a powerful blast of super-heated steam and rock northward and upward. The cause of the eruption was probably the unloading of the overburdened rock mass by the land-slide and the consequent exposure of a magma or hydrothermal reservoir. A few minutes later, a second vertical eruption occurred in the north part of the caldera before the first one was fully developed. This eruption was accompanied by another earthquake.

The extent of the blast zone in the first and lateral eruption has been measured from the devastated area in which all virgin fir trees were blown over. It covers a nearly semicircular northward section of the mountain, 30 kilometers across from west to east and extending outward 20 kilometers from the peak. The eruption killed 65 people, one of whom was a professional volcanologist who was observing gas flow and rock deformations at his post about 10 kilometers from the summit.

The blasts strongly disturbed the atmosphere: airwaves spread out as very long pressure waves around the Earth. Barographs at some weather stations and observatories worldwide recorded the fluctuations in air pressure in the waves; these recordings have been used to compute the rapidity of the eruption. Figure 4 shows the airwaves recorded at the seismographic station at the University of California, Berkeley: the waves following the direct path southeast from Mount Saint Helens to Berkeley, California, and the waves traveling the long path northwest completely around the Earth. The periods of the airwaves range from 2 minutes to

---

°Universal Time (UT) refers to the standard time at the Prime Meridian that passes through Greenwich, England. In order that observatories throughout the world can compare the arrival times of seismic waves, an earthquake's time of occurrence is given in Universal Time.

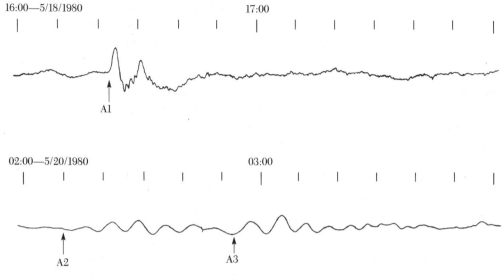

Figure 4 Fluctuations in air pressure at Berkeley after the Mount Saint Helens eruption, May 18, 1980. The top record shows the direct (A1) waves and the bottom shows the two overlapping wave trains (A2 and A3) through the antipodes.

almost 20 minutes. The two most prominent pulses, with widths of approximately 3 minutes separated by about 6 minutes, traveled at speeds of 308 meters per second and 262 meters per second. The onset of the wave around the antipodes (the far side of the Earth) appeared 33 hours later, corresponding to an air speed of 314 meters per second.

Mammoth Lakes Earthquake Swarm, California

The eastern front of the Sierra Nevada, California, provides one of the most spectacular mountain areas of the world. The geological processes that created this scenic beauty have operated for millions of years and are still active today. This mountain range—a huge mass of the Earth's crust, 650 kilometers long and over 30 kilometers wide—has broken free along the great fault system on its eastern front and has tilted westward. Notable along this fault system is the recent volcanism in the Long Valley region within which is situated the ski and holiday resort of Mammoth Lakes, Mono County (see Chapter 2, Figure 2).

On May 25, 1980, at 1633 UT, a large earthquake occurred in the vicinity of Mammoth Lakes. By August 1, a sequence of over 600 smaller earthquakes (see Figure 5) had occurred in the region. During the previous year, several earthquake swarms had occurred along the southern boundary of the Long Valley caldera, and this had prompted seismological research groups and geologists to instrument the area with seismographs and other geophysical devices. The larger earthquakes caused a relatively minor amount of damage from shaking in the town and vicinity, but they led to widespread concern that the seismic sequence heralded a flareup of major volcanic eruptions in the Long Valley caldera. Because of limited access roads to the town of Mammoth Lakes, such sudden violent eruptions could constitute a grave risk. Consequently, steps were taken by government authorities to monitor closely the geological

Figure 5 Seismogram recorded at the University of California station at Priest, California, showing a swarm of hundreds of microearthquakes from the Mammoth Lakes area on May 26, 1980. The epicentral distances are about 300 kilometers, and the time between trace offsets is 1 minute.

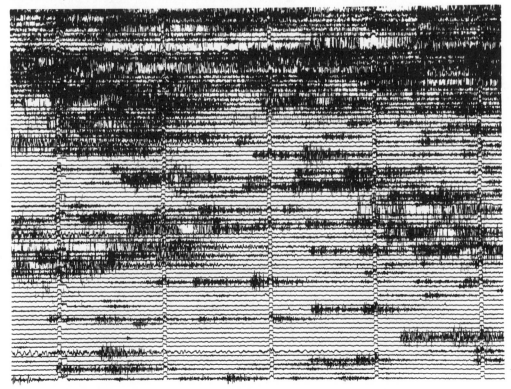

conditions in the Mammoth Lakes area with the aim of building a geological model that could both explain and predict the tectonic events. Was
the 1980 seismic episode a forerunner of a future eruption?

The region of Long Valley and adjacent Mono Basin is one of four
areas in California for which there is well-documented evidence of multi-
ple volcanic eruptions in the past 2 millenia. To begin with, the Long
Valley caldera itself was formed by a gigantic eruption about 700,000
years ago, involving ejection of magma with total volume of about 600
cubic kilometers. Such colossal eruptions are infrequent, and none have
occurred during the written history of humankind. Study of age-dated
volcanic ash in the area indicates that at least 20 such events have occurred in the last 2000 years in this area of east-central California. Such
evidence suggests that the region is in the early stage of caldera evolution.

The most recent volcanic eruption in the region occurred on August 23,
1890, witnessed by only a few people in this remote area. Local earthquakes occurred at the same time. A quotation from the local newspaper,
The Homer Mining Index, gives a colorful perspective:

> Remarkable earthquakes at Mono. The southern end of Mono Lake was
> considerably agitated last Sunday and dwellers in that shaky locality were
> much perturbed. Steam was issuing from a lake as far as could be seen, in
> sudden pops, and the water was boiling fiercely, while high waves rolled
> upon the beach and receded, leaving the sand smoking. In a moment, the
> air was thick with blinding hot sulfurous vapor, and subterranean moans
> and rumblings made the witness think that the devil was holding
> highjinks down below. Fences wobbled up and down and sideways.

To help with modeling the tectonic process, measurements were made
of the tilt and elevation of the ground levels in the vicinity of Long
Valley. The foci of many aftershocks were pinpointed in relation to faults
in the area by a local seismograph network. Ground rupture was mapped
east of Mammoth Lakes along a known fault and its northwestern
branches in a zone 20 kilometers long. Aerial photographs showed significant zones of cracking and ground failure that coincided with other faults.
As well, there was landsliding along zones of weakness on the steep slopes
and older scarps. For a time there was sobering speculation that an episode of dangerous volcanic activity was likely, causing concern among
local inhabitants. But earthquake frequency and steam vent activity began to diminish and by 1985, the Mammoth Lakes area was again quiet.
Because of the ongoing tectonic deformation in this area, structures
should nevertheless be built to resist substantial earthquakes and with
appropriate concern for volcanic hazards.

Tsunamis

Along sea coasts, another disaster may follow large earthquakes. The sudden offset of a major fault under the ocean floor moves the water as if it were being pushed by a giant paddle, producing powerful water waves at the ocean surface. These water waves spread out from the vicinity of the earthquake source and move across the ocean until they reach a coastline. There, their height sometimes increases greatly, and they crash down on the shore with disastrous effects, as shown in Figure 6. Figure 7 shows the effects of the same tsunami further north.

These long water waves are commonly referred to in English as "tidal waves." The name, however, is not really accurate because they do not arise from the attraction of the moon and the sun. In Spanish, the word *maremoto* fits neatly, but, for want of a better word, the names *seismic sea wave* and *tsunami* are used by scientists in English. Use of the Japanese word is particularly appropriate because the islands of Japan have suffered greatly from the destructive effects of tsunamis, some of which have come from as far away as South America.

One of the worst tsunamis in history hit the eastern, or Sanriku, coast of Honshu following a great earthquake centered out at sea on June 15, 1896. The best guess is that this earthquake was produced by a wide area of ocean floor thrusting upward along a submarine fault of the Japan trench. The seismic sea wave washed onto nearby land as much as 25 to

Figure 6   Bore from a tsunami (of April 1, 1946) racing into the mouth of the Wailuku River, Hilo, Hawaii. Note that part of the bridge has already been destroyed—by an earlier wave of the same tsunami. [Plate 8, from G. A. Macdonald, F. P. Shepard, and D. C. Cox, "The Tsunami of April 1, 1946, in the Hawaiian Islands," *Pacific Science*, vol. 1, no. 1.]

Figure 7   The April 1, 1946, tsunami flooding Hakalau Gulch north of Hilo and destroying the Hakalau sugar mill. [Hilo Photo Supply, Ltd.]

35 meters above high tide level. Entire villages were engulfed. More than 10,000 houses were washed away, and 26,000 people were killed. To the east, the tsunami waves spread across the Pacific Ocean (see Chapter 1, Figure 4) and were recorded at Hilo, Hawaii, with an amplitude of 3 meters. The waves then continued to the American coast, where they were reflected back toward New Zealand and Australia. The devastation was repeated on March 2, 1933, when a tsunami, with crests as high as 25 meters, again washed ashore along the Sanriku coast, killing about 3000 people.

References to the devastation of tsunamis can be found throughout recorded history. The earliest description is of a damaging sea wave near the north end of the Aegean Sea in 479 B.C. In the ensuing centuries other tsunamis occurred along the coastal plains and offshore islands of the Mediterranean. Within the last 200 years alone, about 300 tsunamis have produced fatalities. Details on some of the most devastating tsunamis are given in the table on the facing page.

Notable Tsunamis of the World

Date	Source region	Visual run-up height (meters)	Location of report	Comments
1500 B.C.	Santorin eruption		Crete	Devastation of Mediterranean coast
Nov. 1, 1755	Eastern Atlantic	5–10	Lisbon, Portugal	Reported from Europe to West Indies
Dec. 21, 1812	Santa Barbara Channel, Calif.	Several meters	Santa Barbara, Calif.	Early reports probably exaggerated
Nov. 7, 1837	Chile	5	Hilo, Hawaii	
May 17, 1841	Kamchatka	Less than 5	Hilo, Hawaii	
April 2, 1868	Hawaii Island	Less than 3	Hilo, Hawaii	
Aug. 13, 1868	Peru-Chile	More than 10	Arica, Peru	Observed in New Zealand; damage in Hawaii
May 10, 1877	Peru-Chile	2–6	Japan	Destructive in Iquique, Peru
Aug. 27, 1883	Krakatau eruption		Java	Over 30,000 drowned
June 15, 1896	Honshu	24	Sanriku, Japan	About 26,000 people drowned
Feb. 3, 1923	Kamchatka	About 5	Waiakea, Hawaii	
March 2, 1933	Honshu	More than 20	Sanriku, Japan	3000 deaths from waves
April 1, 1946	Aleutians	10	Wainaku, Hawaii	
Nov. 4, 1952	Kamchatka	Less than 5	Hilo, Hawaii	
March 9, 1957	Aleutians	Less than 5	Hilo, Hawaii	Associated earthquake magnitude 8.3
May 23, 1960	Chile	More than 10	Waiakea, Hawaii	
March 28, 1964	Alaska	6	Crescent City, Calif.	119 deaths and $104 million damage from tsunami
Nov. 29, 1975	Hawaii Island	About 4	Hilo, Hawaii	

A comparison of historical earthquakes and tsunamis shows that a large tsunami washing onto a stretch of populated coastline is likely to be much more destructive than the shaking from all but exceptionally large earthquakes (see the description of the 1964 Alaska earthquake in Chapter 2). Only the really great earthquakes, such as the 1556 and 1976 earthquakes in China and the 1908 disaster in Messina (see Appendix A), cause as many casualties as the largest damaging tsunamis. On the average, about one major tsunami occurs each year somewhere in the world; they can occur in most oceans and seas but are particularly frequent in the Pacific, Indian, Mediterranean, Atlantic, and Caribbean. They have also arisen in large inland seas, such as the Caspian and Black seas in Central Asia.

Evidence suggests that most great water waves are caused by fault rupture with vertical displacement along a submerged fault, but there are also other causes. One example is a submarine landslide, such as occurred in Sagami Bay in Japan in 1923. These underwater landslides may themselves be triggered by a nearby earthquake. Sometimes a landslide or avalanche of soil and rock on a mountain into a bay, a large lake, or even reservoir can produce a local water wave that is deadly. A famous landslide-induced sea wave occurred at Lituya Bay, Alaska, after a local large earthquake on July 9, 1958. Water waves rushed into the opposite shores of the bay as far as 500 meters, stripping vegetation in their path. More recently, a giant water wave was produced by a landslide into the Vaiont reservoir in Italy in October 1963. A large volume of water overtopped the Vaiont dam by 100 meters and swept down the valley of the Piave River, killing almost 3000 people. Such incidents are warnings that towns and marinas should not be located around lakes, bays, and reservoirs that may be affected by earthquakes and landslides unless defensive planning measures are taken.

The only other known source of great tsunamis is a major volcanic eruption. The classical example was the wave following the collapse of the top of Krakatoa volcano in 1883, one of the most violent geological paroxysms in historic times. During the summer, numerous earthquakes and considerable volcanic activity had occurred on Krakatoa Island, in the Sunda Strait between Java and Sumatra in the East Indies, with its peak standing to a height of 2000 meters. At the end of August, a series of violent eruptions took place, with great masses of ejecta streaming out from the volcano vent. (By August 28, the cataclysm was essentially over; a total of about 16 cubic kilometers of ash and pumice had been ejected.) On August 27, the central vents caved in: where the island had stood there was now ocean water 250 meters deep. This sudden collapse produced an enormously energetic tsunami. The wave was not high enough in the deep water to sink ships present in Sunda Strait, but when it reached shallow water along the coast, it washed away 165 villages without trace and killed more than 36,000 inhabitants. The wave height was said to exceed 35 meters along the shore, and when it reached Port Alfred in South Africa later, it was still in excess of 30 centimeters. Eventually, it made its way around the African continent into the English Channel, where it was observed to have a surge of 5 centimeters.

In the open ocean, the distance between the crests of a tsunami may be greater than 100 kilometers, and the elevation is seldom more than 1 meter in height. Such waves themselves cannot be detected by ships at sea. As the water depth decreases, the speed of the waves slow down (see the box on page 86). When the tsunami approaches the shoreline, sometimes the water level will first fall, denuding beaches and leaving stranded fish. During this phase of a tsunami at Hilo, Hawaii, in 1923 some persons were drowned by the first wave crest when they unwisely rushed onto the exposed flatlands to pick up the fish.

The local height of a tsunami is affected by the topography of the sea bottom and the continental shelf and by the shape of the shoreline. For example, in open and hook bays, the tsunami can cause the water level of one side of the bay to rise dramatically while the other side is sheltered and shows little change. Coastal regions—such as the Pacific side of the Japanese island of Honshu—that face the source of the tsunami usually suffer the highest run-up of the water, but the lee side of promontories and peninsulas can provide shelter. The tsunami onrush is sometimes amplified in a bay or river mouth, producing an almost vertical wall of water, called a *water bore*. The photograph in Figure 6 shows the wave at Hilo, Hawaii, that formed during the onslaught of the tsunami produced along the deep Aleutian Ocean trench in the great 1946 Alaska earthquake. In the river estuary at Hilo a nearly vertical wave front, about 7 meters high, rushed across the estuary and churned across the roadway and bridge, finally reaching a power plant at the south end of the bay, where it short-circuited the electrical system, plunging most of the island of Hawaii into darkness.

Long-period movements of water can also be produced in lakes and reservoirs by large, usually distant, earthquakes, and sometimes by strong winds. It had been known for centuries that Swiss lakes were apt to rise and fall rhythmically by a few centimeters. The duration of a complete oscillation of the Lake of Geneva, for example, is 72 minutes. In the late nineteenth century, the Swiss professor F. A. Forel made a systematic study of this type of water wave which he called a *seiche* (pronounced *sash*). The term *seismic seiche* was first coined by Anders Kvale in 1955 to describe oscillations of lake levels in Norway and England caused by the earthquake of August 1950 in Assam, India. More recently, the 1964 Alaska earthquake generated water oscillations in wells in the United States, 4000 kilometers away along the Gulf of Mexico.

Properties of a Tsunami

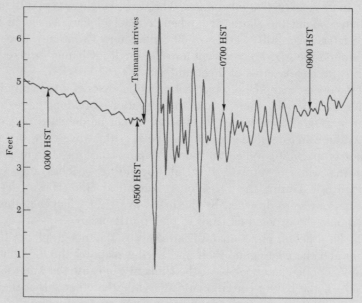

Record of a tsunami in Kuhio Bay, Hilo, Hawaii on November 29, 1975. (HST is Hawaii Standard Time.)

The record shows the following properties of the water waves.

1. The onset was an upward swell of $\frac{1}{2}$ meter.
2. The water level then fell 1 meter below normal.
3. The period between tsunami crests was about 15 minutes.
4. The duration of the tsunami wave action was over 4 hours.

In the deep ocean of depth d, the speed v of a tsunami (long water wave) is equal to $\sqrt{gd}$, where g is the acceleration of gravity (980 centimeters per second squared). For

$$d = 5 \text{ kilometers}$$
$$v = \sqrt{980 \times 5 \times 10^5} \text{ centimeters per second}$$
$$\simeq 800 \text{ kilometers per hour}$$

For a period $T = 15$ minutes from (3) above, the wave length, λ, is:

$$\lambda = v \times T$$
$$= 800 \times \frac{1}{4} \text{ kilometers}$$
$$= 200 \text{ kilometers}$$

Tsunami Alerts

The west coast of North America from California to Vancouver and the northern coast of Europe are not as susceptible to tsunami damage as the coasts of Japan, Alaska, and South America. One reason is that no great subduction zone is present to cause major thrust faulting. In California the motions along the San Andreas fault system are predominantly horizontal, so that where the San Andreas fault or its subsidiaries go under the ocean (as off the Golden Gate Bridge at San Francisco) even *major* horizontal offsets, as in the 1906 earthquake, do not push the sea water enough to generate a seismic sea wave of any consequence. Nevertheless, even where trenches are absent, a tsunami generated by an earthquake source far away can strike almost any coast and can be severe enough to cause heavy damage.

The Seismic Sea Wave Warning System was set up in the Pacific after the devastating Aleutian tsunami of April 1, 1946, in order to reduce the danger from Pacific tsunamis. The system is international: evidence of a large earthquake is immediately cabled, radioed, or phoned in to the Tsunami Warning Center in Honolulu from earthquake observatories

'It sounds like they're saying tsunami — whatever that means'

in the United States, Japan, Taiwan, Philippines, Fiji, Chile, Hong Kong, New Zealand, and Samoa. Then information on variation in water level, obtained from tide gauges at various observatories in the region of the earthquake, is provided. On the basis of this information, tsunami alerts may be issued.°

Although tsunamis travel swiftly (see the box on page 86), there is usually ample time to issue warnings at more distant places. For example, the travel time of a tsunami from the coast of Chile to Hawaii is about 10 hours, and from the Aleutian Islands to northern California, about 4 hours.

Again, the shape of the coastline and the adjacent seafloor topography have a direct bearing on the degree of tsunami risk. The parts of California that have the highest risk are the northernmost coast, above Cape Mendocino, the area near the entrance to San Francisco Bay, Monterey Bay, and several points in southern California from San Diego northward to Point Buchon.[†]

Tragedy at Crescent City, California, 1964

The most recent tsunami of importance along the Pacific coast occurred after the great Alaska earthquake of March 1964. In San Francisco Bay, a wave height of about 1 meter was recorded near the Golden Gate Bridge, and some boats moored at bay marinas were battered. Total damages along the California coast were about 10 million dollars, the largest amount in a century. Of this sum, almost three-quarters was borne by Crescent City, on the far north coast of California.

During the 1964 Alaska earthquake, which occurred at 3:36 A.M. Universal Time, the first alarm was sounded at the Honolulu Observatory at 3:44 A.M. One hour later the position of the focus of the earthquake and its magnitude were accurately determined, but the main communication channels with Alaska had been severed. In California, an advisory bulletin of a possible "tidal wave" was received from Honolulu by the State Disaster Office at 5:36 A.M. UT. A more definite advisory warning was re-

---

°One inherent danger in a tsunami alert is people's high curiosity. For example, an alert was issued at Berkeley, California, during the 1964 Alaska earthquake. Afterward the police chief complained that not only did the tsunami alert cause local people to go to the waterfront to watch the wave come in—but some of his police did the same thing!

[†]Historically, a few small to moderate tsunamis have been generated by movements of the California seafloor—as on December 21, 1812, Santa Barbara Channel, and November 4, 1927, Point Arguello.

ceived at 6:44 A.M. UT and was sent to sheriffs, police chiefs, and civil defense directors of coastal cities and counties. At Crescent City, the county sheriff received the warning at 7:08 A.M. UT, and he notified people in the low-lying areas to begin evacuation. During this time of preparation, long sea waves had been moving across the Pacific Ocean, and they arrived at Crescent City about $4\frac{1}{2}$ hours after they had been generated in Prince William Sound in the Gulf of Alaska. If a large circle is drawn on a terrestrial globe at right angles to the underwater fault from Prince William Sound to Kodiak Island, also in the Gulf of Alaska, it will be found to head toward northern California (see Chapter 1, Figure 4). The seismic sea waves that arrived at Crescent City were particularly large because the topography of the seafloor along the continental shelf at Crescent City is so shaped that the wave heights were amplified.

Several seismic sea waves inundated Crescent City harbor, and the third and fourth waves damaged the low-lying area around the southward-facing beach. The third wave washed inland more than 500 meters. Thirty city blocks were flooded, damaging or destroying one-story wood-frame buildings. After the first two smaller waves had struck, some people returned to the flooded area to clean up. Seven, including the owner and his wife, returned to a tavern at the shore to remove valuables. Because the sea seemed to have returned to normal, they remained to have a drink and were trapped by the third wave, which drowned five of them. This story illustrates the problem inherent in warning systems: too many alerts cause people to become blasé; too few foster ignorance of safety procedures.

The Crescent City disaster had one positive aspect. The town was rezoned afterward and the waterfront area developed into a public park. Businesses previously in the low-lying area were relocated on higher ground. The city is now a more attractive and safer place to live than before the killer tsunami of Easter 1964.

Atlantis and Santorin

Everyone is familiar with the story of the lost continent of Atlantis, the haunting legend of a great island civilization destroyed by a natural catastrophe. The legend comes to us from the writings of Plato, and many scholars have tried to separate the facts from poetic fiction.

Modern scholarship now leans toward the view that if there ever was a highly developed island culture that sank beneath the sea, it was not in the Atlantic Ocean but much closer to Greece and Egypt. In this century, archaeologists have rediscovered the highly accomplished Minoan civilization centered around the island of Crete. There is strong reason to believe that this "first civilization of Europe" suffered a sudden eclipse, and some overwhelming disaster or series of disasters must be sought for an explanation. At this stage of the puzzle, geophysical and geological work has brought to light evidence that the simultaneous abandonment and devastation of many Minoan palaces and villages was due to a powerful geological event, not to foreign marauders. The source of this natural violence is thought to be the volcano Santorin on the island of Thera, situated about 120 kilometers north of Knossos on Crete (see Figure 8). The geological evidence indicates reasonably gentle activity of the volcano about 1500 B.C., with increased violence proceeding to a cataclysmic stage. Indeed, it is suggested that the final eruptive stages of Santorin were similar to the outburst of Krakatoa, Indonesia, in 1883. Minoan cities on the island of Santorin were buried and their ruins preserved to the present time in the pumice and volcanic ash. Few human remains have been found in the ruins, indicating that the populace was probably

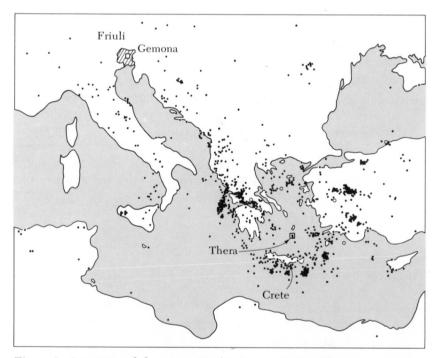

Figure 8   Seismicity of the eastern Mediterranean region. The dots represent epicenters for all earthquakes with magnitudes of 4.5 or more that occurred between 1965 and 1975. [From the hypocenter data file, National Geographic Solar Terrestrial Data Center, Boulder, Colorado. Courtesy of W. Rinehart.]

warned by the early stages of the eruption—perhaps by accompanying earthquakes.

As at Krakatoa, it is highly likely that tsunamis were generated that were large enough to cause destruction on the nearby shores of Crete and to flood lowlands around the eastern Mediterranean. These speculations are supported by direct evidence of the effect of tsunamis in recent years in the Greek islands. For example, a large 1956 earthquake centered near the southeast coast of Amorgos in the Cyclades islands of Greece, was followed by a tsunami that caused damage on Amorgos and on many surrounding islands, including Patmos, Crete, and Milos. More than 80 small ships and boats were wrecked and one person was drowned. On the coast of Amorgos, wave heights of 25 to 40 meters were reported.

Another famous case at the other end of the Mediterranean region occurred around the Iberian peninsula after the 1755 Lisbon earthquake. Then, a series of high ocean waves washed ashore along the west coasts of Spain, Portugal, and Morocco and increased the death toll. The water wave at Lisbon reportedly reached 5 meters above high-tide level. In the Mediterranean Sea it soon died out, but in the North Atlantic it disturbed British, Dutch, and French harbors hours later. Unfortunately, for the mitigation of present-day hazards in smaller oceans and seas like the Mediterranean, the travel time of a tsunami from its source is not long enough for an early warning system to be as effective as it has proved to be in the Pacific Ocean.

Collapse of part of the Arlington Hotel, Santa Barbara, in the earthquake of June 29, 1925. [Photo by Putnam Studios.]

It is not unlikely that every large earthquake might, with proper instrumental appliances, be recorded at any point on the land surface of our globe.

—Professor John Milne, 1893

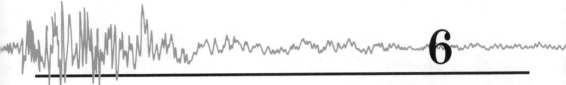

6

Measuring Earthquakes

Strong-Motion and Sensitive Seismographs

What does the ground actually do during an earthquake? To answer this question, *seismographs* have been designed to measure in detail the ground shaking. Because shaking can be quite severe in the meizoseismal zone of a large earthquake, recording instruments within this zone must be designed to withstand the buffeting of the seismic waves so that the recorders will not go off scale.

The first earthquake recorder described in any detail was an artistic device (see Figure 1) invented by the Chinese scholar Chang Heng about 132 A.D. The instrument was a *seismoscope*: unlike a seismograph, it did not give the complete time history of the earthquake shaking but simply the direction of the principal impulse due to the earthquake.°

° Balls were held in metal dragons' mouths that were probably connected by linkages to a vertical pendulum. Shaking released the balls. It was reputed that once, days after a ball fell, a horseman came from a distant place telling of a great earthquake. Use of Chang Heng's instrument seems to have died out in a short time.

Figure 1   An artist's conception of the Chinese scholar Chang Heng contemplating his seismoscope. Balls were held in the dragons' mouths by lever devices connected to an internal pendulum. The direction of the first main impulse of the ground shaking was reputed to be detected by the particular ball that was released. [Courtesy of Texas Instruments Incorporated.]

The first effective seismographs were constructed just before the beginning of the twentieth century. Although the instruments are now more sophisticated, the basic principle employed is the same (see Figure 2). A mass is freely suspended from a frame attached to the ground; the mass is therefore reasonably independent of the frame's motion. When the supporting frame is shaken by earthquake waves, the inertia of the mass causes it to lag behind the motion of the frame, and this relative motion is recorded by pen and ink on paper wrapped around a rotating drum (today the motion is recorded photographically or electromagnetically on magnetic tape). The record is called a *seismogram*. The principle of the

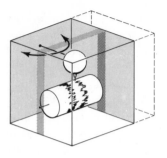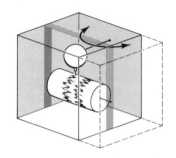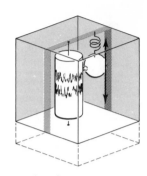

Figure 2 Simple models of pendulum seismographs recording the vertical and horizontal directions of ground motion. The pendulum must be damped in order to separate seismic pulses. [From Bruce A. Bolt, *Nuclear Explosions and Earthquakes: The Parted Veil* (San Francisco: W. H. Freeman and Company. Copyright © 1976).]

pendulum seismograph can be used for both vertical and horizontal shaking of the ground, as illustrated in Figure 2. Vertical motion can be recorded by attaching the mass to a spring hanging from the frame; the bobbing of the mass (as with a kitchen scale) will inscribe a record. For measurements of the sideways motion of the ground, the mass is usually attached to a horizontal pendulum, which swings like a door on its hinges.

If you try to build a simple seismograph° by attaching a mass to the end of a spiral spring or rubber band and shaking your hand, you will find that the mass continues to oscillate after the hand has been brought to rest. This free motion of the pendulum tells nothing about the ground shaking and must therefore be damped by some mechanical or electrical means. In this way, the relative motion between the mass and the frame is a measure of ground motion. However, in most recordings, this relative motion is not the true motion of the ground, so that most seismograms do not give an *exact* picture of what the ground did. The actual ground motion must be calculated by taking into account the physics of the pendulum's motion.

In modern seismographs, the relative motion between the pendulum and frame produces an electrical signal that is magnified electronically thousands and even hundreds of thousands of times before it is used to drive an electric stylus to produce the seismogram. The electrical signals from a seismograph pendulum can also be recorded onto magnetic tape

---

°For instructions on how to build a seismograph, see "The Amateur Scientist," *Scientific American*, January 1963.

(as sound waves are recorded by a microphone onto a tape recorder). In this way, the ground motion can be preserved in a magnetic form and, when required, played out from a tape through some visual recording device or audibly to produce earthquake sounds.

Strong-motion seismographs are specially designed to record the strong shaking of the ground in such a way that the records obtained can be directly read as acceleration, velocity, or displacement of the ground. The most common strong-motion seismographs record the ground acceleration directly and are called *accelerometers* (see Figure 3). Most strong-motion accelerometers do not record continuously but are triggered into motion by the first waves of the earthquake to arrive. This is because, even in earthquake country such as California and Japan, there may not be any strong ground motion from earthquakes to record for months, or even years, at a time. Consequently, continual recording of hundreds of such instruments would be a wasteful exercise. After triggering, the recording continues for some minutes or until the ground shaking falls again to imperceptible levels. These strong-motion instruments are usually capable of recording accelerations of the ground greater than that of gravity.

Strong ground acceleration appears as waves on the accelerogram (see

Figure 3   Photograph of a modern strong-motion seismograph. The starter, pendulum, and timing circuits are at left, the recording drum and film at right.

Chapter 7, Figure 3). It is often difficult to distinguish the regular types of seismic waves—such as P, S, and surface waves—particularly when the observer is near the earthquake source. Seismologists are now making a major effort to understand more of these intriguing and important strong-motion accelerograms.

In this discussion we have emphasized the strong-motion instruments, designed to record the strongest shaking, because these tell us about the felt and damaging motion. However, most seismographs around the world—especially those at the more than 1000 continuously recording seismographic stations—are very sensitive "ears on the world." They can detect and record earthquakes of small size from very great distances.

How to Understand Seismograms

A seismogram appears to be no more than a complicated series of wavy lines, but from these lines a seismologist can determine the magnitude and epicenter of an earthquake. Although experience is essential in interpreting seismograms, the first step in understanding the lines is to remember the following principles: First, earthquake waves consist predominantly of three types—P waves and S waves, which travel *through* the Earth, and a third type, surface waves, which travel *around* the Earth (see Chapter 2, Figure 6). If you look closely enough, you will find that each kind of wave is present on a seismogram, particularly if it is recorded by a sensitive seismograph at a considerable distance from the earthquake source. Each wave type affects the pendulums in a predetermined way. Second, the arrival of a seismic wave produces certain telltale changes on the seismogram trace: the trace is written more slowly or rapidly than just before; there is an increase in amplitude; and the wave rhythm (frequency) changes. Third, from past experience with similar patterns, the reader of the seismogram can roughly identify the pattern of arrivals of the various phases.

Consider the seismogram shown in Figure 4, which is part of a longer paper record made on a rotating drum of a seismograph at the University of California observatory at Berkeley. The earthquake is an aftershock of the 1975 Oroville earthquake in California. The actual line traced on the drum is a spiral, but the lines appear to be straight when the paper is opened out on a table, as in Figure 4. Notice the rows of sharp offsets of each line: these precisely indicate the elapsed time. Accurate timing is a fundamental requirement of seismology, and most observatories today have crystal clocks that keep correct time relative to the standard at

Greenwich, England, within a few thousandths of a second. Further time marks are placed on the records from a radio time service (such as that provided by the station WWV in the United States). The time offsets in Figure 4 are 1 minute apart. The drum movement was such that the time increases from left to right across the paper.

The recorded lines are never without some small wiggles. These occur because this seismograph is so sensitive that it is able to detect the continuous, yet imperceptible, background noise of the Earth. These tiny shakings, called *microseisms*, arise from many local disturbances; traffic on streets, wind in trees, and other natural movements such as the breaking of the surf on the beach. Now examine the trace offset marked by the arrow labeled P in Figure 4. At this point in time, the seismograph detected a significant change in ground shaking. The slightly larger wave seen arriving at this point is the first P wave from an earthquake generated by the fault slip near Oroville, California, at the earthquake focus. Motion following this P wave continued for some 21 seconds. Next you can see a radical change on the seismogram. The amplitude of the wave becomes suddenly larger at the arrow marked S, and the interval between peaks on the waves (the wave period) increases. This point on the seismogram marks the arrival of the first S wave from the earthquake focus. The interval between the arrival of the S wave and the P wave at Berkeley in this earthquake is 21.0 seconds.

Now look a little farther to the right on the record. After the S motion, a long train of waves continues to arrive at Berkeley for about 2 minutes. These waves are mainly surface waves, which have taken longer to reach Berkeley than the body waves. Because the ground motion shown in Fig-

Figure 4   Seismogram at Berkeley from an aftershock of the August 1, 1975, Oroville earthquake. The time between offsets of the traces is 1 minute, and time increases on each trace from left to right.

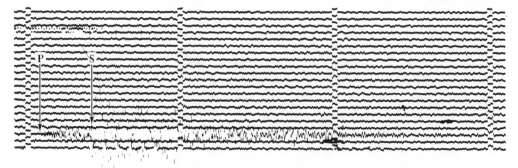

ure 4 is in the vertical direction, the later surface wave train corresponds to Rayleigh waves (see Chapter 2, Figure 6).

The seismic waves in the Earth gradually lose their energy as they spread over greater areas, just as the heights of ripples on a pond decrease as they spread out from the center of a disturbance. P and S waves decrease through spreading more quickly than seismic surface waves, and it is the surface waves that tend to persist at great distances. Even close to the earthquake center, however, a part of the shaking in an earthquake comes from the surface waves.

A closer scrutiny of the seismogram shows that although the wave motion is reasonably continuous, it is somewhat more complicated than can be explained in terms of the arrival of a single P wave, a single S wave, and a Rayleigh wave train. This complexity is due in large part to variations in rock structure along the paths traveled by the waves. Just as sound waves echo back from high buildings or the walls of a canyon, seismic echoes reflect back from rock interfaces in the Earth, and these additional phases cause bumps on the record that, if observed carefully, can be interpreted (see Chapter 8).

A common time standard must be used to compare the arrival times of seismic waves between earthquake observatories around the world. Traditionally, seismograms are marked in terms of Universal Time (UT) or Greenwich Mean Time (GMT), not local time. The time of occurrence of an earthquake in Universal Time can easily be converted to local time, but be sure to make allowance for Daylight Saving Time when this is in effect.°

Let us now briefly summarize the physics of the seismograph. Earthquake shaking produces swings of the pendulum, and these in turn record as a wavelike trace on a seismogram. On seismograms, we observe a series of peaks and troughs, resembling waves on the ocean or vibrations of a violin string. As illustrated in Appendix I, the height of a particular wave above its zero position is called the *wave amplitude*, and the time it takes to complete one cycle of motion (that is, from one peak to the next) is called the *wave period*. The frequency of a wave—measured in units called hertz—is the number of vibrations (cycles) per second, and the wave period is equal to the inverse of the frequency. Humans are able to hear sounds with frequencies of many thousands of hertz down to frequencies of about 15 hertz. In earthquakes the main shaking of the ground that is felt has frequencies of 20 hertz down to 1 cycle per second or even lower.

As mentioned earlier, the amplitudes of the waves recorded on a

---

°California Standard Time is 8 hours behind UT.

seismogram do not constitute the real amplitude of the ground shaking that produced the record. This is because seismographs have amplifying devices that increase the ground motions by a desired factor (perhaps many thousands of times). When the amplifying factor is taken into account, it turns out that the ground motion that produced the S wave marked on the seismogram in Figure 4 had an amplitude of only a fraction of a millimeter.

How to Locate an Earthquake

The seismologist has the unique job of locating the center of an earthquake. At one time, this task was done solely by determining the strength of ground shaking from reports of human reaction and from damage; from these, the position and extent of the source of the wave radiation could be roughly determined (see Chapter 7). In this way, the sources of large earthquakes were found to be spread out across a considerable area, some areas extending many tens of kilometers in length. These methods of locating the *field epicenter* of damaging earthquakes remain valuable because in many areas historical earthquakes that occurred before seismographs were invented are important in the evaluation of seismic risk. Although these field methods give little indication of the depth of the focus of the earthquake, they sometimes define rather well where geologists should search for surface fault rupture.°

Nowadays, for the great majority of earthquakes, the location is determined from the time taken by P seismic waves (and sometimes S waves) to travel from the focus to a seismograph. In some seismic areas, special local networks of seismographic stations have been installed to locate the foci of even very small earthquakes. For instance, around new large dams, sensitive seismographs are routinely operated to detect earthquakes that may have a bearing on dam safety (see Appendix G). Sometimes the seismometers at each station of a network are connected over telephone lines to a central recording observatory where the signals are recorded side by side on film or magnetic tape. This procedure greatly helps seismologists to accurately locate earthquakes not only because the pattern of P and S wave arrivals makes the rough location of the earthquake source

---

°A new twist to "field" location occurred in California recently when a geologist in Sacramento, speaking on the telephone to a colleague in San Francisco, suddenly said, "Wow, I feel the building swaying from an earthquake." After a pause, his San Francisco colleague said, "Wait, so do I." Their conclusion was that the earthquake was to the northeast.

immediately obvious, but also because only one precise crystal clock—at the central observatory—is needed.

Modern methods of locating earthquake epicenters and foci differ in detail, but they essentially depend on a single principle: the travel time of a seismic wave, such as a P wave, from the source to a given point on the Earth's surface is a direct measure of the distance between the two points. Seismologists have been able to determine by trial and error the average travel time of seismic P and S waves, for example, for any specified distance. The times have been printed in tables and graphs as a function of the distance. The appropriate distance between the observatory and focus can be read from the tables of expected travel times by comparing them with those that have been actually measured from any earthquake source to a seismographic observatory.

If arrival times at only one observatory are available, only the distance of the earthquake source from that observatory can be determined reasonably well, and not the geographical location. If arrival times at three observatories are available, then triangulation can be used to determine the latitude and longitude of the earthquake focus and the time of occurrence of the earthquake. Actually, it is common practice now to use the readings from many observatories. The International Seismological Centre in England, for example, might typically locate a moderate-size earthquake on the Mid-Atlantic ridge under the Atlantic Ocean, using the readings from 60 or more seismographic stations from around the world. The arithmetic is carried out with high-speed computers.

To demonstrate how to locate earthquake epicenters, one method that can be easily followed is displayed in the box on page 102. The problem is to determine the location of one of the aftershocks that followed the main 1975 Oroville, California, earthquake (see Chapter 9). Let us suppose that we have available only seismograms from three California stations— Berkeley (BKS), Jamestown (JAS), and Mineral (MIN). We have already scrutinized the seismogram at Berkeley shown in Figure 4. The time interval between the onsets of the P and the S waves at Berkeley was 21.0 seconds. In the same way, time intervals between P and S can be obtained for the stations Jamestown and Mineral. Actual measurements of the arrival times of P and S waves at the three stations are listed at the top of the box.

From past experience, we know the average distance between an epicenter and a seismograph corresponding to each S minus P interval (see the box on page 113). Thus, the appropriate distances between the epicenter and BKS, JAS, and MIN have been figured to be 190 kilometers, 188 kilometers, and 105 kilometers.

Then, applying the distance scale on a map of California, one can use a compass to draw three arcs of a circle, with the three observatories as centers (see Figure 5). The arcs will intersect, at least approximately, at some point. This point of intersection is the estimated location of the earthquake source. (The focal depth is still unknown, and more data are needed to calculate it.) The whole process is now easily performed on a personal computer with graphic screen.

Sometimes, of course, even the use of basic methods such as those described above produces a false location because of a timing error from

Sample Calculation of the Location of the Epicenter of an Earthquake (near Oroville, August 1975)

In this earthquake, P and S waves arrived at the stations Berkeley (BKS), Jamestown (JAS), and Mineral (MIN) at the following times (Universal Time):

	P			S		
	hr	min	s	hr	min	s
BKS	15	46	04.5	15	46	25.5
JAS	15	46	07.6	15	46	28.0
MIN	15	45	54.2	15	46	07.1

The following epicentral distances are estimated from the S minus P times above (from the left column of the box on page 113 in Chapter 7).

	S minus P (seconds)	Distance (kilometers)
BKS	21.0	190
JAS	20.4	188
MIN	12.9	105

With these distances as radii, one can draw three arcs of a circle, as shown in Figure 5. Note that these do not quite intersect at one point, but interpolation from the overlapping arcs yields an estimated epicenter of 39.5° N, 121.5° W, with an uncertainty of about 10 kilometers from these readings.

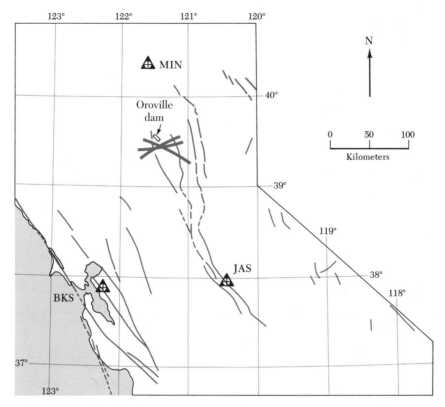

Figure 5 Map of Central California showing three seismographic stations: BKS (Berkeley), JAS (Jamestown), and MIN (Mineral). The arcs near Oroville dam are drawn as described in the text. The thin lines are surface traces of some prominent faults.

the clock, a mistake in identifying a seismic wave type, a blunder in calculation, or a lack of data. Professor Perry Byerly tells of his being called into the Berkeley Seismographic Station at 9:30 P.M., July 17, 1944, in response to a call from a news reporter who said that people had felt an "earthquake" somewhere in the San Francisco Bay area. Byerly painstakingly made an epicentral location from the P and S waves he could see on the seismograms and called back the newsroom to report his rough estimate (somewhere in the north*west* Bay). The janitor answered, saying, "All the reporters are away at Port Chicago (in the north*east* Bay) covering the great explosion at the dock there." "Well," replied Professor Byerly, "please tell them that the epicenter of the disturbance is at Port Chicago."

Seismograph Arrays—The Modern Earthquake Telescope

In some seismic regions, more powerful resolution of earthquake motions is now obtained by clusters of seismographs—called *seismograph arrays*—linked together with a common time-base. The scheme is similar to the use of groups of telescopes by astronomers to scan the sky.

A large seismograph array has been operating since 1980 in Taiwan, a highly seismic area (see Figure 6). As seen in the figure, this array consists of 37 accelerometers arranged in three rings with radii of 100 meters,

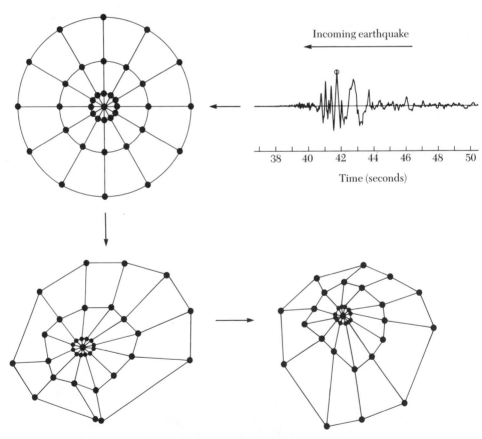

Figure 6   Dots denote sites of strong-motion seismographs operating as a circular array in Taiwan. Incoming seismic waves produce a set of records like that at the top right. Each site is slightly displaced by the wave motion producing distorted rings (highly magnified) plotted by computer graphics at the bottom at two separate times.

1 kilometer, and 2 kilometers, and an additional central recorder. The seismic signals are recorded on ordinary magnetic tape cassettes in the discrete form (*digital*) that enables them to be read at once into the memory of a computer. Then the wave forms can be analyzed and played out in various ways for study.

Consider in Figure 6, an incoming wave front (P or S waves) from a strong earthquake traveling across the array of seismographs, causing each to record the ground motion in turn. One such seismogram is shown in the top right of the figure in the form of the actual displacement of the ground surface. The direction of the seismic source relative to the array can be immediately determined by noting the sequences of arrival times of a wave front at each seismograph of the array. The differences in these arrival times from one side of the array to the other provide a measurement of the velocity of each wave front. In this way, the different types of seismic waves can be distinguished from each other.

Using a desktop personal computer, the set of 37 wave displacements in the earthquake depicted in Figure 6 have been combined to produce a series of snapshots of the actual time-variation of ground displacement. The two frames shown at the bottom of the figure highlight the manner in which strong ground shaking distorts the foundations of large structures in a continuously changing way. In this case, relative displacements of up to 5 centimeters occurred within distances of 200 meters.

The successful exterior-frame reinforcement of the masonry
Church of the Congregation of the Sacred Heart in
Valparaiso, Chile. This church was damaged during a 1971
earthquake. The reinforced section was not damaged in the
great 1985 earthquake, although the unreinforced section (not
shown) partly collapsed. [Photo by Bruce A. Bolt.]

*The earthquake began everywhere with tremors . . . ; then the
great shove of the destructive shock arrived, in some places rather
before, in some a little after, the moment of loudest sound, and
it died away suddenly into tremors again.*

—ROBERT MALLET, The Neopolitan (Italy) earthquake, December 16, 1857

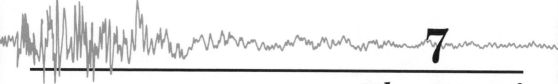

The Size of
an Earthquake

Intensity of Shaking

So destructive was the earthquake in southern Italy in December 1857
that local communications were disrupted and almost a week went by
before news of its extent reached foreign parts. Immediately, Robert
Mallet, an engineer, applied to the Royal Society in London for a travel
grant and proceeded to the Kingdom of Naples, where he spent 2 months
making the first scientific, perceptive field studies of the effects of a great
earthquake.

Mallet's methods included detailed mapping and tabulation of felt reports and damage to buildings and geological movements. In this way he
sought to measure the strength and distribution of the ground motion. By
drawing lines on a map between places of equal damage or of equal *intensity* (he called these *isoseismal lines*), he determined the center of the
earthquake shaking and hence identified the source of the seismic waves.
Also, the patterns of isoseismal lines indicated to Mallet the rate at which

the shaking effects diminished with distance and provided him with an estimate of the relative size of the earthquake.

In the decades that have followed Mallet's work, seismologists have used earthquake intensity as their most widely applicable yardstick of the size of an earthquake. Intensity is measured by means of the degree of damage to structures of human origin, the amount of disturbances to the surface of the ground, and the extent of animal reaction to the shaking. The first intensity scale of modern times was developed by M. S. de Rossi of Italy and Francois Forel of Switzerland in the 1880s. This scale, which is still sometimes used in describing an earthquake, has values ranging from I to X. (The published intensities of the 1906 San Francisco earthquake are based upon it.) A more refined scale, with 12 values, was constructed in 1902 by the Italian seismologist and volcanologist G. Mercalli. A version of it, called the abridged Modified Mercalli Intensity Scale, is given in Appendix D. It was developed by H. O. Wood and Frank Neumann to fit construction conditions in California (and most of the United States). Figure 1 illustrates how the scale was used to evaluate the shaking in the New Madrid, Missouri, earthquake of December 16, 1811.

Anyone who lives in regions where building and social conditions are similar to those of California can estimate the strength of a local earthquake on the Modified Mercalli scale (refer to Appendix D).° For example, suppose the earthquake is felt by all, most people are frightened, and many run outdoors. Suppose too that it shifts heavy furniture (such as refrigerators, large television sets, or sofas) causes plaster to fall, and damages some chimneys. Then it rates VI on the Modified Mercalli scale. Alternative intensity scales have been developed and are widely used in other countries, notably in Japan and in the Soviet Union, where conditions differ from those in California.

The assessment of earthquake intensity on a descriptive scale depends on actual observations of effects in the meizoseismal zone, not on measuring the ground motion with instruments. The descriptive scale continues to be important, first because in many seismic regions there are no seismographs to measure strong ground motion, and second, because the long historical record from seismically active countries is founded on such descriptions. However, the method has one problem that can affect the accuracy of the intensity rating: at a particular town or village the effect reflecting the *greatest* intensity is often chosen, thus increasing the local rating of the earthquake. A particular difficulty is the use of landslides caused by earthquakes. The Modified Mercalli scale gives landslides

---

° After an earthquake in the mountains of northeast California, a householder said that effects in the earthquake "felt like a bear was on the roof." What would be the Modified Mercalli intensity value?

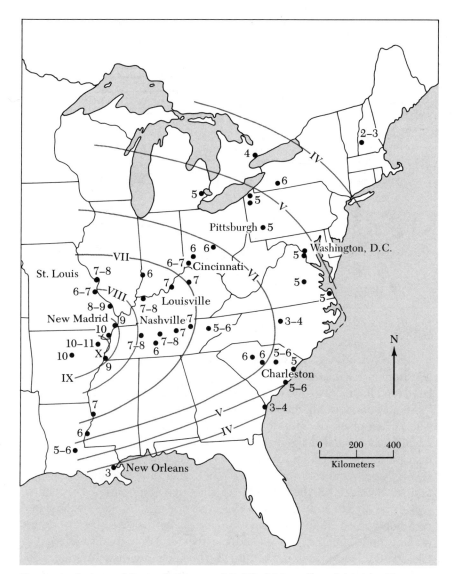

Figure 1 Isoseismal lines of intensity (Modified Mercalli scale) in the New Madrid, Missouri, earthquake on December 16, 1811. The felt radius of the earthquake extended to the East and Gulf coasts. Intensity in the then sparsely populated area west of the epicenter is unknown. Intensity values at specified points are given in Arabic numerals, and the isoseismals are labeled by Roman numerals. [Courtesy of O. Nuttli and *Bull. Seism. Soc. Am.*]

a rating of intensity X, but the fact is that landslides are common in many regions—even nonseismic areas—and quite small seismic shaking is known to be an effective landslide trigger.

FRANK AND ERNEST

HERE'S AN INTERESTING ITEM...

THERE WAS A MEETING LAST NIGHT IN CALIFORNIA...

THE ANNUAL MEETING OF THE EARTHQUAKE RESEARCH SOCIETY.

IT STARTED AT 7:00 P.M.

AT 7:02 IT WAS ADJOURNED BY A MOTION FROM THE FLOOR.

THAVES

[Reprinted by permission of Newspaper Enterprise Association.]

When a study of the intensity of an earthquake is made nowadays, questionnaires (related to the description in Appendix D) are often circulated to inhabitants of the affected region.° Based on the responses to these questionnaires, a map such as that shown in Figure 1 can be drawn. Then areas of equal intensity are separated by isoseismal contours. The resulting isoseismal maps provide crude but valuable information on the distribution of the ground shaking away from the earthquake source, and also they may indicate the effect of the underlying irregular rock layers and surficial soil on the intensity of shaking. The relation between the rock type of San Francisco and the intensity of the 1906 earthquake is commonly cited. Figure 2 shows the correlation between the strength of shaking and damage (part a) and the rock and soil conditions (part b). Clearly, the harder rock in the hills (Kjf) coincides with an area of rather low damage to structures (many chimneys did not fall), whereas high intensities occurred on the filled lands (Qal) around the bay shore.

How to Calculate Earthquake Magnitude

If the magnitudes of earthquakes are to be compared worldwide, a measure is needed that does not depend (as does intensity) on the density of population and type of construction. A strictly quantitative scale that can

---

°Future scale revisions should perhaps include the ubiquitous hamburger and gasoline stations as special items!

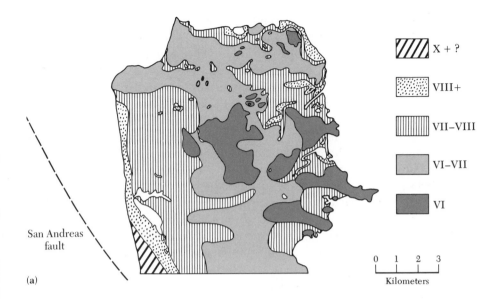

X + ?

VIII+

VII–VIII

VI–VII

VI

San Andreas
fault

0　1　2　3
Kilometers

(a)

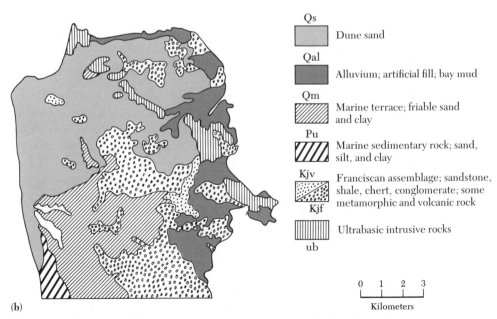

Qs
Dune sand

Qal
Alluvium; artificial fill; bay mud

Qm
Marine terrace; friable sand
and clay

Pu
Marine sedimentary rock; sand,
silt, and clay

Kjv
Franciscan assemblage; sandstone,
shale, chert, conglomerate; some
metamorphic and volcanic rock

Kjf
Ultrabasic intrusive rocks

ub

0　1　2　3
Kilometers

(b)

Figure 2　(a) Isoseismal lines on the San Francisco peninsula (based on the
Modified Mercalli scale) drawn by H. O. Wood after the 1906 San Francisco
earthquake. (b) A generalized geological map of San Francisco peninsula.
Note the correlation between the geology and the intensity.

be applied to earthquakes in both inhabited and uninhabited regions was originated in 1931 by K. Wadati in Japan and developed by the late Charles Richter in 1935 in California. The scheme is to use the wave amplitudes measured by a seismograph. The idea is similar to that of astronomers who grade the size of stars using a stellar magnitude scale based on the relative brightness seen through a telescope.

Because the size of earthquakes varies enormously, the amplitudes of the ground motions differ by factors of thousands from earthquake to earthquake. It is therefore most convenient to compress the range of wave amplitudes measured on seismograms by using some mathematical device. Richter defined the magnitude of a local earthquake as *the logarithm to base ten of the maximum seismic-wave amplitude (in thousandths of a millimeter) recorded on a standard seismograph at a distance of 100 kilometers from the earthquake epicenter.* Using the logarithmic scale, every time the magnitude goes up by 1 unit, the amplitude of the earthquake waves increases 10 times.

The seismograph used as standard for magnitude determinations of local shocks is a simple type with torsion suspension of the mass developed by H. O. Wood and J. Anderson (or its equivalent). The further the earthquake source is from the seismograph, the smaller the amplitude of the seismic wave, just as a light appears dimmer as the observing distance from the source increases. Because earthquake sources are located at all distances from seismographic stations, Richter further developed a method of making allowance for this attenuation with epicentral distance when calculating the Richter magnitude of an earthquake. The procedure is presented graphically in the box. With this scale anyone can easily calculate the magnitude of the small earthquake shown.

The idea behind the Richter magnitude scale was a modest one at its inception. The definition of local magnitude (M_L) was for southern California earthquakes only. The type of seismic wave to be used was not specified; the only condition was that the wave chosen—whether P, S, or surface wave—be the one with the largest amplitude. Richter wrote, "I did the work to provide a purely instrumental scale for rough separation of large, medium and small shocks."

Today, the use of magnitude has expanded beyond recognition from these modest beginnings. The convenience of describing the size of an earthquake by just one number, the magnitude, has required that the method be extended to apply to a number of types of seismographs throughout the world. Consequently, there are a variety of magnitude scales, which are based on different formulas for epicentral distance and ways of choosing an appropriate wave amplitude.

Earthquake magnitudes are used in three main ways. First, they are recognized by the general public, as well as by scientists, engineers, and technicians, as a measure of the relative size of an earthquake; people

Example of the Calculation of the Richter Magnitude (M_L) of a Local Earthquake

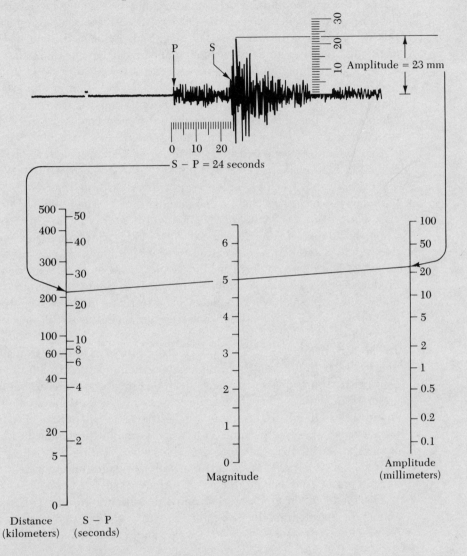

Procedure for calculating the local magnitude, M_L

1. Measure the distance to the focus using the time interval between the S and the P waves (S − P = 24 seconds).

2. Measure the height of the maximum wave motion on the seismogram (23 millimeters).

3. Place a straight edge between appropriate points on the distance (left) and amplitude (right) scales to obtain magnitude $M_L = 5.0$.

correlate a magnitude, at least roughly, with the severity of an earthquake. Second, magnitudes are of significance in the ongoing efforts to draw up a comprehensive nuclear test ban treaty: research has indicated that comparison of different kinds of magnitude is one of the best ways to distinguish between a nuclear explosion and an earthquake due to natural causes.° Third, magnitudes of previous earthquakes are used in an approximate way to predict what the greatest acceleration of the ground shaking may be in an earthquake at a site of an important structure (see Chapter 12). The information is then used by the engineer to design a structure that will withstand such strong motion.†

The magnitude scale has no upper or lower limit, although the largest size of an earthquake is certainly limited by the strength of the rocks of the Earth's crust. In this century, two or three earthquakes recorded on seismographs have had Richter magnitudes of 8.9. The 1906 San Francisco earthquake had a Richter magnitude of 8.25, and the great 1960 Chile earthquake of May 22 was 8.5. At the other extreme, highly sensitive seismographs can record earthquakes with a magnitude of less than minus 2. The energy release in such events is about equivalent to that produced when a brick is dropped from a table onto the ground. Generally speaking, shallow earthquakes have to attain Richter magnitudes of more than 5.5 before significant damage occurs near the source of the waves.

The current practice at earthquake observatories is to use two magnitude scales, both different from the original Richter scale. Two scales are used because earthquakes that have deep foci give very different seismograms from those having shallow foci, even though the total amount of energy released in each event might be the same. In particular, deep-focus earthquakes (see Chapter 1) have only small or insignificant trains of surface waves. It is therefore desirable, when dealing with all global earthquakes, to be able to calculate a uniform magnitude that does not depend on the presence or absence of surface waves.‡

The modification of Richter's original definition is simple. Let us examine the seismogram in Appendix H. An uncomplicated earthquake record clearly shows a P wave, an S wave, and a train of Rayleigh waves.

° Details of this seismological detective work are given in Bruce A. Bolt, *Nuclear Explosions and Earthquakes: The Parted Veil* (San Francisco: W. H. Freeman and Company, 1976).

† This practice is somewhat unfortunate, because near an earthquake source there is no strong correlation between earthquake magnitude and maximum peaks of acceleration.

‡ This problem might be avoided by using a new measure of earthquake strength called *seismic moment* (see the Glossary). Recent resesarch on earthquake size using this measure has suggested revisions in previous estimates of the relative magnitudes of great earthquakes.

(The seismogram shows only the vertical component of the ground motion.) Now, if Richter's procedure for determining local magnitude were followed, we would measure the amplitude of the largest of the three waves and then make some adjustment for epicentral distance and the magnification of the seismograph. But it is just as easy to measure the maximum amplitude of any one of the three waves and hence to find three magnitudes—one for each type of wave.

It has become routine in seismology to measure the amplitude of the P wave, which is not affected by the focal depth of the source, and thereby determine a P-wave magnitude (called m_b). For shallow earthquakes (such as that recorded in Appendix H) a surface wave train is also present. It is common practice to measure the amplitude of the largest swing in this surface wave train that has a period near 20 seconds. This value yields the surface-wave magnitude (M_s). Neither of the magnitudes $(m_b$ or $M_s)$ is the Richter magnitude, but each has an important part in describing the size of an earthquake.

For the shallow-focus earthquake shown in Appendix H, the measurements yield a body-wave magnitude of 5.3 and a surface-wave magnitude of 5.0. Many measurements of this kind for shallow earthquakes have suggested an approximate relation between m_b and M_s. This empirical relation allows the conversion of one type of magnitude into another, at least for moderate-size earthquakes. It turns out, however, that M_s correlates much more closely with our general ideas of the size of an earthquake than does m_b. For example, the 1964 earthquake in Alaska, which was a very strong shallow earthquake, had a surface-wave magnitude M_s of 8.6, whereas the body-wave magnitude m_b turned out to be only 6.5. Thus for this particular earthquake, the magnitude of the P wave (due to its short period) was not a good description of the Alaskan earthquake as a whole, but the M_s value was a better measure of overall size.° Additional magnitude scales, such as the *moment magnitude* (M_w) have been introduced to improve further the uniform coverage of earthquake size (see the Glossary).

Energy in Earthquakes

Today everyone is giving some thought to the energy resources available to mankind. Oil, coal, wind, and the sun, as well as nuclear energy, are all used as sources of energy. In order to discuss energy quantitatively, we

---

°The interested reader might try to explain why this is so. The answer is related to the often repeated observation: the longer the surface fault rupture, the greater the surface-wave magnitude (see Appendix H).

must recognize that energy is the measure of the work that can be done by some machine; in the metric system, common units of energy are ergs. The present total consumption of energy in the United States per annum is about 10^{26} ergs.

From a global perspective, such an amount of energy is really quite small. The amount of heat that flows out of the Earth as a whole, to be lost through the atmosphere into space each year, is about 10^{28} ergs. Earthquakes, too, emit a great deal of energy. As we discussed in Chapter 4, they are the result of the sudden release of strain energy stored previously in the rocks in the Earth. From measurements of the seismic-wave energy produced by the sudden fracture, it is estimated that each year the total energy released by earthquakes throughout the world is between 10^{25} and 10^{26} ergs. When seismograms from various stations around the world are used to calculate the energy in the recorded waves, an earthquake of Richter magnitude 5.5 turns out to have an energy of about 10^{20} ergs. By way of comparison, the energy that nuclear physicists calculate was released in the atomic bomb blast of Bikini in 1946 was about 10^{19} ergs.

It is tempting to correlate the energy release of an earthquake with its size, as measured by the earthquake magnitude scale. Although the correspondence is a rough one, it is nevertheless useful for estimating the amount of energy actually released in earthquakes. The relationship that seismologists suggest prevails between magnitude and energy release is given in Appendix H. This logarithmic relation indicates that an increase in magnitude M_s of 1 unit increases the amount of *seismic energy* E released by a factor of about 30 (not a factor of 10, as is sometimes quoted).°

Earthquake waves, of course, carry energy, and when they encounter buildings some of it is transferred to vibrate the structure. Nowadays, the amount of seismic energy per unit area per second transmitted to the shaking building can be measured by seismographs.

Acceleration of Ground Shaking

We have all felt the considerable forces that arise in a rapidly accelerating or braking car, in a jet aircraft as it takes off, or in the roller coaster at an amusement park. Some have felt similar forces during the hectic moments of an earthquake. The notion of acceleration is of key importance when

---

°If the amount of energy in a magnitude 2 earthquake were represented by the volume of a golf ball, the amount of energy released in the 1906 San Francisco earthquake would be represented by a sphere of radius 33 meters.

trying to measure any type of varying motion such as strong ground shaking. Indeed, as mentioned in Chapter 6, we can think of each portion of the earthquake waves as being associated with a certain acceleration of the ground.

For many years, a widely asked question has been, "How fast and by what amount does the ground move during an earthquake?" Definite answers were hard to find until the development of the modern *strong-motion seismograph*, designed to operate near to the source of an earthquake in such a way that it would not go off scale during the strongest shaking.

It is useful to scale acceleration against a value with which everyone is familiar, because experience does not commonly give us a feel for the magnitude of accelerations when stated in physical terms (often expressed as a centimeter per second or cm/sec², for example). This is the *acceleration due to gravity;* that is, the acceleration with which a ball falls if released at rest in a vacuum (to eliminate wind resistance). We will call this acceleration 1.0g.° It is quite a sizable rate of increase of speed. In terms of automobile accelerations, for example, it is equivalent to a car traveling 100 meters from rest in just $4\frac{1}{2}$ seconds.

Although acceleration of seismic motion is important, a full understanding of vibratory effects also requires an understanding of the velocity and displacement of the ground and of such wave properties as frequency. (The relations between acceleration, velocity, and displacement, as well as the concepts of wave period, wave frequency, and wavelength are explained briefly in Appendix I.)

The farther the waves travel, the more the high-frequency waves are attenuated in comparison with the long-period ones. For example, in 1964, long-surface waves from the Good Friday earthquake in Alaska were recorded at the seismographic station in Berkeley, California, with periods of 17 seconds and maximum ground displacement of 1 centimeter. Yet the length between the wave crests was so long (approximately 50 kilometers) that nobody in Berkeley was aware of moving up and down during the passage of the waves.

Instruments called accelerographs have now provided hundreds of records of seismic shaking, both away from and within buildings, in many countries of the world. Measurements from accelerograms indicate that the highest acceleration in the shaking of firm ground in most moderate earthquakes, at places a few tens of kilometers from the seismic source, lies in the range of 0.05g to 0.35g.

°$g = 980$ cm/s² $= 980$ gals., approximately, the acceleration due to gravity.

Some peaks of high-frequency waves may reach accelerations of half the acceleration of gravity. This usually occurs when the ground motion is measured on firm ground or rock very near the source of the waves.° As discussed in Chapter 2, both vertical and horizontal ground motions are measured in earthquakes. Generally, the vertical acceleration is less than the peak horizontal acceleration, and an average value from many of the available California accelerograms suggests an average ratio of about 50 percent for the vertical compared to the horizontal motions. One of the largest horizontal accelerations recorded thus far was on the abutment of Pacoima Dam in the damaging 1971 San Fernando earthquake— it reached 1.15g. The vertical acceleration was recorded with a peak of about 0.70g.

Studies indicate that damage is often much more attributable to the velocity of the back-and-forth motion of the foundation than to its peak acceleration. In general, the higher the seismic intensity, the higher the average velocity of the shaking. Nevertheless, the mean accelerations have much bearing on the forces affecting a structure (see Appendix D). Consequently, in designing to avert earthquake damage, engineers have come to rely heavily on the estimates of ground acceleration that a structure might be expected to experience in its lifetime.

Because buildings are built to withstand the pull of gravity, even when no special earthquake code is followed, they will usually withstand substantial accelerations in a vertical direction during earthquake shaking. In contrast, experience has shown that it is the horizontal motions of the ground that topple structures and even throw people to the ground. Many types of buildings, such as adobe buildings in South America and the Middle East, are not able to withstand even 10 percent of the acceleration of gravity in a horizontal direction.

The accelerations of the ground recorded during the 1971 San Fernando earthquake are reproduced in Figure 3. Three components of the ground acceleration were recorded: the bottom trace, from left to right, indicates the vertical shaking; the top two traces show the two horizontal components—north-south and east-west ground shaking. At the bottom, a time scale is given in seconds. Acceleration of the shaking has been recorded as a fraction of gravity.

Consider in Figure 3 the structure of the wave form, running from left to right. First of all, the instrument triggered with the arrival of a P wave and, during the first second and a half, a rather high-frequency but small-amplitude P wave shook the ground. The bottom trace shows that the

---

°Oldham, a geologist, was director of the Geological Survey of India. In 1906, he discovered the Earth's massive core using earthquake waves (see Chapter 8).

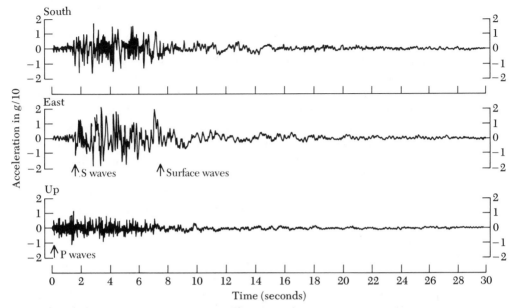

Figure 3 Three components of strong ground acceleration recorded in the parking lot outside the Hollywood storage building about 20 kilometers from the fault rupture in the 1971 San Fernando earthquake, California.

vertical component shaking did not increase very much after this time, reaching a maximum of a little over 0.1*g*. In sharp contrast, however, after about 2 seconds the horizontal components of the ground acceleration became markedly larger with the arrival of S waves and surface waves. On the east-west component, the arrows show the onset of the S and surface waves; the horizontal ground shaking reached a maximum of a little more than 0.2*g* after 3 seconds elapsed.

Although "peak," or maximum, acceleration values are important, another point to recognize is that the damage to structures may be occurring throughout the entire period of strong ground shaking. Indeed, the overall damage may be more closely correlated to the total duration of the strong motion than to any particular peak on the record. For this reason, the second parameter of importance in acceleration records is the duration of strong shaking. A useful measure of duration is called the *bracketed duration*. This is the duration of shaking above a certain threshold acceleration value, commonly taken to be 0.05*g*, and is defined as the time between the first and last peaks of motion that exceed this threshold value. In Figure 3, the bracketed duration above 0.05*g* acceleration is only about 6 seconds.

Upthrow

In earthquake engineering, recent studies suggest that certain structures respond significantly to vertical shaking of the ground, and that design methods that take into account only the horizontal motion are deficient in important ways. The vertical component appears to be particularly important in calculating seismic designs for massive dams and foundations of such surface structures as pipelines. In a number of earthquakes, strong-motion accelerograms have indicated that ground accelerations (both vertical and horizontal) at the basement level of buildings are magnified by considerable factors in the upper floors of the buildings. For example, in the March 22, 1957, San Francisco earthquake (Richter magnitude 5.3), accelerograms in a building in San Francisco showed an amplification in the maximum vertical acceleration of 3 between the basement and the fourteenth floor.

One measure of extreme vertical shaking is the "upthrow" of objects. Reports of such upthrow in large earthquakes, from around the world, have depended upon field observations after the shaking. If the reports are true, do they indicate that earthquake accelerations in the vertical direction exceed the acceleration of gravity? In fact, instrument measurements of vertical ground accelerations greater than gravity have been obtained. For example, near the source of the Gazli earthquake ($M_s = 7.0$) in the Uzbek Republic of the Soviet Union, on May 17, 1976, a vertical acceleration of $1.3g$ was recorded.

One of the earliest dramatic accounts of upthrow is by R. D. Oldham[°] on the great Assam, India, earthquake of June 12, 1897. He reports that loose stones were tossed in the air at Shillong and elsewhere, "like peas on a drum." All the available reports indicate that particularly violent shaking occurred. People were thrown to the ground and injured by the shock. Boulders were displaced, leaving cavities in the earth where they had lain. The ejection was so abrupt that the sides of the cavities were almost unbroken. There were also stories of posts coming out of their holes without cutting the edges of the surrounding soil.

Oldham also writes about the disturbance of the surface soil:

> In the western portion of the southern spur, and all around the civil surgeons' quarters to the distance of a mile down the Nankachar Road

---

[°]Such as in the Bear Valley, California, earthquake on September 4, 1972 ($M_L = 4.7$) the Ancona earthquake in Italy on June 21, 1972 ($M_L = 4.5$), and particularly the San Fernando, California, earthquake on February 9, 1971 ($M_L = 6.5$). In such recordings, horizontal accelerations of $0.6g$ to over $1.0g$ have been recorded independently of the magnitude of the earthquake.

where the soil is sandy and the surface fairly level, the ground looks as if a steam plow had passed over it, tearing up the turf and throwing the clods in every direction, some uphill and some down, and in many cases, turning the sods completely over so that only the roots of grass are visible.

Some Japanese earthquakes have also produced strong upward motion. In the two Imaichi earthquakes (Richter magnitude about 6) of December 26, 1949, some diverse pieces of evidence are mentioned. Near Ochiai village, close to the center of the source area, a stone implement called an *ishiusu*, about 50 centimeters in diameter, was said to have been tossed upward about 20 centimeters a few times, like a rebounding rubber ball. In nearby Imaichi, published studies report that although objects upon the shelves did not fall, iron kettles were thrown off their hooks.

A particularly interesting obeservation on dynamical systems comes from reports of the Kwanto earthquake of September 1, 1923. The disturbances in alluvial material were particularly marked; in fact, near Manazuru Point, the soft ground was so shaken that potatoes were extruded onto the ground. Nearby, large trees sank in the soft soil until only their tops were visible. No doubt liquefaction of the sandy soil was a dominant factor.

In California earthquakes, too, vertical separation has occurred. The rupturing in the 1971 San Fernando earthquake was thrust faulting, and it produced offsets as great as 3 meters. This faulting was evidently an efficient generator of seismic waves, because large ground accelerations were recorded across a fairly wide area. At the Los Angeles County Fire Station 74 in North Dexter Park, San Fernando, a fireman on duty was tossed out of bed onto the floor and the bed fell on top of him. The receiver of a standard wall phone came off its hook and every object in the building was upset. The building was shifted off its foundations and outside "rocks were thrown off the ground and large cracks appeared in both soil and rock."

At the same station, the movements of a fire truck—which must have been due at least in part to the elastic springing system of the vehicle— were also recorded by B. J. Morrill:

A 20-ton fire truck enclosed in the garage moved 6 to 8 feet fore and aft, 2 to 3 feet sideways without leaving visible skid marks on the garage floor. The truck was in gear and the brakes were set. Marks which appear to have been made by the right rear tire were found on the door frame, three feet above the floor, while the metal fender was not damaged. The fender extends several inches out beyond the upper portion of the tire. Four feet above the floor, the hose rack was broken by the rear step of the truck. The step was bent up while the hose rack was broken downwards.

Figure 4 Northwest corner of the quarters building of the Los Angeles County Fire Station in Kagel Canyon, San Fernando, after the 1971 earthquake. Note that a line of shingles that had overlapped the foundation is undamaged. [Photo by B. J. Morrill, 1972; courtesy of USGS.]

Even more striking evidence of vertical separation was the displacement of the building in which the fire fighters were housed. As Figure 4 shows, the building was displaced from the foundations in such a way that the bottom row of shingles—which, prior to the earthquake, overlapped the foundations by 10 centimeters—were undisturbed. This evidence is hard to explain as sliding of the building, but rocking remains an alternative cause.

Disturbed surface soil was also observed after the 1971 earthquake in several places. For example, along flat ground at the top of one ridge, the surficial soil was considerably shattered, giving the appearance of plowed land. One explanation is that the soil was overturned during vertical accelerations that exceeded 1.0*g* during several cycles of the seismic waves. Similar reports had been published already by geologists and seismologists from field studies of numerous other earthquakes around the world.

Although some individual reports can be discounted, apparently certain types of objects do separate vertically in earthquakes, indicating that the acceleration of at least the localized motions exceeds that of gravity. It is possible that one explanation is not sufficient for all phenomena reported; certainly a significant proportion of apparent vertical motions and offsets (for example, of gravestones) can be explained as the consequences of rocking and rotation set up by horizontal accelerations of seismic waves.

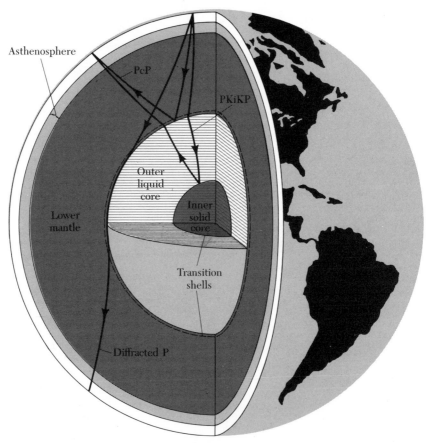

A cross section of the Earth based on seismological evidence.
The paths taken by three major kinds of earthquake waves
are shown. [From Bruce A. Bolt, *Inside the Earth* (San Francisco:
W. H. Freeman and Company, Copyright © 1982).]

The seismograph, recording the unfelt motion of distant earthquakes, enables us to see into the Earth and determine its nature with as great a certainty as if we could drive a tunnel through it.

—R. D. OLDHAM, "The Constitution of the Interior of the Earth as Revealed by Earthquakes," *Quarterly Journal*, Geological Society, 1906.

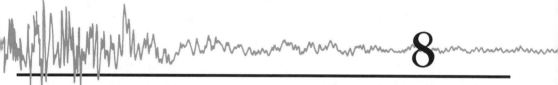

8

Exploring Inside the Earth

Earthquake Waves through the Interior

Seismograms provide most of the detailed knowledge of the Earth's deep interior. Before the turn of the century and the development of the seismograph, the vast region that lies beneath our feet was the subject of much imaginative speculation based on very little information. Only the physical properties of surface rocks and the size and shape of the Earth were known with reasonable accuracy. It was known that the Earth's mean density was about $5\frac{1}{2}$ times that of water and that the density increased toward the center because of the enormous pressures there. Was the material in the center solid, fluid, or gaseous? Was the interior of the Earth like a raisin pudding or was it composed of many shells like the layers on an onion? These questions, as R. D. Oldham pointed out in 1906, could only be answered by measuring earthquake waves that travel through the whole Earth.

The modern era of seismological exploration of deep Earth structure began in 1887 when a German scientist, E. von Rebeur Paschwitz, noticed that ground motions in the form of waves had been registered by delicate horizontal pendulums operating in observatories in Potsdam and Wilhelmshaven in Germany. Some time after a great earthquake was reported in Tokyo, von Rebeur Paschwitz realized that the seismic waves at the two German stations arrived about half an hour after the Japanese earthquake occurred. He then decided that the recordings in Germany were due to the great Japanese earthquake.

By 1900 it had been established that seismographs could detect both P and S waves (see Chapter 2, Figure 6). The presence of both these kinds of waves generated by the slip on the geological fault near the surface of the Earth was of great assistance in unraveling the deep Earth structure. If we think of the Earth as a giant glass spherical lens and the energy released by the fault slip as a light bulb on its surface, the traveling seismic waves resemble the light rays refracting through the lens. The ray picture is shown in Figure 1. Because the Earth is a sphere, it is easiest to plot the distance between the earthquake source and the recording seismograph in terms of the angular distance subtended at the center of the Earth. Thus seismographic stations range from 0 to 180° at the antipodes of the earthquake source.

The first great triumph of the use of seismic rays to x-ray the Earth was in 1906 when Oldham suggested that the best way to explain the travel times of P and S waves from one side of the Earth to the other was to invoke a large central core to the Earth. From suitable seismograms, Oldham plotted the travel times of P and S waves along their ray paths against the angular distance and found that the S waves could be plotted as arrivals out to about 110° of arc, but not beyond it. He explained this change in behavior of the S waves by hypothesizing that they had penetrated a central core in which they traveled at a much lower rate. (It is now believed that S waves do not propagate at all through the liquid core.) In 1914, Beno Gutenberg, a seismologist working in Göttingen, Germany, fixed the depth to the boundary of the separate core rather precisely. Gutenberg found that the direct P waves through the Earth could be traced out to about 105°, after which they rapidly became very weak in energy. Beyond this distance, seismograms showed waves arriving that were delayed by up to a minute beyond that expected for the direct P waves. He also observed waves that could be explained as reflected directly from the boundary of the Earth's core.

It is easiest to think of the penetration of seismic waves to great depth

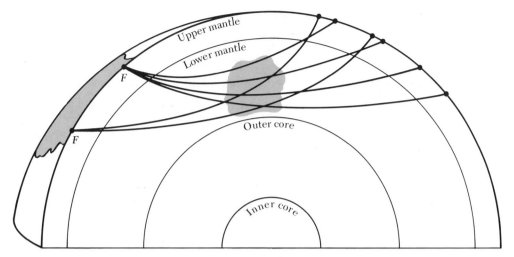

Figure 1   Paths of earthquake waves through the Earth's mantle from earthquake sources at *F* to seismographs at the surface. All the seismic paths pass through the dotted region and provide a tomographic scan of it.

in the same way that one observes rays of light spreading out from a bulb at the point *F* in Figure 1. Because the rocks of the Earth's interior are more compressed toward the center by the great mass of overlying material, the velocity of both P and S seismic waves generally increases with depth from the surface to the center of the Earth. This increase bends the paths of the seismic waves so that they dip down and then refract back to the surface along the paths illustrated in Figure 1. At this surface point they are reflected down again and produce another similar leg. Each time a P or an S wave encounters the surface of the Earth or a boundary between two rock types in the interior, the reflected and refracted seismic waves are, in general, of two kinds (see Chapter 2, Figure 7). In other words, in marked contrast to light waves, at such encounters an incident P wave produces a reflected (and refracted) P and S wave; similarly for incident S waves with vertical motion, called SV waves (but not for the purely horizontal SH waves).° This branching of wave types greatly complicates the groups of seismic waves that move through the Earth and, in due course, arrive at the surface to be felt as an earthquake or to be recorded on a seismogram.

°By considering the directions that the rocks are displaced in the P, SV, and SH waves, the reader should be able to demonstrate that this is so (see Chapter 2, Figure 6).

Seismic Wave Probes

As was explained above, the P and S waves in earthquakes travel down through the body of the Earth like x-rays. In modern medicine, a common technique used by doctors to obtain images of anomalous growths inside the human body is CAT-scanning (for Cathode Applied Tomography): sensors on one side of the body show the way that variations in human tissues affect the intensity of x-rays or atomic particles applied to the other side. By analogy, probing the Earth's interior by P and S waves is called *geophysical tomography* (Figure 1). In the same way, the Earth's outer structure can be resolved by comparing surface wave trains recorded at seismographic stations remote from the earthquake sources. The two types of surface waves, Love waves and Rayleigh waves (see Chapter 2, Figure 6), are seismic companions with separate and distinguishable features. These waves do not penetrate through the whole Earth but are channeled by the Earth's outside surface; their properties depend on the structure and elasticity of the rocks through which they pass. The measurement of the speeds and wave forms of surface waves can be used as tomographic signals; these signals can be decoded to yield a picture of the tectonically complex regions in the upper part of the Earth.

Recordings of seismic Love (LQ) and Rayleigh waves (LR) are illustrated in Figure 2. The Love waves arrive first, followed by the Rayleigh waves; the Love-wave motion is restricted to the horizontal plane, while Rayleigh-wave motion is confined to a vertical plane. Surface waves do not occur as the concentrated pulses typical of P and S waves but are spread out into a train of many cycles of vibrations. This spreading is called *dispersion*. As the surface waves progress around the Earth's surface, they sort themselves out into longer and longer trains of waves according to the period of the motion and the variation in the elastic properties with depth in the Earth. Waves with longer wavelengths travel more quickly than those with shorter wavelengths; because the longer waves penetrate deeper into the Earth, this observation implies that the deeper rocks transmit waves more quickly.

The time of arrival at the recording station of each of the separate wave components in a surface wave train can be measured and the wavelength speeds plotted as a function of the period of the wave. The resulting curve gives the crucial dispersion information on the deep structure and hence the elastic properties of the rocks through which the waves passed. This procedure involves an *inverse problem*. For its solution, the following direct (or forward) problem must first be solved. If the physical properties of the Earth under, say, the North American continent were known, then a computer could calculate the appropriate *theoretical* dispersion curve for the known structure. But in reality, it is the *observed* dispersion curve that is known, and from this cryptic information the

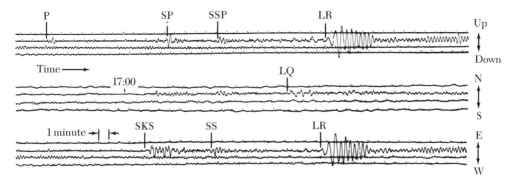

Figure 2   Three components of ground motion recorded by a seismograph in Berkeley at a distance of 88° from a south Pacific earthquake on May 7, 1972. The symbols LR and LQ denote Rayleigh and Love waves, respectively.

elastic properties and layered structure of the rocks underground are inferred. This way of looking at the exploration of remote depths of the Earth is recent. The inverse problem has been solved successfully for the broad average properties of the deep interior, and present research is aimed at refining the observations of earthquakes so that more tectonically complex regions (such as those between the continents and oceans and along the subduction zones) can be unraveled.

Interpretations

Now that the paths of waves that constitute an earthquake have been explained, let us set as a challenge the interpretation of a seismogram recorded at a site remote from the earthquake source. The materials for the puzzle are contained in Figures 2 and 3.

Consider the three records shown in Figure 2. The top record is the vertical motion of the ground recorded by a seismograph at the Berkeley observatory located 88° away from an earthquake in New Ireland in the south Pacific on May 7, 1972. The lower two sets of traces are from the motions of the ground in the north-south and east-west directions, respectively. Several traces are shown in each of the three components because the recorded waves overlap these lines, which are recorded continuously on a revolving drum.

The first-arriving P wave can only be detected in the recorded vertical ground motion. (Why?) It arrived 12 minutes and 53 seconds after traveling through the Earth from the earthquake focus. Along this curved path, the seismic wave penetrated as deep as 2000 kilometers into the Earth.

Interpretation of the various seismic wave onsets marked in Figure 2 can be understood by referring to the examples of types of ray paths drawn in Figure 3. For example, further along the traces on the east-west

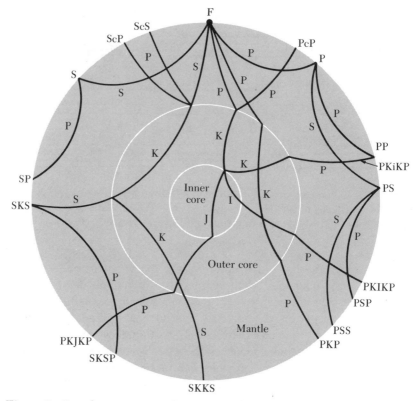

Figure 3 Sample seismic rays through the Earth. Begin at the focus of the earthquake F. The symbol c designates a wave reflected at the outer core's surface; thus PcP is a P wave through the mantle reflected at the core; ScP is an S wave reflected as P. The symbol i designates a wave reflected at the inner core's boundary: PKiKP. The symbols K and I refer, respectively, to P waves that have traveled through the outer and inner core. The symbol SP designates an S wave through the mantle reflected at the surface as P. The ray marked PKJKP, which travels as S through the inner core, has not been observed. [From Bruce A. Bolt, *Inside the Earth* (San Francisco: W. H. Freeman and Company, Copyright © 1982).]

component in Figure 2, the clear onset of waves is marked SKS. As Figure 3 shows, SKS denotes a wave that has traveled first as an S wave and then as a P wave through the center of the Earth before emerging on the other side of the Earth as an S wave again.

Later on the record, onsets of waves are indicated as SP, SS, SSP. These earthquake waves have traveled through the body of the Earth with at least one reflection at the outside surface producing echoes of various types. Each of the ray paths of the New Ireland seismogram can be plotted on a diagram like that in Figure 3.

Similar identifications of thousands of seismograms like that analyzed here have led to the rather sharp resolution of the structure of the Earth's interior. The main results can now be described.

Interior Earth Structure

The Earth has four main shells: the crust, mantle, outer core, and the inner core. This concentric structure (shown in the figure opposite the chapter opening) has been established by many independent analyses of measurements of earthquake waves. Interpretations of the travel times, amplitudes, and other properties of recorded seismic waves of various types have provided the necessary tomographic images described in the first section above.

The *crust* is the worldwide outermost layer of rocks, ranging in thickness from 25 to 60 kilometers under continents and from 4 to 6 kilometers under deep oceans. It has complex internal structures in many places, such as in the tectonically active and transitional areas of the world.

The underlying *mantle* extends from the base of the crust to a depth of 2885 kilometers. It consists of dense silicate rocks. P seismic waves as well as S waves (i.e., shear type) penetrate through almost all parts of the mantle; this demonstrates that the mantle is solid and strong, at least on short time scales. (There is evidence that even mantle rocks flow slowly over geological intervals of millions of years because of their high temperatures and pressures.) The mantle has been subdivided further into shells and anomalous regions, the latter intimately connected with the dynamical geological processes that cause the topographic and tectonic variations on the surface. The behavior of earthquake waves indicates that the outermost 100 kilometers (including the crust) of the Earth, called the *lithosphere*, is relatively rigid, while below it there is a softer layer of about 400 kilometers called the *asthenosphere*. Refined tomographic seismic imaging is now being used to map these geologically important outer layers in more detail.

Further toward the Earth's center, below the solid mantle, is the *outer core* of the Earth, which R. D. Oldham discovered by using earthquake recordings. This enormous shell appears to be liquid and is composed mainly of iron, oxygen, and silicon. Among the crucial arguments for the liquidity of the outer core is that, despite many observations, no seismic waves that have traveled through it as S waves (shear type) have ever been detected on seismograms. Because S waves cannot propagate through materials with no rigidity (see Chapter 2), the strong inference is that the outer core is in a liquid state. Reflections of seismic P and S waves take place efficiently from the outer surface of the core, thus establishing a sharp boundary there.

By 1936, the reality of the crust, mantle, and liquid core was well established. But some major mystery remained when observers attempted to interpret seismograms of very distant earthquakes and found, disconcertingly, clear onsets that had no simple explanation.

Illuminating the Innermost Core

The year 1986 is the 50th anniversary of the discovery of the *inner core* of the Earth. This remarkable achievement was made by Dr. Inge Lehmann, who worked as a seismologist in the Copenhagen Observatory in Denmark. The observatory was well situated to detect the PKP waves (see Figure 3) that pass through the center of the Earth to Europe from earthquakes in the seismically active south Pacific region.

Figure 4 shows some of the seismograms from a 1929 New Zealand earthquake that Lehmann saw at the European stations of Sverdlovsk at a distance of 135° away from the focus and Irkutsk 110.8° away. In 1929 there was no convincing explanation for the arrival of a seismic wave pulse about 19 minutes after the occurrence of an earthquake at these distances. The Earth was at that time conceived as having just three shells—a crust, a mantle, and a single core. The simplified Earth section in Figure 4 (from Lehmann's discussion) shows that for such an Earth model with constant wave speeds in each shell, rays like those marked 1, 2, 3, and 2a were to be expected. However, in order to account for the rays marked 5, 4, and 6 at the observed arrival times, an additional feature was needed. Lehmann stated "we take it that, as before, the earth consists of a core and a mantle but that inside the core there is an inner core in which the velocity is larger than the outer one. The radius of the inner core is taken to be 0.2205 times the earth's radius so that the ray whose angle of incidence at the surface of the Earth is 16° just touches the inner core."

If one assumes an inner core with a sharp outer boundary, a PKP wave (such as path 5 in Figure 4) would be reflected from this boundary back to shorter distances; this would explain the mystery waves from the New Zealand earthquakes.

Inge Lehmann's evidence of the inner core was convincing enough that other seismologists working on the problem of the Earth's structure adopted her hypotheses, and within a few years the reality of the small body at the center of the Earth, with a radius now estimated to be about

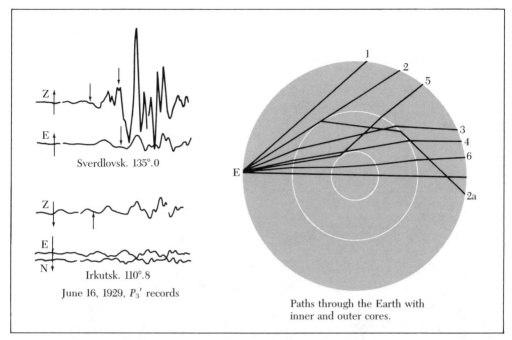

Z

E

Sverdlovsk. 135°.0

Z

E

N

Irkutsk. 110°.8

June 16, 1929, P_3' records

Paths through the Earth with
inner and outer cores.

1
2
5
3
4
6
2a
E

Figure 4 Figures reproduced from I. Lehmann, "P'," Bureau Central
Seismologique International, Series A, *Travaux Scientifique*, 14, 88, 1936.
[From Bruce A. Bolt, *Inside the Earth* (San Francisco: W. H. Freeman and
Company, Copyright © 1982).]

1216 kilometers, became accepted. Of course, there is always uncertainty
in such fundamental research, and Lehmann was careful to state in her
paper° that her argument did not *prove* the existence of an inner core but
merely established it with some degree of probability. A great strength of
Lehmann's Earth model was that it could be tested by independent
means, such as the reflections from its surface. Only in this way can
earthquake probes discover deep structure; indeed, Earth models are not
strictly unique at all.

Additional seismological work over the last 50 years indicates that the
inner core is a solid body in contrast to the liquid outer core. Some of this
recent work involved measurements of the vibrations of the whole Earth
that occur in the very largest earthquakes. The enormous release of energy in such cases causes the entire globe to shake like a bell does after
being struck. The tones of vibration depend on the elastic properties
throughout the Earth.

°Lehmann's paper, "P'," has one of the shortest titles in science. This discovery perhaps
would have rated a Nobel Prize in physics for the analogous detection of a new atomic
particle!

Failure of the earthfill Sheffield Dam due to the Santa
Barbara, California, earthquake of June 29, 1925.
[Photo by Putnam Studios.]

Under the water it rumbled on.

—S. T. COLERIDGE, "The Rhyme of the Ancient Mariner"

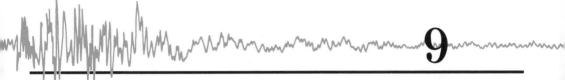

9

Stimulation of Earthquakes by Water

The Effect of Water on Rocks beneath the Surface

If there were no water in the rocks, there would be no tectonic earthquakes. The reasons are many. First, suppose we calculate the pressure at a depth of 5 kilometers in the Earth's crust due to the pull of gravity on the overlying rocks. We would find that it is equal to the strength of granite or similar rock (that is, the pressure it can sustain without breaking) at the pressure (1000 bars°) and temperature (500°C) appropriate for that depth. At greater depths, because the hydrostatic pressure is already greater than the strength of the rocks, we might expect that they would flow and deform plastically under differential pressures, rather than break through brittle fracture (thus producing an earthquake). Indeed, if a sample of hard granitic rock is squeezed in the laboratory under the appropriate temperature and pressure conditions, generally it will flow and not break. But earthquakes happen, and so we have a paradox.

°1 bar equals 10^6 dynes per square centimeter, which is roughly equivalent to 1 atmosphere pressure. Ten bars is about the tensile strength of cement.

135

Experiments on the effect of pressure on minerals containing water of crystallization and on water-saturated rocks do, however, suggest why fracture might occur at depth in the Earth: water acts in such a way that it allows a sudden slip to take place, perhaps by providing a kind of lubrication along slide planes. In these experiments, slips in rock specimens are accompanied by jerks of the pneumatic press that squeezes the rock. These jerks correspond to sudden reductions in the confining pressure. In other words, each jerk signifies an almost instantaneous drop in stress on the slip (fault) surface within the specimen. Out of the laboratory, seismological work on recorded earthquake waves indicates that, in shallow-focus earthquakes, the shearing pressure or stress along faults suddenly drops by amounts ranging from a few tens to a few hundred bars. These rather low-stress drops are much smaller than the strengths of hard rocks, which range up to 1 kilobar. It seems possible, therefore, that the water present in rocks along the fault zone weakens them so that only a small amount of shearing stress is removed during the earthquake rupture.

There is other evidence for the effect of water on earthquake mechanisms. Recall from Chapter 3 that the typical geological section in fault zones shows a succession of gouge, crushed and sheared rock, and clays; hydrological conditions in the fault zone commonly produce hydrous, or water-containing, rocks such as serpentinite. At least near the surface, the gouge and clays often show direct evidence of shear slip associated with wet conditions, with successive smooth striated layers called *slickensides*. In fact, ample ground water appears to be available at depth in most seismically active zones, and the presence of water in springs and deep wells is often quite notable along major faults.

The importance of water in earthquake generation came to the attention of seismologists in 1962 when a series of earthquakes began near Denver, Colorado. Although throughout the years there had been some earthquakes in the area—for example, one of Modified Mercalli intensity VII had occurred in 1882, and a few other local shocks had taken place since—the natural seismicity had always been low. Suddenly, there was a change beginning in April 1962, when a succession of earthquakes was felt: between that month and September 1963 local seismographic stations registered more than 700 epicenters in the vicinity! The magnitudes ranged between 0.7 and 4.3 on the Richter scale.

Most of these earthquakes were within a radius of 8 kilometers of the Rocky Mountain arsenal northeast of Denver, where weapons were being manufactured by the army. One of the by-products of this manufacture was contaminated water, which was at first allowed to evaporate from surface storage. But in 1961 the army switched to what seemed a more environmentally acceptable method of disposal—to pump the waste liquid down a deep well, bored to a depth of 3670 meters. These wastes were injected under pressure into the borehole from March 8, 1962, to September 30, 1963. Injection ceased for a year and then resumed in September 1964 through September 1965. Subsequently, earthquakes were felt in Denver. Inhabitants complained about the possible relation between the pumping and the oubreak of the earthquakes until they eventually succeeded in halting this method of waste disposal.

The correlation between the amount of water injected and the number of earthquakes was indeed quite strong: a high incidence of local earthquakes occurred in early 1963, followed by a sharp decline in 1964, and then another series of earthquakes occurred in large numbers in 1965 when the amount of water pumped, owing to increased injection pressure, was again maximum. A plausible mechanical explanation of the effect is twofold. First, the increased water pressure at the well produced a flow of ground water into crevices and cracks in preexisting faults underground. This increase in pore pressure led in turn to a reduction of the shear strength of the rock and gouge material. Second, because of the fractured condition of rocks in the preexisting fault zones, the preferred flow of water was along microcracks and fault planes, and this interstitial water was an important source of lubrication. The condition was then ripe for the tectonic strain in the crust, built up over many years, to be released in a series of slips, producing earthquakes. Such release of tectonic strain might not have happened for a number of years, or within such a short period, if the extra water pressure had not been introduced.

The Denver information was uncovered by chance, but it was followed up by a planned field experiment under similar conditions. The necessary work was initiated in 1969 by the U.S. Geological Survey at the Rangely Oil Field in western Colorado. Oil wells were already available at the site, and water, therefore, could be regularly injected into the wells or pumped out of them and the pore pressure in the crustal rock measured. At the same time, a specially sited array of seismographs was put into place to monitor fluctuations in local seismic activity. The results showed an excellent correlation between the quantity of fluid injected and the local earthquake activity, as illustrated in Figure 1. When the fluid pore pressure reached a threshold level (1.1×10^4 pascals° in this case), the earthquake activity increased. When the pressure dropped as a result of water withdrawal, the seismic activity decreased. Again, it must be emphasized that the wells at Rangely penetrated preexisting faults and that the crust in the region was already under some tectonic strain, as indicated by the occurrence of small local earthquakes over the previous years.

°3700 psi (pounds per square inch). See Appendix F.

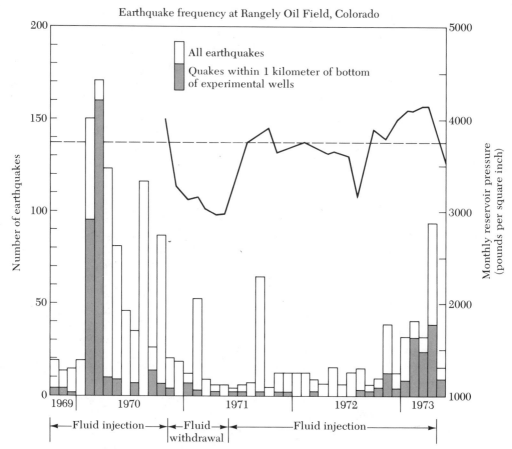

Figure 1 Earthquake frequency at Rangely Oil Field, Colorado, in an experiment in which water was alternately pumped in and out of wells. The reservoir pressure is plotted as a solid line. The threshold of pressure needed to initiate earthquakes is 3700 pounds per square inch (broken line). Those occurring below that threshold were due to natural causes. Each vertical bar represents the number of earthquakes occurring for 1 calendar month. [USGS.]

The Denver and Rangely investigations thus demonstrated the crucial importance of water in triggering sudden ruptures deep in the crust. They also led to the idea of earthquake control. One proposal was to pump water through deep boreholes into faults in a region where natural earthquakes might be particularly hazardous. An outbreak of small earthquakes might be thus induced, thereby reducing the amount of strain energy stored in the crust in the vicinity and reducing the probability of a large earthquake. Tampering with the forces of nature in this way is of course hazardous: if control were attempted along a major active fault, the consequences could be especially damaging. But "destraining" of the crustal rocks by water injection at the site of a future critical structure, such as a massive dam, might be worthwhile. Imaginative schemes of this type may be implemented as practical measures at some future time.

Dam Safety and Earthquakes

A great tragedy was averted in the 1971 San Fernando earthquake just north of Los Angeles in southern California. The lower Van Norman Dam, less than 10 kilometers from the ruptured fault, had been built 30 years before by using the then common method of carrying soil for fill into position by water sluicers. Subsequently, additional hydraulic fill had been placed on the dam. During the 1971 earthquake, a major earth slide took place in the interior portion of the dam, leaving only a meter or so of soil on the downstream side to stop the water from pouring onto a densely populated suburban area. Fortunately, the water in the reservoir was not at the allowable maximum at the time of the earthquake, and the slim earth lip of the dam did not erode but held the water in the reservoir until it could be drawn down. Meanwhile, 80,000 persons were evacuated from the downstream area.

The incident exemplifies the importance of evaluating prospective dam sites for seismic risk. Not only is an earth or concrete dam an expensive structure, but it directly affects the economy of the region through power generation, flood control, and irrigation. As the population grows, structural failure of a large dam poses increasingly greater danger for the sizable numbers exposed to the sudden inundation of the flood plains. Indeed, in various countries major dams are located in areas that in the past have suffered large earthquakes. The likelihood of future damaging earthquakes must be considered—during planning and after construction—to ensure continual safety of downstream habitation. Certainly, geological conditions near the site, including landslides and faulting, must be most carefully studied.

The hazards from normal regional earthquakes aside, however, we must also take account of a curious connection between reservoirs and earthquakes. There have been at least 13 incidents in different countries in which swarms of earthquakes have occurred very near a large reservoir soon after it has been filled.

The idea that earthquakes might be triggered by impounding surface water is not new. In the 1870s, the U.S. Corps of Engineers rejected proposals for major water storage in the Salton Sea in southern California on the grounds that such action might cause earthquakes. The first detailed evidence of such an effect came with the filling of Lake Mead behind Hoover Dam (height 221 meters), Nevada–Arizona, beginning in 1935. Although there may have been some local seismicity before, earthquakes were much more common after 1936. Nearby seismographs in operation since 1940 have shown that following the largest earthquake (magnitude about 5) in 1940, the seismicity declined. The foci of hundreds of detected earthquakes cluster on steeply dipping faults on the east side of the lake and have focal depths of less than 8 kilometers.

In the ensuing years, similar case histories have been accumulated for other large dams, but only a few are well documented. Most of these dams are more than 100 meters high and, although the geological framework at the sites varies, the most convincing examples of reservoir-induced earthquakes occur in tectonic regions with at least some history of earthquakes. Most of the thousands of large dams around the world give no sign of any connection between reservoir filling and earthquakes; of 500 large dams scrutinized in the United States, a poll in 1976 showed that for only 4 percent of them was an earthquake reported with magnitude greater than 3.0 within 16 kilometers of the dam.

Of particular interest are the following four well-studied examples of earthquakes induced by human-made reservoirs. First, Lake Kariba in Zambia began filling in 1958 behind a 128-meter high dam. Although there is some evidence for minor earthquakes in the vicinity before the construction, from 1958 until 1963 when the reservoir was full, over 2000 local shocks under the reservoir were located with the use of nearby seismographs. The largest shock in September 1963 had a magnitude 5.8; since then the activity has decreased.

At Koyna, India, an earthquake (magnitude 6.5) centered close to the dam (height 103 meters) caused significant damage on December 10, 1967. After impounding began in 1962, reports of local shaking became prevalent in this previously low-seismicity area. Seismographs showed that foci were concentrated at shallow depths under Shivajisagar Lake. In 1967 a number of sizable earthquakes occurred, leading up to the principal earthquake on December 10. This temblor caused significant damage to buildings nearby, killed over 200 persons, and injured more than 1500. A strong-motion seismograph in the dam gallery registered a maximum acceleration of 0.63g. The series of earthquakes recorded at Koyna has a pattern that seems to follow the rhythm of the rainfall (see Figure 2). At least a comparison of the frequency of earthquakes and water level *suggests* that seismicity increases a few months after each rainy season when the reservoir level is highest. Such correlations are not so clear in other examples now known.

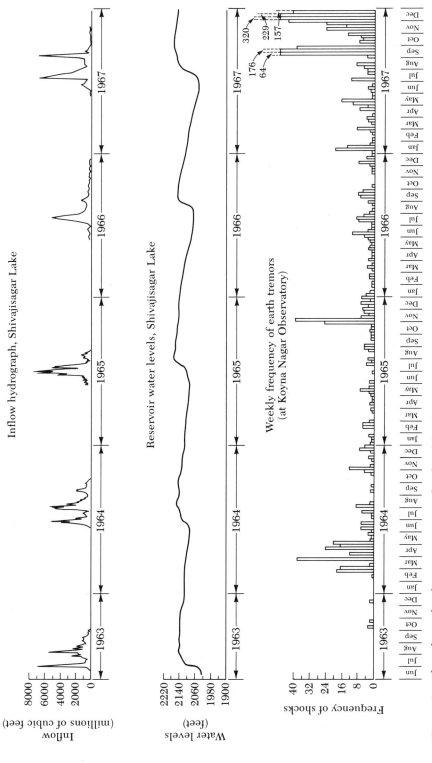

Figure 2 The relationship between reservoir level and local seismic activity at Koyna Dam, India. In September, November, and December, 1967, shock frequency exceeded 40 and at times, toward the end of the year, amounted to 200 or 300. [From data of H. K. Gupta and B. K. Rastogi.]

Another series of earthquakes—which were quite conclusively induced by a reservoir—occurred in China north of Canton. The Hsingfengkiang Dam (height 105 meters) was completed in 1959. Thereafter, increasing numbers of local earthquakes were recorded, the grand total in 1972 amounting to more than 250,000. Most of the earthquakes were very small, but on March 19, 1962, a strong shock of magnitude 6.1 occurred. The energy released was enough to damage the concrete dam structure, which required strengthening. Most earthquake foci were at depths of less than 10 kilometers near where the reservoir was deepest, and some of the foci coincided with intersections of the main nearby faults.

The final example is the massive Nurek Dam (height 317 meters) in Tadzhikistan, Soviet Union, the highest earthfill dam in the world. Even in 1972, before its completion but after water impounding began, increased local seismicity was reported. The full load of stored water was applied onto the crust in 1978; in the years following, no large nearby earthquake has shaken the facility, but many small earthquakes continue to occur.

How does water in a large reservoir stimulate earthquakes? It is hard to believe that it is entirely the effect of the added weight on the rocks; the actual additional pressure a few kilometers below the reservoir is a small fraction of the natural tectonic stresses already present. (Calculations indicate that a few kilometers down the added differential stress available to shear the rock is only about 1 bar.) A more plausible explanation is the trigger mechanism that induced the Denver and Rangely earthquakes discussed earlier in the chapter. In brief, this mechanism would be as follows: Extra water pressure produced by the reservoir-loading spreads out as a pressure wave or pulse into the crustal rocks. Its slow rate of spreading may take it months or years to travel a distance of 5 kilometers, depending on the permeability and amount of fracturing of the rock. But when the pressure pulse finally reaches a zone of microcracks, it would force water into them and so decrease the forces that are preventing the already present tectonic strain from initiating sliding and elastic rebound along the faults.

In an area where there is a likelihood of seismic activity, certain preliminary steps must be taken before construction of a dam. First, whether cause for concern is a natural or an induced earthquake, it is essential at the design stages to estimate the intensity of ground shaking that the structure will sustain during its lifetime. Also, preconstruction geodetic surveys of the region are useful for purposes of detecting any changes in crustal deformations associated with reservoir loading.

Furthermore, in order that earthquake effects can be studied, seismographs and other instrumentation should be installed at an early time. Hydrographs for measuring large water waves (seiches) in the reservoir are also important. In the absence of suitable recording instruments to measure the severity of earthquake motions and of the dam response, the advent of a strong earthquake nearby will pose questions that cannot be answered. If, for example, structural damage has occurred, and no such measurements have been taken, it is impossible to compare behavior with design earthquake conditions and thus to estimate performance for other and perhaps larger shocks, or to make design decisions for repair and strengthening of the dam. (See Appendix G.)

The 1975 Oroville, California, Earthquake

One case history that bears on earthquake forecasting and possible stimulation by changes in ground water level is the sequence of earthquakes near the city of Oroville in northeastern California. The main shock of the sequence, which occurred in the afternoon of August 1, 1975, at 1:20 P.M., did not cause major damage to Oroville and surrounding communities, but it attracted great public interest because it was only 10 kilometers southwest of Oroville Dam (see Figure 3). This earthfill dam near the western foothills of the Sierra Nevada is the largest in North America; it is 236 meters high and has a capacity of 4365 million cubic meters. The filling of the reservoir began in November 1967 and was completed in September 1968.

The region is one of low seismicity, but generally a few minor earthquakes a year take place within 50 kilometers of the dam site. Thirty-five years before, a magnitude 5.7 earthquake occurred about 50 kilometers north of Oroville on February 8, 1940, but caused no damage and aroused little interest. Nevertheless, in 1963, before construction of the great dam, seismographs were installed about a kilometer north of the dam to monitor the background seismicity. These instruments detected no change in the low level of earthquake occurrence within 30 kilometers of the reservoir either during construction, during filling, or after the water was raised to its highest elevation in 1969 through early 1975.

On June 28, 1975, a few small shocks were recorded to the southwest of the Oroville reservoir. It was not known whether these were foreshocks of a larger earthquake or merely an earthquake swarm of small-magnitude events, common in many parts of California. Nevertheless, some additional portable seismographic stations were installed to keep better track of the position of the earthquakes. About 20 small shocks were recorded through July in the same general area, the largest of magnitude 4.7. Then at the end of July the rate of occurrence fell.

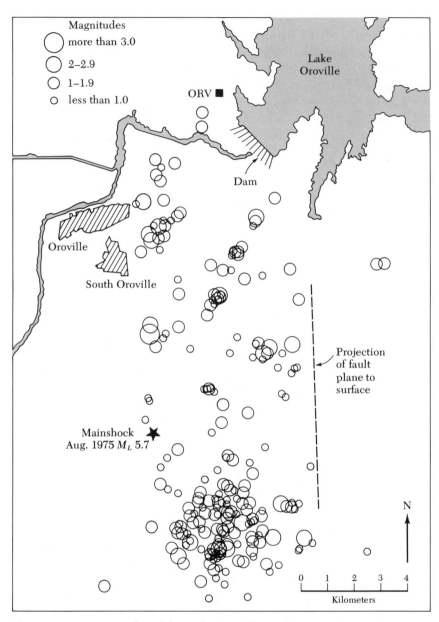

Figure 3 Epicenters plotted from the Oroville earthquake sequence, February through July 1977. The black square designates the location of the seismograph at the Oroville station. The vertical dashed line represents the projection to the surface of the fault plane (see also Figure 4). [Courtesy of California Department of Water Resources.]

However, in the early morning hours of August 1, the seismic alarm system at the University of California Seismographic Station was triggered, and seismogram readings indicated that an earthquake of magnitude 4.7 had occurred near Oroville. Later that morning at 6:30, another minor earthquake occurred nearby.

A personal anecdote may be in order here. Because I was a member of the Consulting Board for Earthquake Analysis of the California Department of Water Resources, the owners of the dam, I had been watching the sequence of earthquakes closely. The reactivation of the sequence on the morning of August 1 led me to call Professor G. Housner at the California Institute of Technology, who was chairman of the Consulting Board. I mentioned to him that the earthquake sequence had reactivated, that there was a small but definite likelihood of a main shock and suggested that he might contact the Department. Subsequently he did so and engineers in charge of operating the dam facilities made a special service inspection of the dam, its facilities and instrumentation.

While the dam inspection was taking place, the principal shock of the sequence, magnitude 5.7, occurred just after lunch on August 1. In a sense, then, this earthquake was forecast. The prediction was based upon a personal hunch that the unusual pattern of small local earthquakes indicated that they might be foreshocks of a larger shock. The incident illustrates that some success in practical prediction is feasible under very restricted conditions, such as when foreshocks occur (which is not always the case—see Chapter 10). A necessary condition for success is that, for whatever scientific, engineering, or social reason, an informed person is aware of a change in local conditions and able to think about the change closely and continuously.

The damage from the 1975 main shock in the meizoseismal area was not severe. Some unreinforced brick chimneys toppled and some weak masonry parapets in the city of Oroville collapsed onto the street. The intensity in Oroville was rated at Modified Mercalli VII. At the dam, most instruments that had been installed some years before for just such an occasion recorded the ground motion. They indicated that the dam itself had not been affected by the shaking. Accelerometers on the dam showed the peak acceleration of the ground to be about 0.15g in a horizontal direction.

Numerous aftershocks occurred. Subsequent careful locations of their foci with portable equipment defined a zone that dipped into the valley at about 60° to the west. These foci varied in depth from 12 kilometers to the west to nearly surface locations to the east (see Figure 4). The directions of the first P waves, recorded from the main shock and the aftershocks, were consistent with normal faulting along a fault striking north-

northwest, with the Sierra Nevada side moving up with respect to the Great Valley of California.

If this fault plane were to be projected to the surface, it would intersect the surface to the south of the dam. Imagine the excitement, therefore, when after a day or two, field geologists found a line of surface cracks in open country at about the place indicated by this intersection. Subsequently, trenches were excavated in several places across the line of cracks, and these confirmed that the cracks in the soil were the surface expression of preexisting fault zone. Fault gouge was present in most of the trenches, and the offsets in soil and rock layers mapped in the walls of the trenches indicated that vertical motions had probably occurred a number of times in the last 100,000 years in a normal dip-slip fashion, causing offsets of a few centimeters on each occasion. Field mapping later established that the total length of surface faulting across the grassy fields was about 5 kilometers.

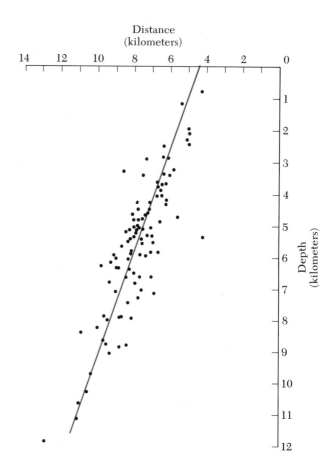

Figure 4   Side view through the Earth's crust southeast of Oroville, California, showing the locations of the foci of some of the larger earthquakes in the 1975 sequence, projected on an east-west cross section. The angle of dip is 62°. [Courtesy of W. Savage, D. Tocher, and P. Birkholm.]

After the Oroville earthquakes there was much speculation on whether they had been caused by the reservoir. However, there is only circumstantial evidence, and no direct causal evidence. The argument against the possibility of reservoir-triggering was that small-to-moderate earthquakes were not unknown in the nearby foothills of the Sierra Nevada, and the regional geological map shows that the line of cracking observed after the earthquake lined up with the extensive system of faults to the south of Oroville. Geomorphic expressions along the zone of cracking indicated that spasmodic movement during the last few thousand years had probably occurred, because small soaks, springs, and subtle changes in elevation were evident.

Further evidence against reservoir induction was that the focus of the main shock lay at a distance in the crust about 15 kilometers away from Oroville Lake. How could the reservoir affect such a distant point? Even the areal extent of the aftershocks defined a zone that intersected the surface of the ground south of the reservoir itself.

On the other side of the question, more quantitative but still circumstantial evidence comes from the measured rate of occurrence of foreshocks and aftershocks. This rate of occurrence of earthquakes above a given magnitude is measured by the factor b given in Appendix H. In most regions, b varies between 0.7 and 1.0; in northern California, b equals about 0.8 if averaged over a few decades. The b values for the reservoir-induced sequences at Kariba and Koyna (discussed in the preceding section) were calculated to be higher than the respective regional values. Yet for the Oroville aftershocks the rate of occurrence gives b a value equal to 0.6—a value *less* than the regional value.

In the end, the strongest argument for triggering at Oroville is simply the presence of the nearby reservoir. Undoubtedly, it sent a pressure pulse through the water in the rocks of the crust. Perhaps, as the pressure pulse spread out by percolation through the crustal rocks nearby, it eventually reached a weak place along an already existing fault zone. Although the pulse weakened as it spread outward, it may have been sufficient to open microcracks just enough to allow fault slip—the straw that broke the camel's back.

Seismicity Induced by Lake Nasser, the Nile River

The Nile River is essential to life in Egypt. Its rise and fall, as recorded by nilometers in Cairo since 622 A.D., has been so regular that Egypt became a food storehouse in time of drought and famine, punctuated by some very high floods and resulting disasters. The river is 16,000 kilometers long with the main stream formed by the confluence of the White Nile and the Blue Nile at Khartoum, 3080 kilometers above its mouth. Below Khartoum, the river reaches Aswan, located on its first cataract (see page 11). In 1902, a concrete dam was built across the river at Aswan for irrigation control. There the river is placid with a strip of green between the water and the rocks of the desert.

A major change to the Nile system occurred in the 1970s when the High Dam was built of earth fill about 10 kilometers south of Aswan—its maximum height is 111 meters and the length of its embankment is 3.6 kilometers. The dam impounded an artificial reservoir called Lake Nasser, approximately 300 kilometers long (exceeded in size only by the Bratsk Reservoir in the Soviet Union). Lake Nasser has a maximum capacity of $164,000 \times 10^6$ cubic meters, which is slightly larger than that of Lake Kariba in southern Africa. Filling of the reservoir started gradually in 1964 and reached a maximum water level of 177.5 meters in November 1978. Since that time, each year the lake has reached a seasonal peak level in October-November; the annual level cycle is approximately saw-toothed in shape. There is a slow decrease from November to a low in July, followed by a more rapid filling. The usual annual variation in level is 4 to 5 meters.

On November 14, 1981, an earthquake (magnitude $M_L = 5.6$) was felt strongly in Aswan. Although its exact hypocenter is unknown (the closest operating seismographic station at the time was at Helwan, about 690 kilometers from Aswan), the intensity data and aftershock locations (recorded by local seismographic stations placed after the main shock) indicate a hypocenter at about 23.55°N and 32.55°E and shallow depth. This location places the earthquake source beneath an extensive bay of Lake Nasser, about 60 kilometers from the Aswan High Dam.

The earthquake was preceded by a few recorded foreshocks and followed by thousands of aftershocks in the same general vicinity (see Figure 5). At Aswan, the Mercalli intensity of the shaking was estimated at VI. Most people rushed out of doors and heard explosionlike sounds, often a sign of very shallow focal depth. Some minor damage was caused to some old buildings in Aswan, but no damage occurred to the dam or to its appurtenant structures. The Aswan area had been considered aseismic; no significant earthquake had been mentioned in historical records anywhere in upper Egypt or located there since the introduction of global seismographic observatories at the turn of the century. The historical record in Egypt might be expected to mention large damaging earthquakes as far back as 3000 years.

It is therefore reasonable to assume that the Aswan area is not the source of significant earthquakes under normal geological circumstances (at least with return intervals of 1000 years). This conclusion makes it very

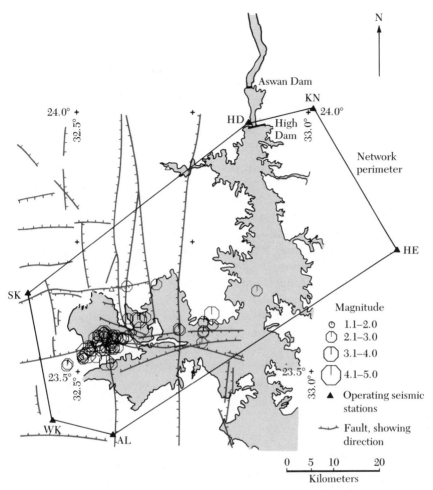

Figure 5 Map of aftershock epicenters of the Aswan sequence from May 7 to June 11, 1982, from the Egyptian Geological Survey and Mining Authority seismographic network. The Kalabsha fault trace passes east-west through the dense epicenter cluster. [From T. R. Toppozada and others, California Division of Mines and Geology, 1984].

likely that the November 14, 1981 earthquake and aftershocks are causally related to the water of Lake Nasser. The Nubian sandstones along the Nile River are very porous, and thus the effective size of the reservoir is much larger than the surface of Lake Nasser itself, with a huge volume of water absorbed undergound in the porous basement. The water load is therefore greater than might at first be calculated, with consequent large changes in water pressure in the pores of the rocks. Calculated models of the hydrology are not sufficiently precise, however, to clearly indicate whether loading of the reservoir in future years will produce similar-sized earthquakes to the one that occurred on November 14, 1981.

A few seismographs had been installed in the Aswan area before the induced earthquake occurred, but their operation was irregular before 1981. Nevertheless, they did enable Egyptian seismologists to identify a few small local earthquakes (M > 2.5), indicating that low-magnitude seismic activity in the area may have begun after the reservoir began filling. The principal earthquake followed the 1981 seasonal maximum in water level. After that time, the water level began to decline because of the widespread drought of the watershed of the Nile River.

Subsequent studies of the aftershock sequence (see Figure 5) indicate that the dense zone of aftershocks was situated close to the surface trace of the Kalabsha fault, which strikes almost east-west across the desert from Libya and terminates close to the west bank of the Nile about 45 kilometers south of the High Dam. Focal depths of the aftershocks indicate two separate clusters. The one nearer the Nile River had shallow depths less than 10 kilometers, and the more westerly cluster had deeper foci at depths of 15 to 25 kilometers.

In the last several years, an extensive geological and seismological study of the Aswan High Dam area has been made. Because strong-motion instruments were not available near the High Dam to record the ground motion during the 1981 main shock, this work depends to some extent on extrapolations from seismic ground-motion recordings made in other countries. All indications are, however, that the dam structures will adequately resist any future induced earthquake.

Moonquakes

Unlike the surface of the Earth, the moon's surface is dry. If water is crucial in the genesis of earthquakes, we might wonder, "Are there moonquakes, and if so, do they resemble those on the primary planet?" Answers have been provided by the space program. Beginning in November 1969, seismographic stations were set up by the United States on the moon during the landings of Apollo 12, 14, 15, 16, and 17 (see Figure 6). Special seismographs—with power from solar energy and nuclear batteries—placed at the five sites operated continuously, sending back a steady stream of geophysical data on the moon's interior. Since 1900, seismologists have used the earthquake waves traveling through the Earth to obtain highly detailed information on the structure of the terrestrial interior (see Chapter 8). Also, the study of the location and mechanisms of earthquakes have revealed a great deal about the way the Earth is deformed. Therefore, from the beginning of lunar exploration, it was expected that seismographs on the moon would provide similar information on its interior and deformation.

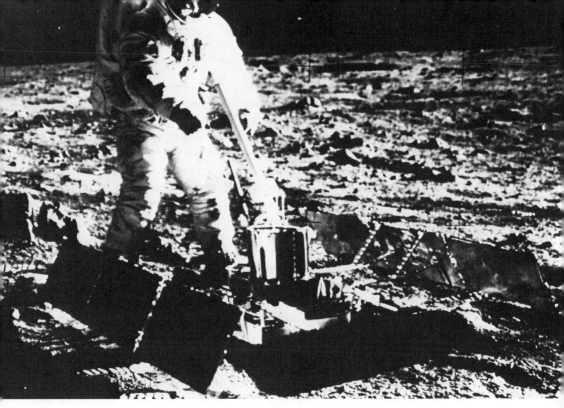

Figure 6 Photograph of a seismograph operating on the moon's surface. [Courtesy of NASA.]

Most earthquakes are a consequence of the movement of tectonic plates. In stark comparison, the moon has, for many millions of years, been a dynamically quiet planetary body with no plate motion, no active volcanoes, and no great ocean trench systems. It was therefore somewhat startling that each lunar seismographic station detected between 600 and 3000 moonquakes every year on the average. Most of these moonquakes were tiny, with magnitudes of less than about 2 on the Richter scale. The microseismic background was very small, and thus the seismographs could be operated with very high magnifications, at least 100 to 1000 times that which is normally possible on Earth. Is the large number of moonquakes detected a consequence of the low level of background noise on the moon (no wind, ocean waves, or traffic), or does it signify the presence of fairly active tectonic processes?

Sample seismograms of typical moonquakes, recorded at the Apollo 16 station, are shown in Figure 7. Three different kinds of events are indicated. First are the deep moonquakes, which have their foci at depths of 600 to 900 kilometers in the moon (radius 1740 kilometers). These deep events are quite surprising. They seem localized at a specific number of places in the moon's interior, of which more than 40 have been identified.

At these active deep centers, moonquakes commonly occur within an interval of a few days during *perigee*, the point at which the moon's orbit is closest to the Earth. About equal numbers of deep moonquakes occur at these centers at opposite phases of this tidal pull, so that the most active periods are 14 days apart. These periodic properties at least suggest that the tidal pull of the Earth on the moon triggers the occurrence of the deep seismic-energy releases. On the Earth, similar conditions of the occurrence of earthquakes with perigee have been sought for many years, but generally without success (see Chapter 10).

The second type of moonquake shown in Figure 7 occurs in the shallower part of the moon. These moonquakes are not as common as the deeper events, and their locations do not exhibit any particularly regular pattern over the surface of the moon. It is thought that, like most earthquakes, they may be due to the release of tectonic elastic strain in the rocks of the moon's crust. If so, then either ground water is present in the moon or some special dry fracturing is occurring in the unusual thermal conditions of the lunar surface.

The third type of seismic event results from the impact of objects, both natural and human-made, on the lunar surface. An example of the seismograms from meteorite impact is also shown in Figure 7. The lunar seismographic stations are efficient detectors of meteorites hitting the surface even at a range of 1000 kilometers. In order to help with the determination of seismic-wave velocities of lunar rocks, parts of the lunar spacecraft were programed to crash back on the lunar surface. These high-speed impacts generated seismic waves strong enough to produce clear recordings at lunar seismographic stations, and because the position of impact is known precisely, the travel times of the seismic waves could be easily calculated. This calculation was the first step to discovering the general architecture and properties of the moon's interior.

The waves recorded by lunar impacts and moonquakes indicated that most of the moon is solid rock. The layered crustal shell on the surface is about 60 kilometers thick, and below lies a denser solid mantle about 1000 kilometers thick. This overlies a central core that seems to be somewhat softer than the mantle but is most probably not liquid. The picture of the Earth's interior obtained by earlier investigations is markedly different (see Chapter 8).

Moonquakes themselves sharply differ from earthquakes. Compare the seismograms in Figure 7 with those from earthquakes shown in Chapter 6, Figure 4. A small earthquake may shake a remote seismograph for a minute or so, but on the moon, the recorded shaking of the lunar surface in a moonquake continues for as much as an hour. (The vertical time marks in Figure 7 are 10 minutes apart.) The wave patterns too are strikingly different: the seismic S waves and surface waves on lunar seismo-

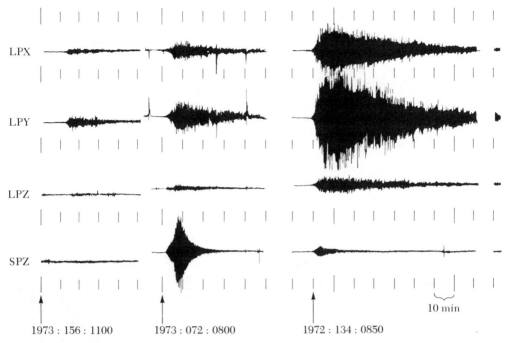

Figure 7 Seismograms from three types of moonquakes recorded at the Apollo 16 station. LPX, LPY, and LPZ are the three long-period components, and SPZ is the short-period vertical component. The first column shows a deep-focus moonquake; the center column, a shallow moonquake; the third column shows records of the impact of a meteoroid on the lunar surface. [Courtesy of NASA.]

grams are not generally as clearly defined and distinct as are those of earthquakes. (In Figure 7, the small P-wave onset for the moonquake can be seen on the SPZ record, and the S wave can be seen best on the LPY record.) After a rapid crescendo the lunar seismogram of a moonquake shows reverberations with a slow decrease in amplitude for many tens of minutes. What is the explanation for this behavior? It is widely believed that both the lack of water and the fractured nature of lunar rocks are contributory causes; the uppermost rocks are so dry the seismic waves attenuate very little, and at the same time the cracks in the lunar rock scatter the seismic waves in all directions.

Seismographs were also placed on Mars by the two Viking crafts sent by the United States in 1976. Unfortunately, the instrument in Viking 1 failed to return signals to Earth, but that on Viking 2 operated as planned, and signals of ground motion on Mars were recorded remotely on Earth. By September 1977, scrutiny of the available Martian seismograms had found only one event that could reasonably be identified as a Marsquake. It is possible, however, that Marsquakes are simply not common, and it is too early to exclude the possibility of notable seismic activity there.

Damage in Charleston, South Carolina, from the earthquake of August 31, 1886. This earthquake is the largest ever reported in the eastern region of the United States. [Courtesy of J. K. Hillers, USGS.]

... after the wind an earthquake; but the Lord was not
   in the earthquake!
And after the earthquake a fire; but the Lord was
   not in the fire; and after the fire a still small voice.

—1 Kings 19:11

10
Events that Precede
an Earthquake

Efforts at Earthquake Forecasting

Can earthquakes be predicted? A variety of prediction methods has been used for centuries, ranging from accounts of "earthquake weather" to arrangements of the planets and odd behavior of animals. Most have been unsuccessful.

Since the 1960s scientific efforts at prediction have grown in an explosive manner, particularly in Japan, the Soviet Union, the People's Republic of China, and the United States. The aim is to establish at least as much reliability in earthquake forecasting as there is in weather forecasting. Most publicity has been given to the prediction of the date and place of a damaging earthquake, especially in a very short time interval. However, there is another aspect of earthquake forecasting: the prediction of *seismic intensity* at a particular site. This is the factor that is emphasized in choosing the sites of important structures such as dams, hospitals, and nuclear reactors and that, in the long run, may provide the greatest mitigation of earthquake hazards. In this chapter, we will examine the scientific prediction of the time and place of earthquakes and defer discussion of prediction of strong ground shaking to Chapter 12.

As pointed out in Chapter 1, studies of the historical world seismicity patterns have made it possible to predict the probable place at which a damaging earthquake can be expected to occur. However, this record does not enable us to forecast a precise time of occurrence. Even in China, where between 500 and 1000 destructive earthquakes have occurred within the past 2700 years, statistical studies have not clearly revealed periodicities between great earthquakes, but they do indicate that long periods of quiescence can elapse between them.

In Japan, where there are also long-term earthquake statistics (see Figure 1), vigorous earthquake prediction research has been under way since 1962 but so far without definite success. (No large damaging earthquake with a focus on the Japanese islands has occurred during recent years, although there have been many smaller shocks.) The Japanese program, drawing on the contributions of hundreds of seismologists, geophysicists, and geodesists, has revealed a rich variety of information and clues. One of the most riveting examples of earthquake precursors ever published comes from the west coast of Honshu, Japan. Here, geodetic measurements of ground elevation, plotted in Figure 2, show that for about 60 years (before 1964) steady uplift and subsidence of the coastline had taken place in the vicinity of Niigata. This rate slowed at the end of the 1950s; then, at the time of the Niigata earthquake of June 16, 1964, a sudden subsidence of more than 20 centimeters was detected to the north adjacent to the epicenter. Although this pattern (see the graphs in Figure 2) was discovered only after the earthquake, a repetition of such decisive level changes would certainly warrant some forewarning.

Most recently in Japan, special studies of historical earthquake cycles in the vicinity of Tokyo, together with local measurements of present crustal deformation and seismicity, have suggested to some Japanese seismologists that a repetition of the great 1923 Kwanto earthquake (see Chapter 4) is not now imminent but that earthquakes in neighboring areas cannot be ruled out. In particular, the Tokai area (see Figure 1) is being closely watched.

At least since the turn of the century, many types of trigger forces that might initiate earthquake ruptures have been postulated. Some of the most serious proposals are severe weather conditions, volcanic activity, and the gravitational pull of the moon, sun, and planets.° Numerous catalogs of earthquakes, including quite complete lists for California, have been searched for such effects without convincing results. For example, in 1974, a popular book suggested that about every 179 years a near alignment of the planets takes place and the extra attraction would trigger

---

° In 1959, a claim was even published that the tiny attraction of the distant planet Uranus induced periodicities in earthquakes.

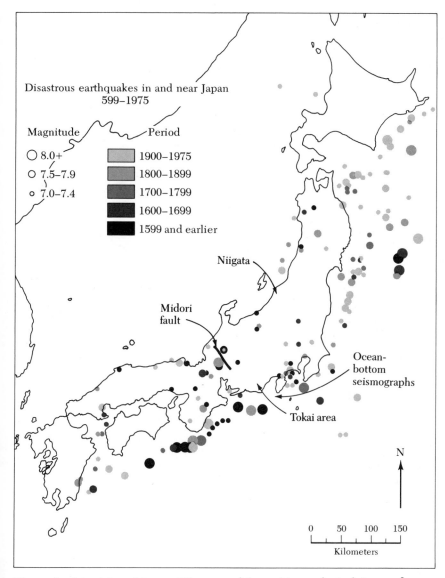

Disastrous earthquakes in and near Japan
599–1975

Magnitude

○ 8.0+
○ 7.5–7.9
○ 7.0–7.4

Period

1900–1975
1800–1899
1700–1799
1600–1699
1599 and earlier

Niigata

Midori
fault

Ocean-
bottom
seismographs

Tokai area

N

0   50   100   150

Kilometers

Figure 1   Seismicity of Japan. [Courtesy of Japan Meteorological Agency.]

great seismicity in California. The next such alignment was due in 1982. Because the San Andreas fault in southern California has not ruptured in a great earthquake since the 1857 Fort Tejon shock, it was surmised that it may be particularly vulnerable to this planetary trigger mechanism in 1982. Fortunately for California, the argument had serious flaws and nothing happened. First, world seismicity catalogs show that the previous years in which this alignment prevailed—1803, 1624, and 1445—were not ones of enhanced seismic activity. Second, the additional pull of the

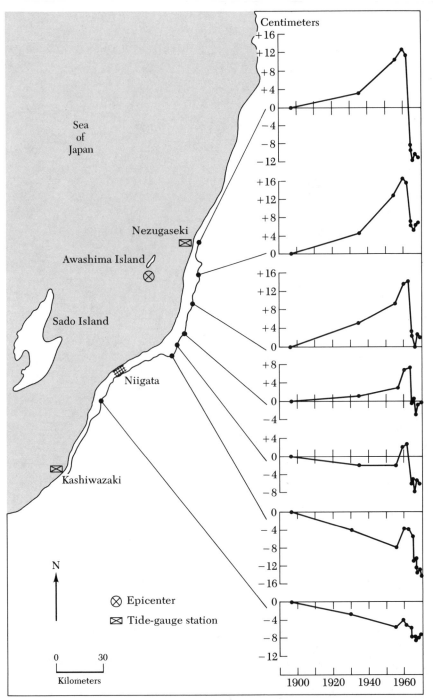

Figure 2 Vertical movements of bench marks along the west coast of Japan near the June 1964 Niigata earthquake, magnitude 7.5. Changes in level (in centimeters) before and after the earthquake are shown on the right. [From data of T. Dambara.]

smaller or more distant planets is insignificant to that between the Earth and the sun. As a consequence, many more periodicities than 179 years would have to be considered, each corresponding to an alignment of the most significant planets.

A strong theoretical basis is usually needed to make reliable predictions, such as in the prediction of the phases of the moon or the results of a chemical reaction. Unfortunately, at the present time there is not yet a precisely formulated theory of earthquake genesis. Nevertheless, limited though our present understanding of earthquake occurrence is, it does allow us to make crude forecasts of when the next great rupture can be expected on a known active fault. In fact, after the 1906 California earthquake, H. F. Reid used the theory of elastic rebound (explained in Chapter 4) to argue that the next occurrence of a great shock near San Francisco would be about a century later.

In brief, Reid's argument was the following: Survey measurements made across the San Andreas fault (see Chapter 2, Figure 2) before the 1906 earthquake indicated that the relative displacement across the fault had reached 3.2 meters in 50 years. After the rebound on the fault on April 18, 1906, the maximum relative displacement along the fault was about 6.5 meters. If we do the arithmetic, we have $(6.5/3.2) \times 50 \approx 100$, therefore about 100 years would elapse before the next great earthquake. For this result we must make the somewhat tenuous assumptions that the regional strain continues uniformly and that the fault properties before the 1906 earthquake were not altered by the earthquake itself. Prudence requires that we do not rule out a series of more moderate earthquakes along the San Andreas fault in the next few centuries rather than another earthquake with a magnitude of 8.25.

At present, many experiments are being conducted, and specific precursory symptoms (listed in the next section) are being tested. (The only "official" prediction in the United States in 1987 is described in the section on the Parkfield experiment at the end of this chapter.) The overall effort, though substantial, gives little reason for optimism that practical prediction schemes will be realized in the near future in most areas of the world. Furthermore, those methods showing most promise require quite elaborate equipment and many workers. The establishment of such networks throughout all zones of high seismic risk would be highly expensive.

Also, there is a fundamental dilemma inherent in earthquake forecasting. Suppose that seismological measurements indicate that an earthquake of a certain magnitude will occur in a certain area during a certain period of time. Now presumably this area is a seismic one, or the study would not have been initiated in the first place. Therefore, it follows that by chance alone the odds are not zero that an earthquake will occur during the period suggested. Thus, if an earthquake occurs, it cannot be taken as decisive proof that the methods used to make the prediction are correct, and they may fail on future occasions. Of course, if a firm prediction is made and nothing happens, that must be taken as proof that the method is invalid.

In response to the recent heightened activity in California on earthquake prediction, in 1975 a scientific panel was set up to advise the State Office of Emergency Services—and hence the state's governor—on the validity of predictions. The panel's important but limited role is to evaluate the data and claims of the person or group (normally a seismologist or seismologists conducting research in a government or university laboratory). The panel does not concern itself with the timing or scope of a public warning that might be issued by state authorities. By 1987, the panel had evaluated only three situations having a bearing on future California earthquakes.°

It has been decided that a valid prediction should be defined as having four essential elements: (1) the period within which the event would occur, (2) the area of location, (3) the magnitude range, (4) a statement of the odds that an earthquake of the predicted kind would occur by chance alone and without reference to any special evidence.

Not only do such panels provide service to state authorities who have responsibility of mitigating earthquake hazards, but their deliberations are also helpful to the scientists attempting the forecast, in that they provide an independent check. In a wider social context, such a scientific jury helps deflect the unsupported predictions of seers and sometimes even the unscrupulous who see a chance for temporary fame or pecuniary gain.

The social and economic consequences of earthquake forecasts are a subject of some controversy. As seismological research continues, numerous earthquake warnings from credible sources will probably be issued in various countries. For example, numerous forewarnings have been issued in China and will be discussed later in this chapter.

In western society, studies on the unfavorable as well as the propitious consequences of prediction have been made. For example, if the time of a large damaging earthquake in California were accurately predicted a year or so ahead of time and continuously updated, casualties and even property damage resulting from the earthquake might be much reduced; but the communities in the meizoseismal region might suffer social disruption and decline in the local economy. The major social and economic responses and adjustments that may occur are summarized in Box 1.

°Two national scientific panels to evaluate evidence on putative earthquakes deserve special mention. The first is the Earthquake Assessment Committee, of six eminent seismologists, advisory to the Japan Meteorological Agency. Each is alerted by a radio pocket beeper if anomalous signals are detected. The second is the U.S. National Earthquake Prediction Evaluation Council, advisory to the U.S. Geological Survey.

Box 1. Types of Socioeconomic Impacts and Adjustments to an Earthquake Prediction

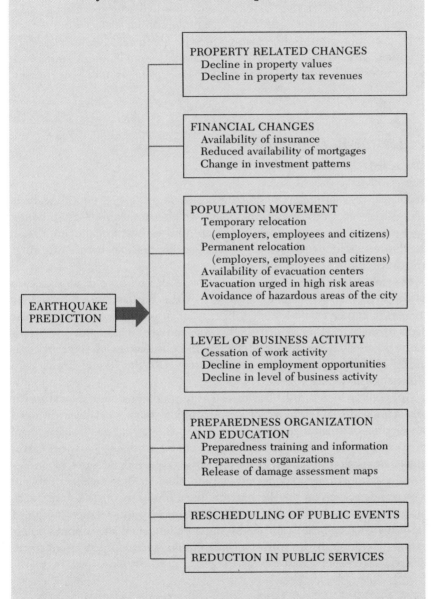

PROPERTY RELATED CHANGES
Decline in property values
Decline in property tax revenues

FINANCIAL CHANGES
Availability of insurance
Reduced availability of mortgages
Change in investment patterns

POPULATION MOVEMENT
Temporary relocation
(employers, employees and citizens)
Permanent relocation
(employers, employees and citizens)
Availability of evacuation centers
Evacuation urged in high risk areas
Avoidance of hazardous areas of the city

EARTHQUAKE PREDICTION

LEVEL OF BUSINESS ACTIVITY
Cessation of work activity
Decline in employment opportunities
Decline in level of business activity

PREPAREDNESS ORGANIZATION AND EDUCATION
Preparedness training and information
Preparedness organizations
Release of damage assessment maps

RESCHEDULING OF PUBLIC EVENTS

REDUCTION IN PUBLIC SERVICES

After J. E. Hass and D. S. Mileti. *Socioeconomic Impact of Earthquake Prediction on Government, Business and Community.* [Institute of Behavioral Sciences, University of Colorado, 1976.]

Without an actual occurrence to draw upon, such assessments are, of course, highly tentative; the total reaction would be highly complex, since responses by the government, public, and private sectors could all vary. For example, if after the scientific prediction and official warning, massive public demand for earthquake insurance cuts off its availability, then temporary but drastic effects on property values, real estate sales, construction, investment, and employment might ensue. Such dilemmas are now imperfectly comprehended by citizens, scientists, and government.

Clues for Recognizing Impending Earthquakes

What are the harbingers of impending earthquakes? A multitude have been suggested,° but it is still not clear which are reliable. Certainly any operative scheme of practical prediction must be based on a combination of clues, so that decisions will be as firm as possible before warnings are issued.

Several of the more promising clues have already been discussed, such as the detection of strain in the rocks of the Earth's crust by geodetic surveys (Chapter 4) and the identification of suspicious gaps in the regular occurrence of earthquakes in both time and space (Chapter 1). And a more precise but not foolproof tool is the observation of foreshocks, as in the 1975 Oroville sequence in California (Chapter 9) and in the 1975 Haicheng earthquake.

To monitor such foreshocks, as well as to predict damaging local tsunamis, a radically different set of seismographic stations has been installed across the continental shelf and ocean trench south of the Tokai special prediction area, Honshu, Japan. The scheme, part of the Japanese earthquake prediction program, is illustrated in Figure 3. A series of ocean-bottom seismographs is connected by more than 200 kilometers of cable to a recording station on the shore. It has been found that if the stations are placed with care, the ocean floor is a seismically quiet place to record earthquakes. The installation of this network launched a new era in observational seismology, in which seismographic stations are no longer restricted to continents and islands.

°One is an unnatural glow in the sky. There were reports, for example, of a luminous night sky to the north of the Friuli region in Italy before and after the May 6, 1976 earthquake. Objective measurements of such "earthquake lights" are needed. Currently, there is no satisfying explanation for such claims.

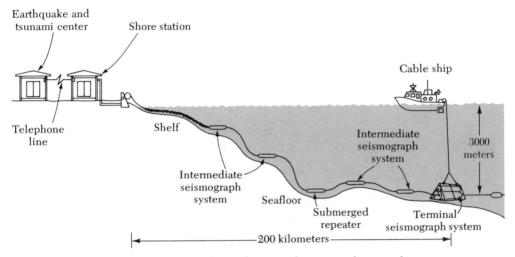

Figure 3   The network of seismographs on the ocean bottom to the east of Honshu, Japan.

In recent years the major earthquake-prediction effort has been more precise measurements of fluctuations in physical parameters in crustal rocks of seismically active continental areas. Special sensing devices have been installed in order that long-term changes in the parameters might be observed. The number of measurements is still limited, and results have thus far conflicted: in some, unusual behavior has been indicated before a local earthquake; in others, nothing significant has been seen before the event, or variations have occurred that are not associated with earthquakes. Five particularly auspicious parameters examined, listed in the left column of Box 2, are seismic P velocities, the uplift and tilt of the ground, the emission of radon gas from wells, electrical resistivity in the rocks, and the number of earthquakes in the region. How can each of these parameters be employed in a prediction scheme?

First, precursory changes in the seismic P velocities in a seismic area are of particular interest to seismologists because seismographic stations are designed especially to measure time very precisely. The idea behind the method is simple. If rock properties change before an earthquake, then the speed of seismic waves might also vary. Suppose for example the P velocity changed by 10 percent through an area 20 kilometers across. Then the travel time of a P wave from one side to the other would change by about 0.4 second. Such changes in time are easily measured with modern seismographs and chronometers. Some of the first information published on precursory changes in travel time of waves in moderate earth-

Box 2. Physical Clues for Earthquake Prediction

Physical parameters	Precursor stages		Stage IV earthquake	
	Stage I	*Stage II*	*Stage III*	*Stage V*
	Buildup of elastic strain	Dilatancy and development of cracks	Influx of water and unstable deformation in fault zone	Sudden drop in stress followed by aftershocks

Seismic P velocity

Ground uplift and tilt

Radon emission

Electrical resistivity

Number of seismic events

After *Predicting Earthquakes*, National Academy of Sciences, 1976.

quakes was gathered as early as 1962 in the Tadjikistan region of the Soviet Union. Measurements there suggested that P velocities changed by about 10 to 15 percent before the occurrence of local earthquakes. Field work in the Soviet Union and elsewhere since that time has indicated that the velocity of P waves in the focal region decreases by about 10 percent for a time and then increases again to a more normal value just before the main shock occurs, at least under some circumstances.

More detailed checks of the scheme have now been accomplished in a number of countries with mixed results. In the United States, work along these lines at Lamont-Doherty Geological Observatory in 1971 was based on quite small earthquakes in the Adirondacks in New York. Increases were detected in the travel time of P waves before three small earthquakes; and on the night of August 1, 1973, this method was used to predict that an earthquake of magnitude 2.5 to 3.0 would occur within a few days. The forecast was in part successful, but it lacked the fourth criterion for validity—a statement of the odds.

A different type of study was made by seismologists at the California Institute of Technology. From readings of seismograms at their stations, they concluded that before the 1971 San Fernando earthquake in southern California, there had been a precursory decrease of P velocity lasting about 30 months. They found that the velocity had subsequently returned to normal, followed quickly by the earthquake. They inferred that the volume in which the travel times of the P waves had been affected extended over a radius of about 30 kilometers in the neighborhood of the earthquake focus. Such a study cannot of course be used to predict, because it occurred after the earthquake was over.

In contrast, other tests of the method carried out in central California at the University of California at Berkeley, the U.S. Geological Survey, and Stanford University have independently indicated that fluctuations in travel times before a number of small to moderate earthquakes along the San Andreas fault have not been significant. One difficulty is that when the source of the P waves is an earthquake, the earthquake focus has to be located precisely from the travel times themselves. Then small changes in the estimated focal depths of successive earthquakes, arising from migrations of foci along a fault zone (see Chapter 9, Figure 4), are sufficient to explain some of the variations seen in the measured P travel times. A more promising procedure is to use travel times from seismic sources with known positions and times of origin, such as chemical explosions or quarry blasts. So far, measurements of travel times from timed quarry blasts through seismic areas before earthquakes have revealed few convincing changes in the travel times. This negative result indicates that any precursory changes in the velocity of the rocks before small-to-moderate earthquakes are probably highly localized around the focal region.

The second parameter listed in Box 2 that can be used in prediction is precursory change in ground level, such as ground tilts in earthquake regions (see Figure 4). One most encouraging study of this kind, made after the 1964 Niigata earthquake in Japan, has already been described in the first section of this chapter. How then should we interpret a rapid uplift of a considerable area around Palmdale in southern California, which apparently began around 1960? The uplift, according to one study, amounted to a maximum of 35 centimeters and extended 150 kilometers along the San Andreas fault southward into the transverse ranges. To date no significant earthquakes have been produced in the area. So few uplifts of this scale have been studied that no firm inference can be drawn about

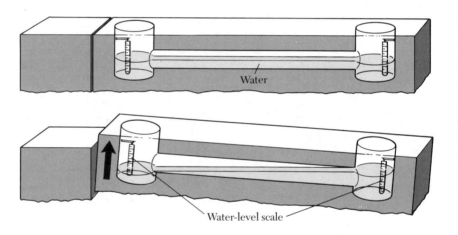

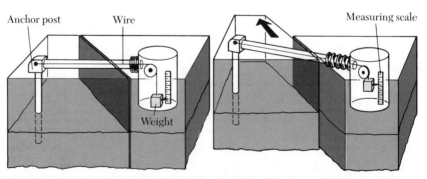

Figure 4 Diagrammatic models of a water-tube tiltmeter (top) and a simple wire-displacement meter (bottom). The arrows indicate ground movements or fault slip.

correlation with future earthquakes. The area is, of course, one in which major earthquakes have occurred in the past and are likely to occur again in the future. The best response for the time being is to greatly intensify various types of measurements in the region.

The third parameter is the release of radon, an inert gas, into the atmosphere along active fault zones, particularly from deep wells. For example, it has been claimed that significantly increased concentrations of radon were detected just before earthquakes in some parts of the Soviet Union. Because so few measurements of radon concentration in various geological circumstances are available, however, it is currently impossible to determine whether observed increases are exceptions to the normal variations in the concentration of this gas.

The fourth parameter, to which a good deal of attention has been given, is the electrical conductivity of the rocks in an earthquake zone. It is known from laboratory experiments on rock samples that the electrical resistance of water-saturated rocks, such as granite, changes drastically just before the rocks fracture in a high-pressure device. A few field experiments to check this property in fault zones have been made in the Soviet Union, the People's Republic of China, Japan, the United States, and elsewhere. From these studies, some workers have reported decreases in electrical resistance before earthquakes. Again, more studies of this kind are needed to check this method, but at present it seems encouraging.

Variation in the seismicity rate is the fifth parameter. More information is available on this method than on the other four, but the present results are not definitive. In brief, a strong change in the normal background earthquake occurrence is noted—usually an increased rate of small earthquakes. Such changes were observed in 1975, before the Oroville earthquake (discussed in Chapter 9) and the Liaoning earthquake (to be discussed later in this chapter). Another forecast that seems to have been successful has been described by Italian seismologists. After the tragic principal shock of May 6, 1976, in the Friuli region (see Chapter 1), the aftershocks were monitored. In early September 1976 it was noticed that the number occurring per day in the region had increased significantly. On this basis, authorities issued a general warning that people living in buildings of dubious strength might be advised to sleep elsewhere, even in tents. On September 15, 1976, a major aftershock ($M_s = 6.0$) occurred at 5:15 P.M., collapsing many weakened buildings. Yet few were killed in this earthquake. The method of measuring the rate of occurrence using a b value has already been discussed while considering the Oroville earthquake sequence (Chapter 9). It has been suggested that if the b value for a region is continually recalculated as more earthquakes occur, it might be found that it does not remain constant. Such temporal changes in the b value may signify the advent of a major shake.

We can think of the variations in these five parameters or properties as taking place in five stages, which are manifest in the strained rocks of the crust before, during, and just after a large earthquake.° Consider the occurrence of an earthquake in five stages, as set out in Box 2. The first stage is a slow buildup of elastic strain due to the underlying tectonic forces. During this period all the seismic parameters have their normal values. At Stage II, cracks develop in the crustal rocks in the fault zones, and this causes the whole volume to swell or dilate. As the cracks open, the speed of compressional P waves through the dilatant volume falls, the ground surface rises, radon gas escapes, the electrical resistivity decreases, and there may be a change in the level of microearthquakes in the vicinity. At Stage III, the water diffuses from the surrounding rocks into the pores and microcracks, leading to unstable conditions. As the water fills the cracks, the speed of P waves through the region begins to increase again, the uplift of the ground ceases, emission of radon from the fresh cracks tapers off, and the electrical resistivity decreases further. Stage IV is the onset of the earthquake. This is immediately followed by Stage V, during which numerous aftershocks occur in the area.

It should be stressed that the details and even the direction of some of the variations in parameters in Box 2 are partly speculative because of limited field measurements. Available measurements do suggest, however, that the precursory period leading to Stage IV depends on the volume of rock involved in the ultimate fault rupture of the main shock. Rough estimates are that the precursory events may continue for several months for earthquakes of Richter magnitude 6; from 1 to 3 years for magnitude-7 earthquakes; and from 3 to 10 years for magnitude-8 earthquakes. But other types of precursors may be short-term, even for large earthquakes.

Earthquakes and Prediction in China

On February 4, 1975, officials of the Manchurian province of Liaoning decided the evidence was sufficient for them to issue an urgent warning to the populace that a strong earthquake would probably occur within the next 24 hours. Persons in the cities of Haicheng, Yingkow, and nearby towns and villages (see Figure 5) were urged to remain outdoors even though it was cold winter weather.

° It would be advisable to review the discussion on dilatancy of the crustal rocks in Chapter 4.

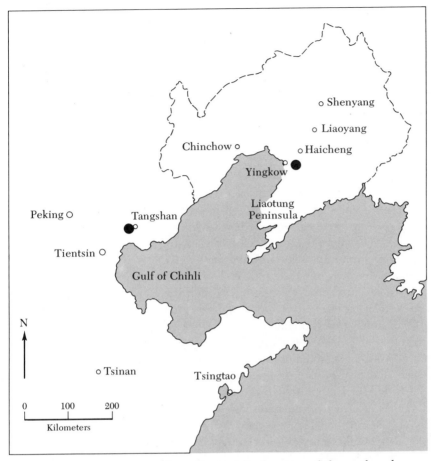

Figure 5 Map of northern China, showing the locations of the earthquakes near Haicheng (February 4, 1975) and Tangshan (July 27, 1976).

Then, at 7:36 P.M. a strong earthquake of magnitude 7.3 shook the Haicheng-Yingkow region. The event was described as follows in a later Chinese report:

> Most of the population had left their houses, big domestic animals had been moved out of their stables, trucks and cars did not remain in their garages, important objects were not in their warehouses. Therefore, despite the collapse of most of the houses and structures during the big shock, losses of human and animal lives were greatly reduced. Within the most destructive area, in some portions more than 90 percent of the houses collapsed, but many agricultural production brigades did not suffer even a single casualty.

Chinese reports, as well as those by western observers who visited the area subsequently, confirmed that damage had indeed been widespread and that large-scale reconstruction was taking place. In one Yingkow commune of 3470 people, most of the 800 dwelling houses were severely damaged, and 82 had completely collapsed. Yet, according to reports, there were no casualties. In Haicheng, 90 percent of the structures were destroyed or seriously affected: entire buildings fell into the streets, and factories and machinery were damaged. In the countryside, dams, bridges, irrigation works, and houses were damaged. Without the prediction, a significant number of the 3 million people in this densely populated province would have died inside collapsed buildings. The exact number of dead is not known but may have reached some hundreds.

We have here a milestone in seismology. The first effective forewarning of a destructive earthquake was issued, preventing many deaths and injuries. What does this remarkable success imply? Is routine earthquake prediction on a large scale imminent?

In answer, it is only fair to cite the failures as well as the successes of the Chinese prediction program. Although there are claims that the time of several Chinese earthquakes has been forecast correctly—such as the 1975 Haicheng earthquake, and a pair of earthquakes 97 minutes apart, magnitude 6.9, near the China-Burma border in western Yunnan on May 29, 1976—others have not (although specific statistics have not been published). Also, forecasts of impending earthquakes have been made in China that turned out to be false alarms. One was issued in August 1976 in Kwangtung province (normally not very seismically active) near Kwangchow (Canton) and Hong Kong. During the earthquake alert many people slept outdoors in tents for nearly 2 months and concern spread to Hong Kong for a time. No earthquake occurred.

The most publicized lack of forewarning was the tragic earthquake of July 27, 1976, which almost razed Tangshan (see Figures 5 and 6), an industrial city of 1 million people situated 150 kilometers east of Peking. Official reports estimated a death toll of about 250,000 in the meizoseismal area. About 100 persons were killed as far away as Peking, where some mud walls and old brick houses collapsed. It is estimated that an additional 500,000 persons were injured. When the enormous industrial loss is added to this human calamity, the economic aftermath on the country was severe. (The Tangshan earthquake also had political implications: a traditional Chinese view maintains that natural disasters are a mandate from heaven, and earthquakes have been claimed to mean trouble for governments as far back as the Sung dynasty.)

After a particularly lethal earthquake in 1966 about 300 kilometers southwest of Peking in Hsingtai, Hopei province, Premier Chou En-lai called for an earthquake prediction program "applying both indigenous and modern methods and relying on the broad masses of the people."

Such a narrow but specific seismological goal is particularly appropriate for this country with its over 900 million people. Many structures are

Figure 6   Horizontal and vertical offsets in a schoolyard of the fault that produced the 1976 Tangshan earthquake. [Photo by Bruce A. Bolt.]

not earthquake resistant so that the only effective short-term way of counteracting earthquakes is to evacuate people from their unsafe dwellings ahead of time. Second, the linking of seismological research to earthquake prediction enables scientists to work in a framework with approved, and indeed admirable, social ends. Third, earthquake prediction programs can be developed in a structured rural society, so that tens of thousands of peasants take part in discussions of earthquake hazards and report such physical phenomena as variation in water level of wells and any abnormal behavior of animals. A beneficial effect of this approach is the widespread education of masses of people (if it is done in an objective way).

In Liaoning province, the subsequent site of the 1975 Haicheng shock, some observational programs of possible precursory phenomena were begun as early as 1970 by seismologists and nonprofessional but interested people. In late 1973 and 1974 a number of changes and variations in physical parameters were reported. For example, in the region of the Jinzhou fault in Liaoning province, the ground surface rose at 20 times its normal rate, an elevation increase of about 2.5 millimeters in 9 months.°
Unusual fluctuations in the Earth's magnetic field were reported, as were

---

° A line of fresh *en echelon* cracks, extending into the shallow basement rock, was observed after the earthquake; the line is approximately parallel to the largest dimension (about 60 kilometers) of the aftershock zone but only about 5.5 kilometers long. Some Chinese geologists conjectured that a new fault was created. The Jinzhou fault did not rupture.

changes in the elevations of the shorelines of Liaotung Peninsula. Similar phenomena, *not* associated with earthquakes, have been reported in many parts of the world, but those in Liaoning were evidently considered symptomatic enough to warrant the cautious speculation, at the end of June 1974, that a local earthquake of moderate size might strike within the next 2 years. The entire set of symptoms gathered by December 1974 apparently caused authorities to declare at least one abortive short-term emergency.

In early February of the following year, more impressive clues came from seismographic stations near Haicheng, which reported that many small earthquakes had begun to be recorded. The specific prediction was mostly based on this increase in background seismicity (compare the Oroville earthquake story in Chapter 9). Throughout the region, people recounted incidents of peculiar animal behavior (see Figure 7). In addition, there were numerous reports, mainly from amateur observers, of changes in ground water level. Tiltmeters showed that the ground had changed direction of tilting in some places but not others.

On February 3, the Shihpengyu Seismographic Station, east of Yingkow, suggested that the small earthquakes were the foreshocks of a large earthquake. As a result, on February 4, the party committee and the revolutionary committee of Liaoning province alerted the entire province. Special meetings were held at once to ensure that precautionary measures would be taken. The people were mobilized to build temporary living huts, move patients from hospitals, concentrate transportation facilities and important objects, organize medical teams, induce people to evacuate their homes, and move the old and weak to safety.

In retrospect, the efficacy of the mobilization speaks for itself. But the process of arriving at the decision to do so is less clear-cut. Some of the observations on which decisions were based were less than scientific. There is no firm scientific evidence, for example, that animals can sense the advent of an earthquake.° Also, variations in the ground levels occur in many places throughout the world without being accompanied by earthquakes. Even the occurrence of the foreshocks is not an infallible indicator, since there is no way of knowing that an earthquake is a foreshock of a large one until the large one occurs. In addition, some sizable earthquakes—like that in San Fernando, California, in 1971—have not been immediately preceded by foreshocks. Also, swarms of earthquakes, unac-

---

°However, accounts of similar animal behavior before a major earthquake have previously been reported from various countries, e.g., before the 1906 San Francisco earthquake, before the 1923 Tokyo earthquake, and recently, before the 1976 Friuli earthquake. Fine sensing of variations in magnetic and electric fields, radon gas concentrations, aerosol particles, and so on have been suggested as explanations, but no controlled experimental evidence has been published.

companied by any principal shock, are common in earthquake country. From a psychological perspective, the Liaoning foreshocks must have prepared much of the population for an official warning; it is known that many persons were already staying out of their weak adobe and stone houses before February 4 because of the repeated shaking. Thus, remarkable as the 1975 prediction was, there were other factors as well, such as continuous and widespread local and provincial government concern, telltale foreshocks, social discipline—and a modicum of good fortune.

Fossil Earthquakes

Seismologists have for a long time sought ways of detecting the occurrence of great prehistorical earthquakes. Several methods have been tried. The first uses the uplift of seashores produced by sudden fault slip, which results in a change in the levels at which seashells and mollusca live in tidal regions. For example, after the 1964 Alaska earthquakes, tidal benches were dated from the fossil sea life, and the sequence of uplifts of the land surface associated with previous major earthquakes was determined. Another scheme is the measurement of growth rings in large trees of great antiquity growing in earthquake country. Severe shaking of the ground sometimes damages the root system of a tree, causing retarded growth in the following year. However, even after correlating the growth rates through a wide area, the range of uncertainty is large because of

Figure 7 Cartoon in Chinese seismological textbook, suggesting that animals may give forewarnings of earthquakes. "Chickens fly up to trees and hogs stay quiet. Ducks go out of water and dogs bark wildly." [Courtesy of W. Lee and Francis Wu.]

Figure 8   Near-vertical slip plane of the San Andreas fault, Pallett Creek, California, exposed on the side of a trench. Dark bands are horizontal layers of sand and peat. [Courtesy of K. E. Sieh.]

climatic variations. More precise procedures that have been recently developed can, under favorable circumstances, rather reliably track sequences of great earthquakes back in Holocene time. These procedures depend on the geological field studies of fault movement (see Chapter 3, Figure 2).

Detailed stratigraphic mapping has been successful along the San Andreas fault in California, where dated features are ascribable to specific large historic earthquakes. About 50 kilometers northeast of Los Angeles, the trace of the San Andreas fault transects a low-lying area that becomes a swamp from the waters of Pallett Creek during a rainy season. Trenches excavated by geologists across the fault in this area exposed a well-marked sequence of silt, sand, and peat (marsh-plant remains) layers (see Figure 8). The motivating hypothesis for the work was that the displacement and liquefaction effects of great paleoearthquakes might be preserved in such beds of sand and peat. The theory is as follows: During the strong shaking of the ground, water-saturated sand layers at some depth below the surface become liquefied (see Glossary). The overpressure of the rocks and soil above then causes the water and sand to rise to the surface, forming "sand blows" or "sand fountains" (see Figure 9). As the cycle of wet and dry seasons continues, Pallett Creek and other neigh-

Figure 9 Cemented sand-liquefaction column or pipe. A system of cemented sand columns or pipes was exposed during trench excavations in the Tanlu fault zone in Anhui province. [Photo by Bruce A. Bolt.]

boring streams carry down gravel and silt, which cover up the sand blows formed in the intense shaking; after the passage of time, another great earthquake occurs, producing further liquefaction and resulting sand blows at the surface; these are, in turn, also covered up. Thus the sand blows, silt and peat layers form a conformable sequence, with the younger layers lying over the older ones. The plants or other organic materials within each layer are dated by radiocarbon methods.

At Pallett Creek, evidence was found for at least nine paleoearthquakes extending back more than 1400 years to A.D. 545. The dates, all but one of them approximate, are as follows:

1857, 1745, 1470, 1245, 1190, 965, 860, 665, 545

The key year, 1857, marked the directly documented Fort Tejon earthquake of January 9 (see Appendix B), which is the last great earthquake produced by rupture of the southern section of the San Andreas fault. There is thus a direct check on the method. (There is some independent evidence also that the 1745 marker bed was the result of shaking from a rupture of the San Andreas fault southward from the city of San Bernardino.)

Two conclusions follow from the work at Pallett Creek. First, large earthquakes along the southern reach of the San Andreas may break different segments of the fault at different times. Second, the average time between these past earthquakes is approximately 160 years, but there is a large variation. The greatest time interval was nearly 300 years and the smallest as short as 55 years.

It should be noted that the Pallett Creek site gives information on earthquakes caused by rupture along only one large section of the San Andreas fault in Southern California and not its whole extent even there. Also, damaging earthquakes may occur where ground water conditions are not always appropriate to produce significant liquefaction by even a large earthquake in the vicinity (such as during a very dry season). Similar studies on liquefaction have since been carried out across other active faults in places such as China and Japan (see Figure 9). Difficulties arise in very wet and very dry climates; for example, long-lived organic material (such as from redwood trees) emplaced in the sand layers by water or animal action can produce spurious dates in the statistical analysis.

The Parkfield, California, Earthquake Prediction

There are now two classes of credible earthquake predictions in California. The first involves general forecasting that gives probabilities over a considerable time span. The second type is more specific, stating the time span, region, and magnitude range; at present, there is only one such definitive prediction.

The historic seismicity record in California is too short for finely tuned forecasting; however, geodetic and geologic information, when considered with the 180-year earthquake record, leads to the conclusion that a damaging earthquake of magnitude 7.0 or greater in California is immi-

Box 3. Odds of Seismicity for Northern and Central California

The *Bulletin* of the Seismographic Stations of the University of California lists 3638 earthquakes ($3.0 \leq M_L \leq 6.9$), which occurred in the 280,000 square kilometer area of northern and central California from 1949 through 1983. The cumulative number of earthquakes (N) expected with an assigned magnitude M_L is

$$\log N = 4.23 - 0.815\, M_L,$$

normalized to earthquakes per year per 280,000 square kilometers.

The annual rate of seismicity ($r = 10^{\log N}$) in earthquake sequences per year and the percent probability of one or more earthquakes of magnitude M_L or larger occurring in one day, week, month, year, or decade is:

$M_L \geq$	r (eq/yr)	Percent probability in one				
		day	week	month	year	decade
3.0	60.0	15.0	69.0	99.0	100.0	100.0
3.5	24.0	6.3	36.0	86.0	100.0	100.0
4.0	9.2	2.5	16.0	54.0	100.0	100.0
4.5	3.6	0.99	6.7	26.0	97.0	100.0
5.0	1.4	0.39	2.7	11.0	76.0	100.0
5.5	0.55	0.15	1.1	4.5	43.0	100.0
6.0	0.22	0.059	0.42	1.8	19.0	89.0
6.5	0.085	0.023	0.16	0.71	8.1	57.0
7.0	0.033	0.009	0.064	0.28	3.3	28.0

nent. From such joint data, a probability assessment[*] in 1979 demonstrated that when all sections of major earthquake-producing faults were considered, the odds were about even (50–50) that an earthquake with a magnitude greater than 7 would occur in California in the next decade. It was further pointed out that with every passing year, these odds slowly increase. Indeed, considering the historic earthquake record for the whole state going back to 1800, these 50–50 odds could be viewed as perhaps a conservative appraisal. Since 1979, seismologists have refined this prediction, particularly by subdividing the state into regions, but the results have been consistent overall with the above estimate (see Box 3).

---

[*]Made by the late R. H. Jahns of Stanford University and myself for the State Seismic Safety Commission.

The one definitive prediction is that a moderate earthquake is likely to occur near the town of Parkfield, California (see Chapter 2, Figure 2), between 1987 and 1993. In this rural region of rolling, open ranch land, remote from highly populated developments, the San Andreas fault trace is clearly visible, and its seismological properties along a 25-kilometer-long section are among the best understood in the world. The long-term seismographic record of the University of California observatories, installed in 1887, established that moderate-sized earthquakes (M_L 5.5 to 6) occurred near Parkfield in 1901, 1922, 1934, and 1966. There is also evidence from felt reports of similar earthquakes in 1857 and 1881. In addition, available seismograms have permitted quantitative estimates of size and location for the earthquakes of March 10, 1922; June 8, 1934; and June 28, 1966.

A simple plot (see Figure 10) of the earthquake dates immediately suggests a cyclical pattern. There is an almost constant recurrence time of about 22 years. The exception is the 1934 fault slip (but note that 44 years elapsed between 1922 and 1966). If this cyclic pattern is repeated, the next Parkfield earthquake might be expected about 1988. With an allowance for statistical variation, the window of occurrence is approximately 1987 to 1993.

More information is needed if much reliance is to be placed on such correlation. Indeed, some confirmatory evidence has been marshaled. The starting place is the last earthquake in the area on June 27, 1966, which was well recorded on seismographs in California and around the world. These seismograms yielded a magnitude $M_L = 5.5$ and indicated a rupture southeastward from a focus near Parkfield for a distance of approximately 16 kilometers. The fault rupture zone was confirmed by the presence of fresh cracks along the mapped fault trace south of the earthquake epicenter. Secondly, instrumental locations of the epicenters of the earthquakes of 1922 and 1934 indicate that they have an almost common epicenter with the 1966 earthquake at the northwest of the above rupture zone. Further, a cluster of foreshocks occurred in the 6 months before June 27, 1966 within about 3 kilometers of this epicenter. A similar foreshock pattern occurred in 1934. The foreshock cluster area has been called the *preparation zone,* on the theory that release of strain energy there occurs preparatory to a major rupture to the southeast.

After a common location and rupture mechanism is established as a basis for the prediction, an explanation for a cyclic release of seismic energy must be sought. Seismograms of the 1922, 1934, and 1966 Parkfield earthquakes indicate that similar amounts of energy were released. The elastic rebound theory (see Chapter 4) states that the sudden fault slip is a consequence of the strength of the contacts between rock surfaces being exceeded after a period of slow strain accumulation. If the strain

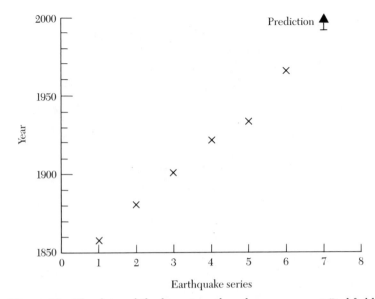

Figure 10 The dates of the largest earthquake sequences at Parkfield, California, since 1850. The linear trend is clear. The arrow predicts the next similar event. [After W. H. Bakun and T. V. McEvilly, 1984.]

accumulates at a constant rate and the rock strength remains the same, it follows that there will be a constant time interval between the earthquakes. The 1934 Parkfield earthquake is an exception to the argument, but the other interoccurrence times are supportive.

As a consequence of the overall evidence and the favorable situation of the Parkfield area (low population, accessible fault zone, open countryside), a prediction experiment is being conducted at Parkfield. A network of sensitive seismographs has been placed around the postulated preparation zone. Surface-fault movements are being monitored continuously by creep meters (see Figure 4) in the form of 10-meter-long devices across the San Andreas fault trace. Geodetic surveys are being made with special laser geodimeters that measure the distance across the fault between points that are 5 to 8 kilometers apart. Dilatation of the rocks is being measured by balloonlike devices installed in boreholes; as the volume of the rock changes, the strain is measured as a change in pressure. The usefulness of watching for such precursors was suggested by reports of possible fault slip before the 1966 earthquake. An irrigation pipeline that crosses the San Andreas fault near Parkfield was found broken about 9 hours before the main earthquake; a tectonically related explanation is supported by sightings of fresh cracks along the fault about 10 days before the main shock. There are thus several lines of diagnostic evidence that may identify forerunners of the next Parkfield earthquake. Seismologists are now on tenterhooks as 1993 comes nearer.

Interior damage over the altar in the church of Monte di Buia from the Friuli earthquake, Italy, on May 6, 1976. [Courtesy of James Stratta.]

I remember when (Britain) was shaken with an earthquake some years ago, there was an impudent montebank who sold pills which (as he told the country people) were very good against an earthquake.

—JOSEPH ADDISON, *The Tatler*

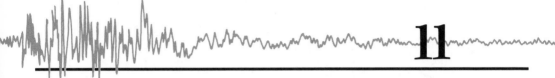

11

Self-Protection in an Earthquake

Types of Risks

We might call 1976 the year of killer earthquakes. The reports of the dreadful loss of life from around the world were alarming. As many as 300,000 people may have died: the Guatemala shock of February 4 killed 23,000; the Italian earthquake on May 6 near Friuli caused over 900 deaths; the July 28 shock (local time) near Tangshan, China, probably killed over 250,000 people; on June 25, a magnitude 7.1 shock killed perhaps 6000 persons in West Irian; an earthquake and accompanying tsunami in the Philippines on August 16 resulted in 2000 fatalities; and over 4000 were killed in an earthquake near Muradiye in Turkey on November 24. In addition, hundreds of thousands were injured, and the earthquakes produced enormous economic losses. Most casualties were directly caused by the collapse of weak houses and buildings. (The Guatemala, Tangshan, and Friuli earthquakes all occurred at night when people were in their structurally hazardous homes.)

Paradoxically, despite these grim statistics, 1976 had slightly less than the average number of large earthquakes. Global statistics show that each year there are, on the average, about 100 earthquakes of magnitude 6 or greater, that is, about 1 potentially damaging earthquake every 3 days (see Appendix A). About 20 earthquakes with magnitudes of 7 or greater occur annually; this is about 1 severe earthquake every 3 weeks. Thus, the misfortune of 1976 was not that more large earthquakes than normal occurred, but rather that more than usual occurred by chance in susceptible highly populated regions.

Earthquake risks must be balanced against other everyday risks. In the United States, the principal noncatastrophic risk in day-to-day life is posed by the automobile: about 300 of every million people are killed per year. Much farther down the scale come the main catastrophic risks such as fire (0.5 deaths per million per year) and tornadoes (0.4 deaths per million per year). The risk from earthquakes is lower still, and it can be further reduced if we protect ourselves from earthquakes. Of course, the methods of doing so will vary with the circumstances. Let us look first at the main hazards produced by earthquakes, summarized in Box 1.

By far the most important hazard is the shaking of the ground. This in turn shakes buildings, causing objects to fall and structures to collapse partially or totally. A great deal can be learned about building safer structures by studying these effects as soon as possible on the spot, and many valuable studies of this kind have been published.

Unfortunately, structural damage in historical earthquakes is usually

Box 1. The Main Earthquake Hazards

Ground shaking
Differential ground settlement
Land and mud slides
Soil liquefaction
Ground lurching
Avalanches

Ground displacement along a fault

Tsunamis and seiches
Floods from dam and levee failure

Fires

Figure 1   Artist's impression of damage to Basel after the October 1356 earthquake, shown on a woodcut from the "Basler Chronik" of Christian Wurstisen, 1580. [From *Basel und das Erdbeben von 1356*, Rudolf Suter, Basel, 1956.]

not easy to evaluate. One intriguing debate centered on the Biblical account of the falling of the walls of Jericho (Joshua: 6). Some compilers of historical earthquake catalogs speculated that this event had been caused by an earthquake. A contrary opinion was voiced by the famous French seismologist, Montessus de Ballore. He argued that the walls should be the strongest structures of the city, and yet Joshua's army had crossed the ruined walls to "destroy and burn the city"—hardly necessary if strong shaking had already taken its toll.

For some major historical earthquakes, the effects have been recorded in other ways. For example, the damage resulting from one that struck Basel, Switzerland, on October 18, 1356 is represented for posterity in a woodcut done 2 centuries later (see Figure 1).

The ground shaking also damages the soils and foundation materials under structures, and much of the destruction in earthquakes is a consequence of this ground failure° (see Figure 2); the relation is particularly evident in the measures of intensity given in Appendix D.

°Considerable detail on these earthquake effects is given in B. A. Bolt, W. L. Horn, G. A. Macdonald, and R. F. Scott, *Geological Hazards* (Berlin: Springer-Verlag, 1975).

Figure 2 An example from the Niigata earthquake of June 16, 1964, in Japan of liquefaction in the foundation soils under a building. This structure was not damaged from the shaking but, after the earthquake, leaned at an angle of about 20°. [Courtesy of Takeshi Minakami, Earthquake Research Institute, University of Tokyo, Japan.]

A few structures will be damaged because they happen to straddle an active fault that ruptures and causes displacements in the soil above the fault. This type of hazard can be minimized by taking care to construct buildings off the fault traces, as specified by geological information. To this end, special geological maps have now been drawn for various areas throughout the world. For example, a recent map of California published by the Division of Mines and Geology shows all known active faults (historical rupture, Quaternary displacement, and so on) in the state. Such broad maps are, of course, not foolproof because some active faults may not have been detected at the time of publication (such as the 1971 San Fernando faulting, the 1975 faulting south of Oroville and the 1983 Coalinga faulting), and some faults marked as active may not again be the source of large earthquakes.

The 1971 San Fernando earthquake north of Los Angeles provided firsthand observations of the effect of surface rupture on various types of structures. Flat-lying San Fernando is almost entirely built up with single-story wood-frame houses. The fault offset (up to 1 meter vertically and 1 meter laterally) produced no structure collapses, no deaths, and few serious injuries. Damage to houses along the fault scarp ranged from minor to that requiring expensive repairs, and a few homes were completely demolished. Water and gas pipes crossing the fault rupture were often compressed and ruptured, and concrete road beds were crushed and overthrust.

Sometimes floods are produced by earthquake shaking. Along the ocean, tsunamis can cause more death and damage than the shaking itself; in lakes and reservoirs, water oscillation (seiches), the collapse of retaining walls, or landslides can be serious secondary hazards for people living downstream. As mentioned in Chapter 5, an earthquake (magnitude 7) on July 9, 1958 shook Lituya Bay, Alaska, and triggered a massive landslide into the bay that produced a water surge 60 meters high.

Finally, there is the formidable threat of fire, such as resulted from the 1906 San Francisco and the 1923 Tokyo earthquakes. Soon after the San Francisco earthquake, fires broke out in several places and spread for 3 days, burning 508 blocks of the city. The main problems were the highly combustible nature of many buildings, the lack of fire protective devices such as sprinklers, and the narrow streets. The ground shaking caused the city water-pipe system to break in hundreds of places so that, although there was ample water in the distribution reservoirs, little was available in the burning areas. In the 1923 Japanese earthquake, over 140,000 lives were lost in Tokyo, Yokohama, and other centers in Kwanto province, many in the fire storms in Tokyo which were fanned by high winds.

The fire scourge is one hazard that can be sharply reduced by action and planning. Fire drills should be conducted in homes, schools, hospitals, and factories. Community fire-fighting services and regulations should be strong. In most cities the trend is encouraging. Certainly both Tokyo and San Francisco now have better equipment and water supply, and fewer vulnerable buildings than at the time of their conflagrations.

The best protection advice for an individual to keep in mind is to be prepared and not to panic. Remember that earthquakes are strong vibrations of the ground that will greatly subside in less than a minute, often in less than 15 seconds. In this brief period of severe shaking, quickness of wit can prevent injury. People are often surprised by how calm they have been.

Box 2 lists suggestions for protection before, during, and after an earthquake. If you are in an open area in the countryside or even in the city, or if you are in a car or other vehicle on the open road, you will have little to

Box 2. Protection in an Earthquake

Before an Earthquake

At home

Have a battery-powered radio, flashlight, and first-aid kit in your home. Make sure everyone knows where they are stored. Keep batteries on hand.

Learn first aid.

Know the location of your electric fuse box and the gas and water shut-off valves (keep a wrench nearby). Make sure all responsible members of your family learn how to turn them off.

Don't keep heavy objects on high shelves.

Securely fasten heavy appliances to the floor, and anchor heavy furniture, such as cupboards and bookcases to the wall.

Devise a plan for reuniting your family after an earthquake in the event that anyone is separated.

At school

Urge your school board and teachers to discuss earthquake safety in the classroom and secure heavy objects from falling. Have class drills.

At work

Find out if your office or plant has an emergency plan. Do you have emergency responsibilities? Are there special actions for you to take to make sure that your workplace is safe?

During an Earthquake

Stay calm. If you are indoors, stay indoors; if outdoors, stay outdoors. Many injuries occur as people enter or leave buildings.

If you are indoors, stand against a wall near the center of the building, or get under a sturdy table. Stay away from windows and outside doors.

If you are outdoors, stay in the open. Keep away from overhead electric wires or anything that might fall (such as parapets and cornices on buildings).

Don't use candles, matches, or other open flames.

If you are in a moving car, stop away from overpasses and bridges and remain inside until the shaking is over.

At work

Get under a desk or sturdy furniture. Stay away from windows.

In a high-rise building, protect yourself under sturdy furniture or stand against a support column.

Evacuate if told to do so. Use stairs rather than elevators.

At school

Get under desks, facing away from windows.

If on the playground, stay away from the building.

If on a moving school bus, stay in your seat until the driver stops.

After an Earthquake

Check yourself and people nearby for injuries. Provide first aid if needed.

Check water, gas, and electric lines. If damaged, shut off valves.

Check for leaking gas by odor only. If it is detected, open all windows and doors, shut off gas meter, leave immediately, and report to authorities.

Turn on the radio for emergency instructions. Do not use the telephone—it will be needed for high-priority messages.

Do not flush toilets until sewer lines are checked.

Stay out of damaged buildings.

Wear boots to protect against shattered glass and debris.

Approach chimneys with caution.

At school or work

Follow the emergency plan, or instructions given by someone in charge.

Stay away from beaches and waterfront areas where tsunamis could strike, even long after the shaking has stopped.

Do not go into damaged areas unless authorized. Martial law against looters has been declared after a number of earthquakes.

Expect aftershocks: they may cause additional damage.

fear from even a high-intensity earthquake. If you are indoors when the shaking starts, get under the strongest structure in the room, perhaps an inside doorway or a strong table or chair. These help protect you from falling objects, such as light fittings and ceilings. Evacuate the building as soon as possible because it might be damaged, and aftershocks may collapse weakened buildings many hours after the main shock. If you are in city streets during the shaking, move to the center of the street or into a doorway to avoid falling broken glass and building walls.

Householders and apartment dwellers should have a fire extinguisher easily accessible in the home. Then if a fire breaks out from, say, cooking oil on the stove, it can be dealt with. Even if water mains are ruptured, liquid can usually be found for minor fire-fighting purposes, first aid, and even drinking in toilet cisterns, water heaters, canned drinks, and elsewhere. A flashlight should always be on hand at night, because the power supply often fails immediately. A first-aid kit may be needed, particularly for injuries due to broken glass. Leaking gas from broken connections to overturned gas heaters or even broken gas mains can produce dangerous fires and explosions; therefore, open flames should not be used to explore damaged basements. Electric power should be shut off if any gas is smelled. Finally it is advisable to keep informed about the nature and extent of damage throughout the area: keep a battery-powered radio in the house. The telephone may be dead, and even if it is not, it should be used only for emergency calls.

The odds are high (over 60 in 100) that a damaging earthquake will occur when most persons are at home. Where the standard of home construction is high or timber frame is used, this is to the good. But unfortunately, in many places, construction materials and methods are seismically hazardous. For example, in China, as well as regions of the Mediterranean, Turkey, Iran, South and Central America, and Asia, the types of housing almost guarantee heavy death tolls during an even moderate earthquake shaking (see Figure 3). As described in Chapter 3, this was what happened in the 1976 Guatemala earthquake. The economic resources to bring the present rural housing in most earthquake-prone countries up to adequate earthquake-resistant levels in a short time are just not available.

A disaster is less serious if most of the people in a damaged area survive, because the local labor force can immediately undertake reconstruction and repairs without undue burden on the economy. This is one reason why so much effort is being poured into earthquake prediction in China where several hundred million workers are in jeopardy. However, as pointed out in Chapter 10, practical prediction activities, despite some successes, may, *on the average*, produce social and economic dislocations.

Figure 3   Destruction of weak wood and masonry structures in Biwajimi, Japan, in the Mino-Owari Earthquake, October 28, 1891. [From *Imperial Earthquake Commission Report*, no. 19, 1904.]

Inexpensive modifications of rural and urban housing designs (such as the use of corrugated iron and simple wood and metal reinforcement) are the best long-term measures to prevent injury.

In contrast, the single- and two-story wood-frame houses typical of the United States and New Zealand, and the light wooden buildings of Japan are examples of places that are among the safest to be in an earthquake. These buildings can suffer damage, as shown in Figure 4, but it is minor in comparison with the total collapse that can and does occur elsewhere (see Figure 3). But even in these countries the trend is to experiment with new materials and change the design of ordinary buildings, so that the increase in seismic risk may not be recognized until an earthquake occurs. For example, the 1971 San Fernando earthquake in California demon-

Figure 4   Interior damage in a wood-frame house at Inangahua following the earthquake of May 23, 1968. Note that cupboard doors and drawers have come open, fixtures have moved from walls, and the electric range has fallen on the floor (becoming a possible fire hazard). [Courtesy of *New Zealand Weekly News* and R. D. Adams.]

strated that well-constructed concrete-block structures, unlike older weak masonry, have a high seismic resistance. However, some newly completed wood-frame houses of split-level design, presumably built to code, collapsed. Unlike the older houses with quite small windows and a separate garage, there was insufficient shear bracing in the narrow garage walls at ground level. Shaking collapsed the garage, causing the rooms above to drop into the garage, many on the family cars.

The 1983 Coalinga, California, Earthquake

In the United States, since the early 1970s, the tempo of federal and state government programs related to earthquakes has increased. In large measure, the stimulus was the February 9, 1971, San Fernando earthquake in southern California, which was the first of significant size to occur in a modern urban environment in the United States.

Starting in 1971, hearings were held and several bills related to seismic risk and hazard reduction were introduced into Congress. The culmination of these activities was the National Earthquake Hazards Reduction Act of 1977. In contrast to earlier versions, which stressed earthquake-prediction research, it was largely successful because it focused on practical questions of mitigation of earthquake hazards. The act initially authorized the allocation of 205 million dollars to be shared by the Federal Emergency Management Agency, the U.S. Geological Survey, the National Bureau of Standards, and the National Science Foundation over a 3-year period beginning in 1978. Responsibilities were assigned to various federal departments and agencies, with significant parts being played by state and local government, universities, private organizations, and individuals. In this way, the appropriated funds, continued in succeeding years through 1987, have had a far-reaching effect on every level of society touched by seismic dangers.

In California, government reaction to the 1971 San Fernando earthquake was quick. In 1972 the legislature created the Seismic Safety Commission° to be responsible for establishing state goals and priorities on earthquake-hazard reduction. The Commission has broad independent powers of recommendation and coordination, including the proposal of needed legislation. The establishment of this commission is among the most significant accomplishments on earthquake-hazard mitigation in

---

°The author has been a member of the commission from 1980 through 1988.

the United States, and specifically in California, since the study of the 1906 earthquake by the State Earthquake Investigation Commission (see Chapter 2).

One activity of the commission has been to study the aftermath of each damaging earthquake in California. One recent case, which has direct lessons for the general public, is the magnitude 6.7 earthquake that struck Coalinga, an isolated town in the San Joaquin Valley, on May 2, 1983 (see Chapter 2, Figure 2). At that time, the population of the town was about 6500. The community was relatively young, yet had a significant number of residents 65 years of age or older. It was not prosperous or particularly poor. Most residents lived in single-family, wood-frame residences of various ages.

The position of this earthquake is a reminder that damaging seismic shaking can occur in places not associated with major or even known active faults. (Surface faulting was observed in a large aftershock but not in the main shock. The latter fault mechanism was unusual: it was thrust, not strike-slip.) The catalog of historical seismicity did show that moderate earthquakes were pervasive along the eastern front of the coast ranges of California running northwest through Coalinga; in 1982 and 1985, there had been sequences of felt earthquakes centered about 30 kilometers from the town. Nevertheless, Coalinga was essentially unprepared for an earthquake of even moderate magnitude. Nearly 200 people were injured and approximately 1000 were left homeless. The earthquake caused over 30 million dollars in damage. Production in the surrounding oil fields was disrupted and downtown business premises generally were severely damaged and had to close. The town was faced with replacing or repairing two-thirds of its housing and rebuilding essentially the entire 12-square-block business district.

The Seismic Safety Commission had hearings on the postearthquake recovery and cataloged all the available information and studies. There were problems with recovery that may be common to many communities, including early demolition of damaged downtown structures that lead to controversy and lawsuits. There were dilemmas related to financing the long-term economic recovery (as opposed to earthquake-damage repairs), and there were debates concerning the design of the new business district. The effect of the earthquake on sales and prices of houses was small, but it caused many rents to increase. The exodus of residents and businesses predicted after the earthquake failed to materialize, and employment actually rose above 1983 levels. Some of the residents reported having earthquake-related problems, both emotional and financial, but most residents were generally satisfied with the manner in which various government agencies responded to their needs in the postearthquake period.

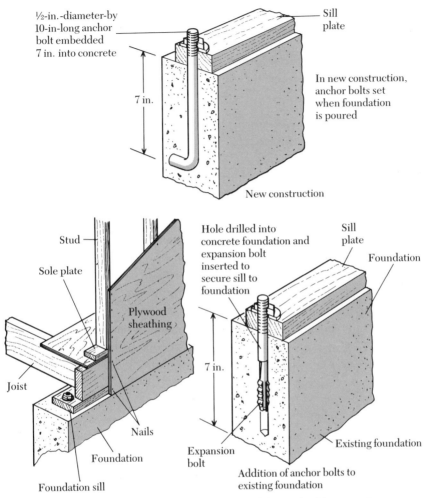

½-in.-diameter-by 10-in-long anchor bolt embedded 7 in. into concrete

Sill plate

7 in.

In new construction, anchor bolts set when foundation is poured

New construction

Stud

Sole plate

Plywood sheathing

Joist

Nails

Foundation

Foundation sill

Hole drilled into concrete foundation and expansion bolt inserted to secure sill to foundation

Sill plate

Foundation

7 in.

Expansion bolt

Existing foundation

Addition of anchor bolts to existing foundation

Figure 5 Detail of connections of existing wood-frame buildings to the foundation. Plywood sheathing should be securely nailed to sills and studs. Anchor bolts ($\frac{1}{2}$-inch in diameter) can be embedded into concrete or masonry foundation no more than 6 feet apart and within 12 inches of the end of each sill board.

One of the major lessons of the earthquake was the importance of bolting timber-framed homes to their foundations to prevent separation (see Figure 5). Surveys showed that about 15 percent of one-story wood-frame houses were damaged when they fell off their foundations, mostly those more than 20 years old and often those with no lateral bracing. The maximum Modified Mercalli Intensity in Coalinga was estimated to be VIII, yet the large majority of houses with adequate foundation connections were hardly damaged; newer homes of all types showed no indication of significant structural damage, although some chimneys fell or cracked.

Steps to Reduce Hazards to Homes

Basic structural design aside, a householder can make certain innovations to minimize earthquake hazard, such as the following:

1. Exterior sheathing of timber-framed houses should be waterproof plywood of 1 centimeter minimum thickness adequately nailed. Because garage doors and large windows weaken the shearing strength, bracing such as plywood sheathing should be added.

2. Internal lighting fixtures and utility equipment (water heaters, refrigerators, wall stoves) should be fastened to structural elements securely enough to withstand large ground accelerations.

3. Brick chimneys should be adequately reinforced and braced to structural elements to prevent collapse into the living area; if they are not reinforced, the flues should be lightweight. Reinforcement with only 4 rods of vertical steel does not provide sufficient safety in high earthquake-risk zones.

4. The frame and sill plate should be inspected periodically to assure that the wood structure, built to resist lateral forces and *tied to concrete foundations*, has not been damaged by termites or fungus.

5. Since unreinforced brick and concrete-block walls often collapse during seismic shaking, all masonry walls should be reinforced and tied to adequate footings.

6. Roofs and ceilings should be of as light a construction as the climate allows.

7. In high seismic-risk zones where foundation soils may move, flexible joints should be provided between the utility lines (particularly gas and water lines) and the outside mains.

8. Closets and heavy furniture should be fastened or strapped to the wall studs wherever these constitute a danger or contain valuable property.

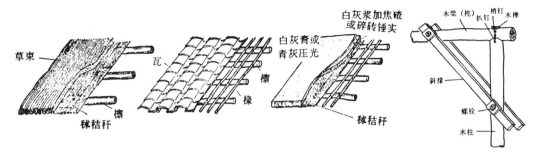

Figure 6 Diagrams showing how to build roof supports in Chinese peasant dwellings. [From a popular booklet on earthquakes distributed in the People's Republic of China.]

In fact every seismically active country could benefit from large-scale programs of instruction on how to make the home more earthquake resistant. Already in China the people are being taught how to strengthen ordinary rural dwellings (see Figure 6).

Even in small-magnitude earthquakes, such as the 1975 Oroville and the 1983 Coalinga earthquakes in California, the destruction and economic loss caused by falling objects can be high.[°] Attachments of light fixtures often need strengthening, and the catches on cupboard doors and the way items are stocked on the shelves should be effective (see Figure 7). Inexpensive restraining bars and supports should be placed on countertops and shelves, particularly in hospitals where the drugs, chemicals and equipment on shelves are vital and, if broken, can be lethal.[†] Also the invaluable and irreplaceable art objects in museums and galleries should be secured to withstand lateral shaking. (Small hinges of strong transparent adhesive tape provide some protection.)

Despite the ample descriptions of the effects of earthquakes on buildings and the Earth's surface around the world throughout many centuries, there is surprisingly little information on the human reaction and social results. The folklore of earthquake countries such as Japan and China reflects numerous complexities and contradictions of the human mind when under the influence of sudden and uncontrollable natural forces. Thus, the Japanese woodblock prints of catfish (see the illustration facing page 1) contain conflicting themes; sometimes the catfish is the destroyer,

---

[°]So many bottles were broken in liquor stores in Oroville in 1975 that the state legislature passed a special bill providing reimbursement for the owners from state funds!

[†]Helpful ideas on preventing nonstructural damage can be found in R. Reithermann, *Reducing the Risks of Non-Structural Earthquake Damage: A Practical Guide*, Second Edition (Oakland, Calif.: Bay Area Regional Earthquake-Preparedness Project, 85–10, 1985).

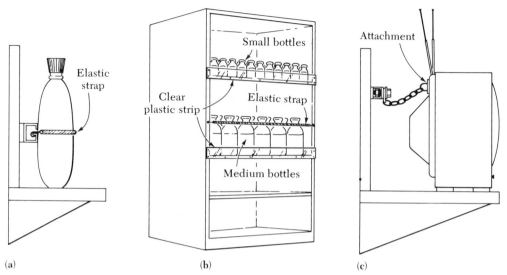

Figure 7 Methods of securing items on shelves. (a) Countertop items are secured by an elastic strap extending around the item. (b) Small items, such as those on the top shelf, can be affixed by a vertical strip, and the medium-sized bottles below by a strip and a horizontal elastic strap. (c) Large items on shelves can be attached at the rear by a chain that connects to a bolt or hook at the back of the shelf.

attacked by the people who have suffered from the earthquake calamity. In others it is a benefactor who has, by damaging the homes of the wealthy, provided work for the artisan classes. Some namazu-e have political, humorous, or social content in the same spirit as modern cartoons.

After the San Fernando earthquake in 1971, the generally calm response of the population in the meizoseismal area was impressive. During the subsequent balmy nights, many residents slept on lawns and in cars, as a sensible precaution against damaging aftershocks. Fortunately, unlike some other earthquake episodes, such as the Friuli sequence in Italy in 1976, aftershocks of the 1971 San Fernando and 1983 Coalinga earthquakes in California caused little additional damage. As time went on, however, there were disquieting reports of children showing significant emotional disturbances, particularly related to the unpredictability of the aftershocks. In modern society, after great natural disasters, the veneer of scientific and logical thought gives way to more primitive reactions and explanations that were connected in earlier times with superstitious beliefs and folklore. One cannot help wondering what the personal responses will be to future great earthquakes° in a society where the roots to folk legends and beliefs have been much attenuated.

Earthquake Insurance

Availability of insurance coverage against earthquake damage varies a great deal from country to country. From an insurance company's point of view, earthquake insurance is not comparable to automobile insurance or life insurance but is rather like a stowaway that has crept into the business. The insurer is used to taking a calculated risk, but earthquake risk does not follow the usual rules: the insured event must occur with some predictable regularity; the probability of sustained damage and its magnitude must be calculable; risk must be spread geographically; and the amount of damage must be limited.

Yet, in a number of countries, such as New Zealand, Japan, the Soviet Union, and the United States, workable insurance schemes covering earthquake risks have been instituted. In general, the cost of earthquake coverage is moderate in relation to the value of a dwelling and the protection provided, although there is frequently a substantial deductible sum that the insured must bear personally.

In the United States, earthquake coverage is available from many private companies. For example, in one typical 1985 scheme made available to homeowners, coverage for $100,000 cost annually $200, with 10 percent deductible allowance. There are also policies providing insurance against tsunamis, landslides, and other geological hazards not necessarily related to earthquakes. It is common, however, for insurers to exclude secondary damage caused by earthquakes, such as fire, when policyholders do not have an earthquake insurance rider.

In California, the insurance premium depends on the zone in which the building is located. For a typical modern, wood-frame dwelling, the coverage is usually written as an addition to a regular homeowner's policy, with a deductible amount calculated separately for the dwelling and contents. Earthquake insurance on poorly built dwellings may be quite expensive and is not common. But in seismically active areas, such as the San Francisco or Los Angeles regions in California, any homeowner

---

°In the damaging San Salvador earthquake of May 3, 1965, the handyman at the seismographic station of El Salvador became so disturbed by the violent shaking that he grabbed a pistol and fired it at the seismograph!

©1977 Universal Press Syndicate 2/26

should give serious thought to the advisability of earthquake insurance (see Figure 8). In 1984, a state law required insurance companies to offer earthquake coverage as a special rider to homeowners' policies. Nevertheless 80 percent of owners do not have such insurance, perhaps because of the substantial deductible amount. The type of construction, the location of the dwelling, and the amount of damage that must be sustained before the policy becomes applicable, are all factors that must be considered before a decision is made.

In Japan, where seismic risk is similar to that of California, local insurers divide the islands into 12 earthquake zones according to earthquake frequency and degree of hazard. Zone 5, consisting of the prefectures of Tokyo, Chiba, Kanagawa, and Yokohama, is considered the highest risk area. Although earthquake coverage is available, it is granted only as an extension of fire coverage. For the individual homeowner, the maximum coverage available is 30 percent of the sum insured for fire.

New Zealand has a government-backed scheme of indemnity for earthquake shaking and fire damage, as well as other geological hazards, such as landslides. Under the government act, private insurance companies have the responsibility of collecting the premium of 5 cents for each $100 of coverage. One-half of this premium may be claimed from a mortgagee, and property owners must bear 1 percent of the loss incurred from earthquakes, with a minimum of $10 and a maximum of $100. All insurance policies in New Zealand include this earthquake coverage, even those on automobiles, and the only way to avoid it is to be totally uninsured.

For Europe generally, the availability and cost of insurance reflects the generally low risk and low demand. In the United Kingdom, where small-to-moderate earthquakes have occurred in historic times in some areas,

Figure 8 Collapse of masonry walls of the Californian Hotel in the Santa Barbara, California, earthquake on June 29, 1925. No one was injured. Rebuilt and reinforced, the hotel stands today. [Photo by Putnam Studios.]

coverage is readily available under comprehensive policies and is included within the overall rate. This overall rate varies, but for the average family home, the rate for buildings is in the region of £1.25 for £1000 of the house value; and the contents, £2.5 for £1000 again on value. The insured has to bear the first £5 of earthquake damage. Earthquake coverage is not available in West Germany or Holland, nor in the seismically quiet areas of Belgium, Denmark, Sweden, and Norway. In France, coverage is not usually available, although insurers may grant it on request as an extension to a fire policy at a minimum rate of 1 franc for 1000 francs on house value.

Spain and Switzerland have compulsory earthquake coverage incorporated in general policies, and premiums are paid into a special government fund. In Spain, earthquake coverage is part of a package for catastrophe perils. The premium for the entire package is 15 percent of the premium for the basic policy. The government must meet any claims, provided the earthquake damage results from intensities exceeding VII on the Modified Mercalli scale. In Italy, with its belt of seismicity in the north and south, coverage can be added to a fire policy, but terms are subject to individual negotiation. In Greece, earthquake coverage is written separately from fire insurance. In Portugal, coverage is available as an extension to the fire policy. The country is zoned for rating purposes, the highest rates being in the south and west, and the lowest in the north and east.

In Canada, coverage is available as an extension of fire policies in all provinces, and the rates vary according to seismic zone. Examples of rates for brick or stone dwellings range from $1.00 per $1000 on value in Manitoba, to $2.00 per $1000 on value in eastern Newfoundland. In both areas, policyholders have a deductible of 4 percent on the value of the property insured. In Australia, earthquake insurance rates reflect the saying that the continent is "quiet but not silent." In Melbourne or Sydney, the rates for buildings are in the region of $1.50 per $1000 on building value, and $4.00 per $1000 on contents. The rate does not vary from one type of construction to another.

The capacity of private companies to handle large-scale earthquake loss is limited. One solution is for governments to take the initiative. This can be done in two ways: the institution of compulsory insurance like that in New Zealand; or the dispensation of emergency funds, as was done after recent earthquakes in California, Nicaragua, and Guatemala. In particular, some kind of ongoing insurance plan will be necessary if reliable earthquake prediction is ever attained (lest thousands of people suddenly rush out to purchase an earthquake policy in response to the first forewarning). Thus governments fostering work on earthquake prediction become more responsible for guaranteeing that people throughout the nation are adequately and consistently protected.

Finally, remember that any insurance scheme—no matter how well planned and executed—is at best short-term; it is no replacement for the mitigation of earthquake hazards by such preventive measures as applying current knowledge to the design and construction of new buildings and improving old buildings to make them more resistant.

Aerial photograph of the uncompleted but damaged freeway
and overpass system at the foot of the San Gabriel Mountains
after the February 9, 1971 San Fernando earthquake,
California. [Courtesy Lloyd S. Cluff.]

Who builds his house on sands deserves a fool's cap.

—ALEXANDER POPE, *An Essay on Man*

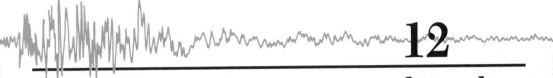

12

Environmental Studies for Earthquake-Resistant Design

Improvements in Planning

Structures in many earthquake countries are now being designed more safely. Not only have building owners become more conscious of the financial reasons for adopting earthquake-resistant design in construction and renovation but also public concern has increased.

This concern is due partly to the growing awareness of environmental issues, and partly to the recognition that it is the public that will bear the cost of reconstruction. Modern social developments are such that most industrial losses must be met by government programs, which are funded by taxes. As a consequence of these developments, regulatory agencies have been established by local, state, and central governments in many countries to protect individuals and general economic well-being.

The first step in a regulatory code is to draw up an appropriate set of rules. Since 1971, for example, cities and counties in California have been required by law to include a seismic-safety element in their general development plans. Although the procedures worked out in response are inconsistent in hazard assessment, the overall results appear to be worthwhile. Technical studies assess the consequences of the historical seismicity and activity of any local faults, the soil conditions and likelihood of landslides, subsidence, and liquefaction. Land use and emergency response plans are developed based on these assessments.

The observational bases for many of these special assessments are regional geological maps of various kinds. The fundamental maps show the geological structure, with emphasis on faults for which there is evidence of movement in Quaternary time. They may be supplemented by maps of the type and thickness of surficial material such as alluvium, filled areas, and so on. Seismic-intensity maps, showing reported intensities of historical earthquakes and isoseismal lines (see Chapter 7, Figure 1) are also used if they are available.

From this basic geological and seismological information, seismic-zoning maps can be constructed on a variety of scales. On the largest scale, these identify the regions of a country or province in which various intensities of ground shaking may have occurred or may be anticipated. If they are showing anticipated intensities, the probability or odds of occurrence of a given intensity are implicit in the map. At present, the zoning maps that exist in North America, Europe, the Balkans, the Soviet Union, China, Japan, New Zealand, Australia, and elsewhere are based on geological factors, earthquake occurrence rate and magnitude, historical intensities, and subjective extrapolations from earthquakes in other parts of the world. In spite of their uncertainties, local seismic-hazard zoning maps are becoming more common; and some show even the blocks or streets in a number of cities, such as Tokyo.

On the maps, risk is conceived as either *relative* or explicitly *probabilistic*. Most maps of relative risk mark zones with an arbitrary numerical or alphabetic scale; for example, a now superseded seismic-risk map for the United States had four zones ranging from no hazard (zone 0) to most hazard (zone 3). Maps of *probabilistic risk* give an idea of the underlying statistical uncertainty, as is done in calculating insurance risk. These maps give the odds at which a specified earthquake intensity would be exceeded at a site of interest within a given time span (typically 50 or 100 years).

Recently, some radical changes have been made in the broad seismic zoning of the United States. New probabilistic maps have been developed as the basis of seismic-design provisions for building practice (see Figure 1). It gives the expected intensity of ground shaking in terms of the *effective peak acceleration*. The effective peak acceleration can be thought of as the maximum acceleration in earthquakes on firm ground

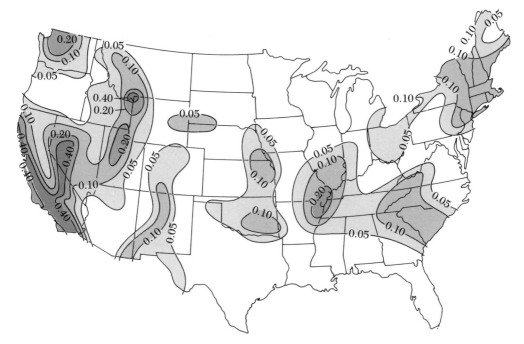

Figure 1 A new seismic-risk map for the United States, prepared for the Applied Technology Council in 1976 to 1977. The contours indicate effective peak, or maximum, acceleration levels (values are in decimal fractions of gravity) that might be expected (with odds of only 1 in 10) to be exceeded during a 50-year period.

after high frequencies that do not affect sizable structures (high-rise buildings, factories, bridges, dams, and so on) have been discounted. As explained in Chapter 7, ground acceleration has been correlated with seismic intensity in earthquake-engineering practice.

The acceleration values plotted on the map contours have certain odds of occurrence, thus accounting for the caprice of earthquakes. Each value plotted has roughly a 90 percent probability of not being exceeded in 50 years. For example, the highest values are found in seismically active California, where near the contour marked 0.4 the chance is only one in ten that active peak ground acceleration of 0.4g or greater will occur within 50 years.

Another factor that must be considered in the plotting of any seismic-risk map is the *attenuation*, or decrease in average intensity of shaking with distance from the earthquake source, as illustrated in Figure 2. It is important because attenuation of seismic waves varies in different parts of the country.

In order to avoid the drawbacks of previous zoning maps of the United States, the following general principles are followed in producing the new ones (such as that shown in Figure 1).

1. The map takes into account not only the size but also the frequency of earthquakes across the country.

2. The zoning pattern is based on the historical seismicity, major tectonic trends, intensity attenuation curves, and intensity reports.

3. Regionalization is defined by contours rather than numbers in zones so that the map shows the "risk surface" for the whole country, with valleys of low seismic risk and mountains of high seismic risk.

4. The map is simple and does not attempt to subdivide the country into microzones. For this reason, only four highly smoothed contours have been selected.

5. The contours must be continuous.

The effective peak-acceleration map is intended for zoning, design, and site evaluation purposes; engineers can read expected accelerations by interpolation directly from the map. Thus it is hoped that, if precautions in construction are taken, the exposure to seismic hazard over the years will be approximately equal throughout the country.

Seismic-risk maps are usually translated into building codes for application to construction. The seismic resistance of a structure is developed by engineers who follow the instructions in a building code and analyze the design specified by the code. All structures in a seismic region should conform to the local building code and, in general, more detailed analyses are applied only to the larger and more costly buildings. The codes are usually keyed to the risk zone or a ground-shaking parameter such as the acceleration plotted in Figure 1.

Since the 1960s a number of techniques have been developed to implement earthquake-resistant designs that are compatible with modern architecture. The more that seismologists understand earthquakes and engineers understand the response of buildings, the more formidable the protective measures will be. As we have seen in the previous chapters, scientific understanding of earthquakes has advanced to a stage at which the causes of earthquakes and the types of ground shaking are reasonably well explained. More critical observations from the strong-motion seismographs are becoming available, each throwing more light on the intensity of seismic shaking under various circumstances. Thus the studies of the 1971 San Fernando earthquake, the 1976 Guatemala earthquake, the

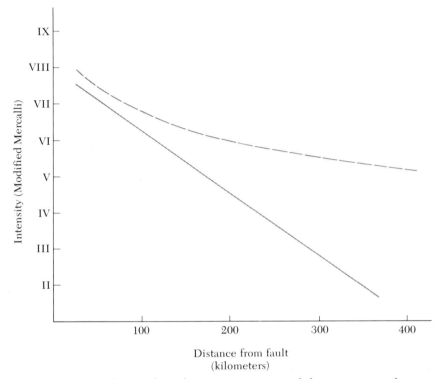

Figure 2 Graph showing how the average intensity of the strong ground shaking from seismic waves decreases with distance from the earthquake source. The intensity values refer to effects on firm ground. The solid line is the attenuation for California and the dashed line is that for the eastern United States.

1985 Mexico earthquake, and many others around the world have all helped to improve earthquake-resistant design.

Engineers working on earthquake problems have also improved their abilities to analyze building motions, often using high-speed computers. Already, some dynamic analyses not only are supported by a strong theoretical basis but have been verified in actual earthquakes, such as the 1971 San Fernando earthquake in the Los Angeles area. A number of high-rise buildings designed according to earthquake-engineering codes were found to have shaken during the earthquake close to the way the designer had predicted. Sometimes, structural designs are proven inadequate, particularly if the architectural form is unusual or the materials untried (see, for example, the failure at Olive View Hospital shown in Figure 7).

Seismic risk to most critical structures is often carefully reduced these days. The methods used to predict what the ground might do in a large earthquake vary in detail from site to site and from country to country. Obviously, the amount of work and expense invested in making geological-hazard studies for any site in order to minimize risk depends very much on the type of facility. Some large facilities hardly affect the population directly, and the main task is to minimize the cost of structural damage. But others, such as large hospitals, must be functional through the aftermath of a damaging earthquake in the region. Consequently, in most preliminary studies, difficult decisions have to be made; and consulting seismologists, in offering advice to design engineers, usually wish they had much more observational material.

Sometimes, because of this lack of certainty, the criteria for the site evaluations are much stricter than warranted by the level of risk accepted in everyday life. Fortunately, as long as devices to measure strong ground motion are in place, an earthquake in one country will produce knowledge that can be applied throughout the world. In this sense, the science of seismology and the practice of earthquake engineering are global enterprises that transcend national boundaries for the benefit of humankind.

The Mexico Earthquake of September 19, 1985

In comparison with California, which has had 5 earthquakes with magnitude greater than 7 in this century, Mexico has had 42, many of which brought great toll in human lives. The tragic earthquake of September 19, 1985, with a magnitude of 8.1, had its source in the subduction slab under the Pacific coast of Mexico (see Chapter 1, Figure 4). It occurred in a seismicity gap that had been pointed out by seismologists for over a decade. It is enlightening to compare the cause and effects of the Mexico earthquake with the Chile earthquake (see Chapter 2) of comparable size in the same year, which was also produced in a subduction zone.

Fortunately, the Mexico earthquake struck in the early morning, at 7:17 A.M. local time when businesses and schools were not fully occupied, because many structures were severely damaged in Mexico City. Even so, casualties in Mexico City, over 350 kilometers away from the focus, amounted to over 8000 deaths, with 30,000 injured and about 50,000 homeless. Severe damage or destruction occurred to about 500 buildings (see Figure 3), with an estimated 4 billion dollars worth of total damage. From one point of view, because Mexico City has a population of over 18 million people and about 800,000 buildings, these statistics indicate that

Figure 3 Removal of debris from a collapsed reinforced concrete building in the Lake Texcoco zone of Mexico City, September 1985. [Photo by V. V. Bertero.]

the shaking affected severely only a small fraction of the city.° The damage along the coast nearer the source was significant but much more limited, partly because of the types of buildings and geological conditions there.

Extensive measurements of the strong ground motion of this earthquake were provided by a network of accelerometers of the National Autonomous University of Mexico (UNAM). Under cooperative arrangements with the University of California at San Diego, strong-motion instruments had also been placed along the Pacific coastline most affected by the shaking.

This cooperative effort arose from an international workshop in Hawaii in 1978, which recommended that to obtain quickly essential missing data on strong shaking of the ground for scientific and engineering purposes, arrays of accelerometers should be placed in the most seismic areas of the world, including Mexico. About 7 months after the workshop, a magnitude 7.8 earthquake occurred along the coast of Mexico. The senior seismologists in the cooperative Mexican-United States program then re-

---

° A commissioner of the California Seismic Safety Commission, Mr. L. Cluff, was staying overnight in Mexico City and experienced only moderate shaking; he went to breakfast in his hotel and became aware of major destruction in the city only about 10 A.M. that morning.

evaluated the hazard probabilities and decided to install additional accelerometers in the states of Guerrero and Michoacán northwest of Acapulco, where there were seismic gaps. When the 1985 earthquake occurred, the stations that had been installed provided 16 digital records of strong ground motion very near the seismic source.

The intervening distance between the earthquake source near the coastal region and the Valley of Mexico greatly reduced the amplitude of seismic waves in Mexico City so that few structures built on firm soil and rock suffered damage. However, the near-surface geology in part of Mexico City created different conditions. Over recent geological time, rains had carried gravel, sands, and clays into the valley and had deposited them in Lake Texcoco. This lake was drained by the Spanish after the conquest of the Aztecs to allow development of the city. Modern Mexico City is to a large extent built on the higher ground surrounding the old lake bed, but near the city center, there are parts underlain by a thick deposit of very soft, high-water-content sands and clays. This zone contained most of the buildings that collapsed during the September 19 earthquake. The map in Figure 4 shows the striking concentration of structural damage. (A similar pattern of damage occurred previously in Mexico City during a 1957 earthquake.)

What is the explanation? Let us start with the radiation of the seismic waves from the sudden movement along a fault in the subduction zone of the west coast in the Michoacán area. Locally, seismic waves radiated upward to the surface through distances of 20 kilometers or more. Accelerometers along this part of the coast showed moderate ground shaking amounting to 16 percent of gravity in a horizontal direction. This intensity is moderate for such a large-magnitude earthquake. As the waves traveled outward through the crustal rocks toward Mexico City, they spread out in time and space, and their amplitudes decreased somewhat overall. Those that shook the firm surface materials in the higher parts of Mexico City, such as at the National University of Mexico, were reduced to horizontal accelerations of only 4 percent of gravity and no damage resulted. In the lake zone, however, surface waves of about 2-second period were preferentially amplified by the clay layers. Moreover, these surface waves had become extended over time so that now there were over 10 cycles of this motion in the dispersed wave train (see Chapter 8, Figure 2). In this area, strong-motion instruments on the surface measured peak horizontal accelerations of up to 40 percent of gravity. This resonance was again amplified by the vibrational properties of buildings between 10 and 14 stories high, which have characteristic vibrational periods of between 1 and 2 seconds. Such buildings, when their foundations are pushed sideways, sway back and forth like inverted pendulums,

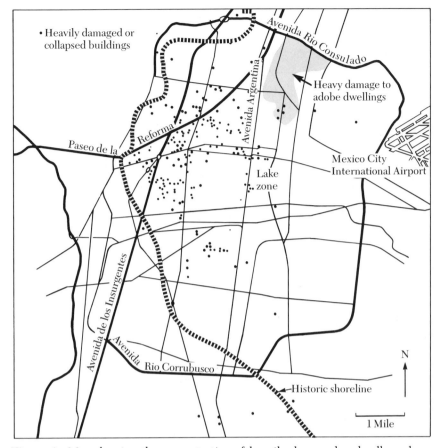

Figure 4 Map showing the concentration of heavily damaged and collapsed major structures in the old lake zone of Mexico City.

and resonance leads to large displacements and a variety of structural failures (see Figure 5). Even in the most heavily shaken zone, most buildings in Mexico City were generally not structurally damaged. These included most shorter buildings and higher "skyscrapers," such as the Latin American Tower of 37 stories which was constructed in the 1950s. Its extreme height produced a vibration period of 3.7 seconds—above the period of the most intense seismic surface waves.

Explanation of the detailed damage in Mexico City will be sought for many years, with engineers studying building designs and running computer simulations of the building vibrations, using as input the actual recorded ground motions. In these ways, the disastrous 1985 Mexico earthquake and the "twin" 1985 Chilean earthquake provide valuable lessons for seismically resistant design of structures in earthquake country.

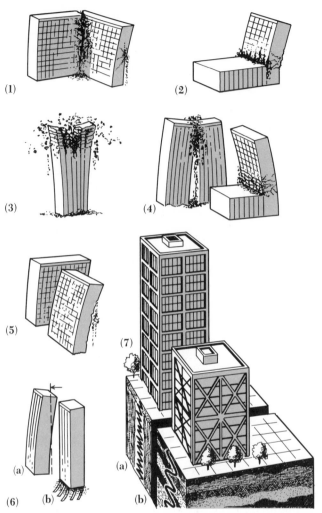

Figure 5   Diagram showing the effect of strong ground shaking on high buildings with differing shapes. (**1**) Two wings at right angles with different motions causing damage at the connection points. (**2**) Building of varying height producing different resonance frequencies. (**3**) As the waves move up the building, the shaking is amplified at the top. (**4**) Pounding between adjacent buildings because of different phases of the motion. (**5**) Enhanced swaying because of alignment of structures relative to the direction of incoming wave motion. (**6**) Flexible high-rise buildings with different architecture: Design (a) remains elastic, while "soft" ground floor in (b) has no shear resistance. (**7**) Pair of buildings on different soils: (a) on rock which transmits higher frequency waves; (b) on softer soil layers which set up wave resonance requiring special bracing of the structure.

Major Engineered Structures and Earthquake Risk

Simplified regional seismic-risk maps (such as that shown in Figure 1) are adequate for designing a majority of structures and zoning and planning purposes. However, in earthquake country, much more specific seismic site evaluation should be carried out for such structures as large dams, bridges, freeways, offshore oil drilling platforms, high-rise buildings, and nuclear reactors (Figure 6). The costs of erecting them, and their importance to the surrounding community or nation are too great to permit reliance solely on broad regional risk maps. In the recent decade, numerous special studies on these structures have been made in the United States, Japan, the North Sea, and elsewhere by teams of geologists, seismologists, soil engineers, and others. Consequently, a great deal has been learned about earthquake occurrence and planning to mitigate earthquake hazard. The main points of such studies are listed in the box on page 214. In most projects, the study begins with analysis of the geological history of the region. The last steps are to calculate numerical values for the maximum accelerations (or velocities) and durations of the predicted seismic waves appropriate for the design.

Figure 6   An example of the collapse of a major lifeline in a major earthquake. This highway bridge in Alaska collapsed in the great Good Friday earthquake of March 27, 1964. [Courtesy of U.S. Army.]

Consider, for example, the geological and seismological procedures that are followed in order to establish a firm basis for the engineering design of a nuclear reactor at a particular site. Increasing numbers of nations are now constructing and operating nuclear power plants to produce electric power. Because of the particular nature of nuclear reactors, the location and design are subject to strict government regulations so that public health and safety are not endangered. Where earthquakes are more than a remote possibility, such as in Spain, Taiwan, Japan, Italy, and the United States, government agencies have developed detailed siting criteria.

Seismicity Risk Studies for a Particular Site

Geological studies

Regional tectonics and patterns of deformation

Mapping of significant capable faults within 100 kilometers

Determination of fault types (strike-slip, dip-slip, and so on)

Evidence for and against recent displacements along faults

Field location of any landslide, ground settlement, or water inundation problems

Soil engineering studies

Field report on foundation soils

Special treatment of slope instability and subsidence when necessary

Modification of strong-motion parameters when necessary

Seismological studies

Study of local historical earthquake records

Mapping of earthquake epicenters

Determination of earthquake intensity and magnitude recurrence relations over time in the region

Study of all historical intensity information near site

Correlation of earthquake locations with mapped faults

Estimation of future seismic intensities (acceleration, velocity, duration) near the site with stated odds of recurrence

Selection of strong-motion records from past earthquakes that best represent the probable intensities

In the United States since 1971, the Nuclear Regulatory Agency (previously the Atomic Energy Commission) has been responsible for determining the validity of the seismological evaluations made by the power companies proposing to build nuclear power reactors. The earthquake history of the region must be examined and an assessment made of the probability of ground motions occurring in the vicinity. Generally, the siting report must establish—from the long-term tectonic history, from the earthquake record, and from what is known of the properties and probable behavior of the local soil and rock layers—those strong ground-shaking parameters that define two earthquake types. The first is called *the safe-shutdown earthquake.* This type is defined as one producing the maximum ground shaking for which the structures and components of the reactor must be designed in order to remain in operating condition during and after the strong motion. Such stringent requirements are necessary to ensure the integrity of the reactor containment walls and the ability to shut down the reactor safely if necessary. The second, less severe type is called the *operating-basis earthquake.* The design of the plant must ensure that this ground shaking would not be enough to prevent the continued operation of the plant without undue risk to the health and safety of the operators and the public.

The decisions stemming from geotechnical studies of this kind aim at maximum prudence—well beyond that deemed necessary for other types of structures. In the United States, the steps required to obtain approval for a reactor take sometimes over 5 years, cost many tens of millions of dollars, and are often unproductive (applications to build have been withdrawn because no firm decisions on risk could be reached).

No comparative evaluation of the objectivity and correctness of decisions in siting nuclear reactors throughout the world has yet been made. Indeed it may be premature until a few substantial earthquakes have occurred at reactor sites. As yet, no major modern power reactor has been shaken by an earthquake of intensity above VII or so.° When a large earthquake does take place near a reactor without dangerous consequences, a more confident attitude—at least toward seismic hazards—will prevail.

Earthquakes can also affect energy production in other ways. In some parts of the world, such as Alaska, California, and the North Sea, huge oil-drilling platforms may be subject to large-amplitude seismic waves. The

---

°On June 7, 1975, a 5.3 magnitude earthquake shook the Humboldt nuclear power station in northern California. This moderate earthquake was centered 25 kilometers away from the site and was felt with Modified Mercalli Intensity VII there. There was no ensuing structural damage, but soon after the station was permanently closed down.

present exploitation of the oil reserves under the North Sea has raised the question of hazards from earthquakes there. The region is a considerable distance away from the active edges of the Eurasian plate, and geological and historical records indicate earthquakes should be minor. Nevertheless, in the past, mildly damaging earthquakes have been centered in Scotland and under the sea off the shore of southern Norway. The strongest regional shock of this century, with a moderate magnitude of about 5.5 on the Richter scale, was in the North Sea on June 7, 1931. Also, numerous earthquakes have occurred along the Great Glen fault in Scotland. Because the fault extends northeastward into the North Sea, small-to-moderate earthquakes can be expected to occur there occasionally.

The design of drilling rigs for use in the North Sea therefore requires checking to test effects of earthquake shaking. The consequences of earthquake damage to an oil rig are, of course, not likely to be as widespread as to a nuclear reactor. Yet seismic-risk evaluation is still prudent and economically desirable for protection of workers' lives, capital investments, and the environment.

Oil pipelines too may be subject to earthquakes. Thus the 1260-kilometer trans-Alaska pipeline had to be designed to withstand seismic hazards. This pipeline crosses a number of earthquake-prone areas on its way from the Arctic Sea to Valdez port in Prince William Sound. The pipes are designed to resist large horizontal ground offsets at fault crossings, liquefaction of the ground supporting them, and various levels of shaking intensity appropriate to the section traversed.

Safe Operation of Hospitals and Schools

One grave result of the February 9, 1971 San Fernando earthquake in southern California was the damage to hospitals. Some wings of the old Olive View Hospital of masonry construction collapsed but, fortunately, were unoccupied at the time. More disturbing were structural failures at the new Olive View Hospital built of reinforced concrete: the first floor of the psychiatric ward caved in completely (see Figure 7), and the main hospital facility was heavily damaged and later demolished (although only two persons were killed at Olive View). The committee of the Structural Engineers Association of Southern California gave the following opinion:

> The lateral force design of the [new] Olive View hospital structures generally complied with the building codes in existence at the time. Failures in both units occurred in columns due to increases in vertical loads as a

Figure 7 Looking west at the new Psychiatric Clinic at the Olive View Community Hospital after the 1971 San Fernando, California, earthquake. The reinforced concrete building was originally two stories, but the ground level, which was used for office space, was entirely crushed. The second story is now resting on the debris near the ground. No serious injuries occurred, although the upper wards were occupied. [Photo by Bruce A. Bolt.]

result of vertical accelerations of the ground and high lateral accelerations causing severe shear and bending stresses.

To the southeast of Olive View, in the northeastern San Fernando valley, also in the meizoseismal zone of the 1971 shock, was a Veterans Administration hospital. The facility opened in 1926, and in February 1971 consisted of 47 separate buildings and 6 more facilities, which constituted a 456-bed general medical complex. The buildings were located within 5 kilometers of the fault rupture observed in the 1971 earthquake. Later studies established that damage resulted from ground shaking and not from any localized crustal faulting. Engineering surveys at the hospital indicated that 26 buildings and additions constructed before 1933 suffered the greatest structural damage. Four of these buildings totally failed during the shaking, killing 38 persons. Buildings that were constructed after 1933 and had masonry or reinforced concrete shear-resisting walls generally did not collapse. In 1972 it was decided to abandon the site, and most buildings have since been demolished.

In all, four major hospitals were seriously damaged in 1971. As a result, an urgent drive was launched to ensure that more adequate seismic resistance was incorporated into hospital structures in the United States. One program was the seismic-risk evaluation and strengthening of all Veterans Administration hospitals in the country.° Geotechnical consultants made geological and seismological evaluations of sites, both in use and proposed, following procedures similar to those listed in the box. The purpose of these studies was to locate any special geological hazards at the site as well as establish seismic parameters describing the strong ground motion that the site might experience. These seismic parameters were used as the basis for engineering studies and analysis.

Some well-maintained and valuable Veterans Administration facilities did not receive acceptable grades, and difficult decisions to evacuate and demolish had to be made. The determining criterion for retaining a facility was that, after any alterations or strengthening, it must be able to resist without collapse the level of ground shaking that could be reasonably expected during its lifetime, although some structural and architectural damage was allowable. Certain buildings in California did not meet this rule and could not be corrected economically, so they were evacuated and demolished.

A special requirement for hospitals is that they—perhaps more than any other public facilities—must remain operational after an earthquake for the treatment of injured and sick persons. Often not much attention is given to certain mechanical, electrical, and architectural elements, which—although not part of the structural frame—are crucial to the maintenance of a working system: these include facades, parapets, power systems, switching gear, elevators, alarms, sprinklers, medical equipment, and boilers. Also, all heavy suspended items such as ceilings must be braced to prevent swaying. In short, a hospital need not be completely functional in all aspects after the shaking, but adequate post-earthquake emergency services, utilities, and access facilities must be available.

Consider, for example, electrical power. Post-earthquake electrical systems should be designed to supply the essential electric demand of the hospital, including ventilating units but not necessarily laundry and cleaning equipment. Several days' emergency supply of fuel oil should be stored in standby tanks that have been designed to resist the same seismic intensity as the hospital buildings. Air-conditioning systems should be capable of servicing at least one operating room and (where available) one intensive-care unit. Similarly, water service for the hospital must be provided by several independent systems.

°The author was a member of the four-person advisory board.

The safety of certain critical smaller items in medical facilities is too often overlooked. Medical supplies, for example, should be protected from breakage during the earthquake shaking. Much of the same advice mentioned in the previous chapter for family homes applies to hospitals. The problem in hospitals is not so simple, however, because all protective measures must be weighed against the extent to which normal hospital activities might be disrupted by installation of securing devices. Glassware that is used constantly can rarely be secured, and some loss of fragile items must be expected in an earthquake. But wheeled hospital equipment can be stored in nonhazardous positions or restrained by brakes or connections to beds and other units fixed to prevent overturning and rolling during the earthquake. Above all, because significant earthquakes, even in seismically active areas, are infrequent, safety in hospitals and similar public service facilities requires constant training and vigilance by staff and continued revision of emergency plans.

Finally, the problem of schools should be mentioned. Chance has played too great a role in recent years in many seismic countries. Earthquakes have caused school buildings to collapse, but they have often occurred on weekends or at night (see Figure 8). One of the most famous examples of such an occurrence was the magnitude 6.3 earthquake near Long Beach and Compton in southern California on March 10, 1933. The local time of the shock was 5:54 P.M. Fortunately, by this hour most of the schools and colleges were vacant, for many of them suffered extreme damage and several collapsed. Only about 120 fatalities are listed for this earthquake, but 3 were teachers killed in the high school at Huntington Beach.

This event provoked such public resentment against shoddy construction that the California legislature passed an act the same year to control the construction of new public schools thereafter. The Field Act set firm standards for mitigating the earthquake risk in the public schools in California. It applied primarily to new public schools. Since then, regulatory standards for other categories of buildings, such as private schools, places of public assembly, colleges, and public service buildings have also been set in various ways, but generally without the strict supervisory control or penalties that pertain to the public schools.

The Field Act requires supervision and enforcement by the Office of the State Architect of the State of California. This office oversees the plans of any proposed school and can act against school districts if they fail to meet design standards. The efficacy of the Field Act has been tested several times, and generally the results have been most satisfactory. The recent test with the 1971 San Fernando earthquake was particularly gratifying because this shock was of the same magnitude as the 1933 Long Beach earthquake. A special study in the San Fernando valley area after the earthquake showed that of some 568 older school buildings that did not satisfy the requirements of the act, at least 50 were so badly damaged that they had to be demolished. But almost all the 500 or so school buildings in the district that met seismic-resistance requirements suffered no structural damage. The odds of children suffering injury if these schools had been in session would have been very small.

Throughout the years in California, several steps have been taken to reduce hazards posed by older school buildings not dealt with in the Field Act. The favorable publicity derived from the confirmatory statistics in the 1971 San Fernando earthquake further encouraged the legislature and school districts to push ahead with the urgent task of replacing substandard school buildings. The California law is now such that nearly all unsafe public school buildings in the state have been closed, demolished, or repaired. Because bond issues for loans to strengthen or rebuild structurally deficient schools were not passed, substantial amounts came from the state budget. Nevertheless, by 1980, most children in California were able to attend earthquake-resistant public schools.

The same cannot be said for many other earthquake countries—Mexico and Chile, for example. As mentioned in Chapter 2, many school build-

Figure 8 Wrecked modern school building in Government Hill slide area, Anchorage, Alaska (1964). The building withstood the shaking but not the landslide. The earthquake occurred during a school holiday. [Courtesy of USGS.]

ings were heavily damaged in the great 1985 earthquake in central Chile, fortunately again not occurring during school hours. Most knowledgeable observers feel that, had the earthquake occurred on a weekday, the number of injured students and teachers would have been high. The positive aspect is that many other school buildings, particularly of recent vintage, suffered little damage beyond a few broken windows, showing that the necessary engineering knowledge is available.

Worldwide, it is generally accepted that if a government requires people, especially children, to congregate in certain buildings during certain hours, it has the responsibility to ensure that the buildings are resistant to geological hazards such as earthquakes. Although it is almost impossible in practice to guarantee that any building will be totally earthquake-proof, experience shows that buildings can be built, in a variety of styles and with a variety of materials, so that they will provide maximum protection for people inside during severe shaking. It has been demonstrated in California and elsewhere that the application of earthquake regulatory codes to school buildings and other public buildings is effective when supervision is vested in a capable organization with clear guidelines and the power to impose penalties.

In countries where school buildings do not meet earthquake design standards, successful forecasting might be one of the only ways loss of life can be minimized. Given the uncertainty of prediction methods (see Chapter 10), it is more satisfactory in the long term to develop a situation in which school buildings at least are earthquake-resistant. Then, rather than a community's having to evacuate children and close schools as the predicted date approaches, well-designed school buildings could become centers of community life where children and others could congregate during the danger period.

There is still much to be done in earthquake lands.

World Earthquakes and Seismicity Rates

Table 1 Notable World Earthquakes and Seismicity

Year	Date (UT)	Region	Deaths	Magnitude	Comments
856	December	Greece, Corinth	45,000		
1038	January 9	China, Shensi	23,000		
1057		China, Chihli	25,000		
1268		Asia Minor, Silicia	60,000		
1290	September 27	China, Chihli	100,000		
1293	May 20	Japan, Kamakura	30,000		
1531	January 26	Portugal, Lisbon	30,000		
1556	January 23	China, Shensi	830,000		
1663	February 5	Canada, St. Lawrence River			Maximum intensity X. Chimneys broken in Massachusetts
1667	November	Caucasia, Shemakha	80,000		
1693	January 11	Italy, Catania	60,000		
1737	October 11	India, Calcutta	300,000		
1755	June 7	Northern Persia	40,000		
1755	November 1	Portugal, Lisbon	70,000		Great tsunami
1783	February 4	Italy, Calabria	50,000		
1797	February 4	Ecuador, Quito	40,000		
1811	December 16	Missouri, New Madrid	Several		Intensity XI. Also January 23, February 7, 1812.
1812	December 21	California, offshore Santa Barbara	Several injuries		Maximum intensity X. Reported tsunami uncertain
1819	June 16	India, Kutch	1543		
1822	September 5	Asia Minor, Aleppo	22,000		
1828	December 18	Japan, Echigo	30,000		
1857	January 9	California, Fort Tejon			San Andreas fault rupture. Intensity X–XI
1868	August 13	Peru and Bolivia	25,000		

Year	Date	Location	Deaths	Magnitude	Remarks
1868	August 16	Ecuador and Colombia	Ecuador 40,000 Colombia 30,000		
1872	March 26	California, Owens Valley	About 50		Large-scale faulting
1886	August 31	South Carolina, Charleston-Summerville	About 60		
1891	October 28	Japan, Mino-Owari	7000		
1896	June 15	Japan, Riku-Ugo	22,000		Tsunami
1897	June 12	India, Assam	1500	8.7	
1899	September 3 and 10	Alaska, Yakutat Bay		7.8 and 8.6	
1906	April 18	California, San Francisco	700	8.25	San Francisco fire
1908	December 28	Italy, Messina	120,000	7.5	
1915	January 13	Italy, Avezzano	30,000	7	
1920	December 16	China, Kansu	180,000	8.5	
1923	September 1	Japan, Kwanto	143,000	8.2	Great Tokyo fire
1932	December 26	China, Kansu		7.6	Much damage
1935	May 31	India, Quetta	60,000	7.5	
1939	January 24	Chile, Chillán	30,000	7.75	
1939	December 27	Turkey, Erzincan	23,000	8.0	
1948	June 28	Japan, Fukui	5131	6.9	
1949	August 5	Ecuador, Pelileo	6000	5.9	
1960	February 29	Morocco, Agadir	14,000	8.5	
1960	May 21–30	Southern Chile	5700	7.3	
1962	September 1	Northwest Iran	14,000	6.0	
1963	July 26	Yugoslavia, Skopje	1200	8.6	
1964	March 28	Alaska	131	7.4	Damaging tsunami
1968	August 31	Iran	11,600	7.8	Surface faulting
1970	May 31	Peru	66,000	6.5	$530 million damage. Great rock slide
1971	February 9	California, San Fernando	65		$550 million damage

Table 1 *(continued)*

Year	Date (UT)	Region	Deaths	Magnitude	Comments
1972	December 23	Nicaragua, Managua	5000	6.2	
1975	February 4	China, Liaoning Province	few	7.4	Predicted
1976	February 4	Guatemala	22,000	7.9	200-kilometer rupture—Motagua fault
1976	May 6	Italy, Friuli (Gemona)	965	6.5	Extensive damage. No surface faulting
1976	July 27	China, Tangshan	About 250,000	7.6	Great economic damage, also perhaps 500,000 injured. Not predicted
1977	March 4	Romania, Vrancea	2000	7.2	Damage in Bucharest
1977	August 19	Indonesia, South of Sumbawa Island	100	8.0	Tsunami at Sumbawa Island and northern Australia
1979	December 12	Near coast of Ecuador	600	7.7	20,000 injured
1980	October 10	Algeria, El Asnam	3500	7.7	Extensive damage
1980	November 23	Southern Italy	3000	7.2	About 2000 missing, 7800 injured
1981	June 11	Southern Iran	3000	6.9	
1981	July 28	Southern Iran	1500	7.3	
1982	December 13	Yemen	2800	6.0	About 300 villages badly damaged
1983	May 26	Japan, Oga Peninsula	107	7.7	Tsunami caused extensive damage
1983	October 30	Turkey	1342	6.9	
1985	March 3	Chile, Valparaíso	177	7.8	Extensive damage. 2575 injured
1985	September 19	Mexico, Michoacán	9500	7.9	More than $3 billion damage. 30,000 injured. Small tsunami

Source: U.S. National Oceanic and Atmospheric Administration.

Table 2
Worldwide Earthquakes per Year

Magnitude M_S	Average Number Above M_S
8	2
7	20
6	100
5	3000
4	15,000
3	More than 100,000

Important Earthquakes of the United States and Canada

Year	Date (local time)	Place	MM intensity	Remarks
1638	June 11	Massachusetts, Plymouth	IX	Many stone chimneys down. Chimneys down in shocks in 1658 and probably other years
1663	February 5	Canada, Three Rivers, lower St. Lawrence River	X	Chimneys broken in Massachusetts Bay area
1732	September 16	Canada, Ontario	IX?	7 killed at Montreal
1755	November 18	Massachusetts, near Cambridge	VIII	Many chimneys down, brick buildings damaged, stone fences generally wrecked. Sand emitted from ground cracks. Felt from Chesapeake Bay to Nova Scotia
1769	July 28	California, San Pedro Channel area	X	Major disturbances with many aftershocks
1790	?	California, Owens Valley	X	Major shock with appearance of fault scarps
1811	December 16	Missouri, New Madrid	XI	Three principal earthquakes. New Madrid destroyed, extensive changes in configuration of ground and rivers, including the Mississippi River. Chimneys down in Cincinnati and Richmond. Felt in Boston. Several killed. The three shocks had Richter magnitudes of about 7.5, 7.3, and 7.8
1812	January 23			
1812	February 7			
1812	December 8	California, San Juan Capistrano	IX	Church collapsed, killing 40
1812	December 21	California, near Lompoc	X	Churches and other buildings wrecked in several towns including Santa Barbara
1836	June 10	California, San Francisco Bay area	X	Ground breakage along Hayward fault from Mission San Jose to San Pablo
1838	June	California, San Francisco	X	Fault rupture phenomena along San Andreas rift. This earthquake is probably comparable with the earthquake of April 18, 1906
1857	January 9	California, Fort Tejon	X–XI	One of the greatest historical Pacific coast shocks. Originated on San Andreas fault in northwest corner of Los Angeles County. Buildings and large trees thrown down

Year	Date (local time)	Place	MM intensity	Remarks
1868	April 2	Hawaii	IX–X	The largest historic Hawaiian earthquake. Occurred off the southern tip of the Big Island and was felt for over 350 miles. Generated a tsunami, maximum height 65 feet. 148 lives lost
1868	October 21	California, Hayward	X	Many buildings wrecked and damaged in Hayward and East Bay. Severe damage at San Leandro and San Francisco. 30 killed. Rupture of Hayward fault
1870	October 20	Canada, Montreal to Quebec	IX	Widespread. Minor damage on coast of Maine
1872	March 26	California, Owens Valley	X–XI	One of the greatest earthquakes in Pacific coast area. 7-meter scarp formed. 27 killed at Lone Pine out of 300 population. Adobe houses wrecked
1886	August 31	South Carolina, Charleston	X	Greatest historical earthquake in eastern states. 102 buildings destroyed, 90 percent damaged, nearly all chimneys down. $5.5 million damage. About 60 killed. Felt in Boston, Chicago, and St. Louis
1887	May 3	Mexico, Sonora	XI	Widespread in border states. Chimneys down in several towns, including El Paso and Albuquerque
1895	October 31	Missouri, near Charleston	IX	Felt in Canada, Virginia, Louisiana, and South Dakota. Acres of ground sank and lake formed. Many chimneys demolished
1899	September 10	Alaska, Yakutat Bay	XI	Great earthquake. Widely felt. Slight damage because area uninhabited. Shoreline rose 15 meters
1899	December 25	California, San Jacinto	IX	Nearly all brick buildings badly damaged in San Jacinto and Hemet. Chimneys down in Riverside. 6 killed. Another severe shock in 1918
1900	October 9	Alaska, Kenai Peninsula	VII–VIII	Felt from Yakutat to Kodiak. Severe damage in Kodiak
1906	April 18	California, San Francisco	XI	Great earthquake and fire. About 80 percent of estimated $400 million damage due to fire. 700 killed. Greatest destruction in San Francisco, Santa Rosa. Horizontal slipping along San Andreas fault, 6.5 meters. Greatest damage on poorly filled land

Year	Date	Location	Intensity	Description
1909	May 26	Illinois, Aurora	VIII	Many chimneys down. Felt over wide area
1915	June 22	California, Imperial Valley	VIII	Nearly $1 million damage. 6 killed. Well-constructed buildings were cracked
1915	October 2	Nevada, Pleasant Valley	X	Widespread. Adobe houses and water tank towers wrecked. Fault break 35 kilometers with 3.5 meters vertical throw in one place
1925	February 28	Canada, Murray Bay	VIII	Felt in many eastern and central states. Damage less than $100,000
1925	June 27	Montana, Manhattan	IX	Landslide blocked entrance to railroad tunnel. Some buildings wrecked and many chimneys fell. $300,000 damage
1925	June 29	California, Santa Barbara	IX	$6 million damage. 13 killed. 70 buildings condemned
1929	August 12	New York, Attica	IX	250 chimneys toppled
1929	November 18	Canada, Grand Banks, off Newfoundland	X	Submarine shock broke 12 transatlantic cables, some breaks 240 kilometers apart. Some deaths by tsunami along Burin Peninsula. Some chimneys in Canada toppled
1931	April 20	New York, Lake George	VIII	Chimneys fell
1931	August 16	Texas, near Valentine	VIII	All buildings damaged, many chimneys fell
1932	December 20	Nevada, Cedar Mountain	X	In sparsely settled region
1933	March 10	California, Long Beach	IX	$41 million damage, 120 killed. Fire damage insignificant
1934	March 12	Utah, Kosmo	VIII	Marked changes in terrain north of Great Salt Lake. 2 killed
1935	October 18 October 31	Montana, Helena (strong aftershock)	VIII	$3.5 million damage, 4 killed, less than 50 injured. More than half of buildings damaged from 2.5 to 100 percent. Second shock strongest of many aftershocks
1935	November 1	Canada, Timiskaming	IX	Widespread. Landslide near origin
1940	May 18	California, Imperial Valley	X	$6 million damage, 8 killed, 20 seriously injured. 65-kilometer fault appeared with maximum horizontal displacement of 4.5 meters

Year	Date (local time)	Place	MM intensity	Remarks
1941	June 30	California, Santa Barbara	VIII	$100,000 damage
1941	November 14	California, Torrance, Gardena	VIII	About $1 million damage. 50 buildings severely damaged
1944	September 5	Canada-New York, Cornwall and Massena	IX	On St. Lawrence River, $1.5 million damage reported. 90 percent of chimneys in Massena destroyed or damaged
1946	April 1	Alaska, Aleutian Islands	?	Great earthquake. Tsunami destroyed a light station and caused severe damage in Hawaii. Estimated damage $25 million
1947	October 16	Alaska, Nenana	VIII	Rock slides and damage to Alaska railroad
1949	April 13	Washington, Puget Sound	VIII	$25 million damage. 8 killed directly and indirectly. Damage confined mostly to marshy, alluvial, or filled ground. Many chimneys, parapet walls, and cornices toppled
1952	July 20	California, Kern County	X	$60 million damage, 12 killed, 18 seriously injured. Railroad tunnels collapsed and rails bent in S-shape. Surface faulting with about 0.5 meter of vertical, as well as lateral, displacement
1952	August 22	California, Bakersfield	VIII	2 killed, 35 injured. Damage $10 million
1954	July 6	Nevada, Fallon	IX	Extensive damage to irrigation canals. Several injured
1954	August 23	Nevada, Fallon	VIII	Surface ruptures. Damage more than $91,000
1954	December 16	Nevada, Dixie Valley	X	Surface ruptures along 88 kilometers linear distance and up to 4.5 meters vertical throw in sparsely populated desert
1957	March 22	California, San Francisco	VIII	Damage in Westlake and Daly City area
1958	April 7	Central Alaska	VIII	Severe breakage of river and lake ice, pressure ridges and mud flows
1958	July 9	Alaska, Lituya Bay	XI	Major earthquake. landslide created water wave that denuded mountain side as high as 540 meters. Long fault break. Cables severed. 5 killed by drowning

Year	Date	Location	Intensity	Description
1959	August 17	Montana, Hebgen Lake	X	Huge landslide dammed river and created lake. Fault scarps with 4.5-meter throw. Maximum vertical displacement 6.5 meters. 28 killed. $11 million damage to roads alone
1964	March 27	Alaska, Prince William Sound	X–XI	Great (Good Friday) earthquake. Damage to public property $235 million; real property $77 million. In Anchorage, extensive damage to moderately tall structures (45 meters or less) and to poorly constructed low buildings. Landslides and slumps caused total damage to many buildings. Docks in several ports destroyed by submarine slides and tsunami. Sea-wave damage on U.S. coast and elsewhere. 131 lives lost. Shorelines rose 10 meters in places and settled 2 meters elsewhere
1965	April 29	Washington, Puget Sound	VII–VIII	Property loss $12.5 million, mostly in Seattle. Felt over an area of 350,000 square kilometers. 3 persons killed and 3 died apparently of heart attacks
1969	October 1	California, Santa Rosa	VII–VIII	Property loss of $6 million. Felt over an area of 30,000 square kilometers
1971	February 9	California, San Fernando	VIII–XI	$500 million direct physical loss, 65 killed, more than 1000 persons injured. Felt over an area of 230,000 square kilometers
1975	August 1	California, Oroville	IX	3.8 kilometer-long fracture zone. Felt over 120,000 square kilometers. $2 to 3 million property damage
1975	November 29	Hawaii	VIII	Largest earthquake to strike Hawaii since 1868. Tsunami reached heights of 14.6 meters above sea level 25 kilometers west of epicenter. Dislocations of faults along a zone 25 kilometers long. Subsidence as much as 3.5 meters. $4.1 million property damage
1979	February 28	Southeastern Alaska	VII	First major earthquake since 1899 to occur between Yakutat Bay and Prince William Sound. M_s 7.1. Ground acceleration at 73 kilometers distance was 0.16g
1979	August 6	California, Coyote Lake	VII	Ground displacement along Calaveras fault. Maximum horizontal displacement was 5 to 6 millimeters. 16 injuries and $500,000 property damage

Year	Date (local time)	Place	MM intensity	Remarks
1979	October 15	California, Imperial Valley	IX	91 injured. 1565 homes and 450 businesses damaged. Estimated $30 million damage including heavy agricultural damage. Felt over 128,000 square kilometers. Maximum acceleration recorded 27 kilometers from epicenter was 1.74g. 25 kilometers of fault displacement along the Imperial Valley fault. 55 centimeters maximum lateral displacement and 19 centimeters of vertical displacement
1980	January 24 January 26	California, Livermore	VII	50 injuries. Estimated $11.5 million damage. Felt over 75,000 square kilometers. 1500 meters of discontinuous surface rupture showing a maximum of 5 to 10 millimeters of right lateral displacement
1980	May 18	Washington, Mount Saint Helens	IV	This earthquake occurred seconds before the explosion that began the eruption of Mt. St. Helens volcano. The eruption killed 31, left 33 missing, and caused between $500 million and $2 billion damage
1980	May 25 May 27	California-Nevada Border, Mammoth Lakes	VII	Four earthquakes occurred with M_L 6.1; M_L 6.0; M_L 6.1; and M_L 6.2. Total of 13 injured. Felt over approximately 250,000 square kilometers. $2 million estimated damages. 17-kilometer long zone of discontinuous surface rupture associated with the Hilton Creek fault, with maximum vertical displacement of 50 millimeters and 200 millimeters of slip on a single fracture. Many landslides and rocks falls in snow-covered unpopulated area
1980	November 8	California, off coast of northern California	VII	6 injured. $1.75 million property damage. Highway overpass collapsed. Small landslides and some liquefaction occurred. Although the source was under the Pacific Ocean off the coast, it was felt over 97,000 square kilometers
1983	May 2	California, Coalinga	VIII	45 injured with no loss of life. Heavy property damage in Coalinga and broken oil pipelines in area. Felt over all of central California. Thousands of aftershocks. Estimated $31 million in damage

Source: U.S. National Oceanic and Atmospheric Administration.

Important Earthquakes of Central and South America

Year	Date (local time)	Place	Magnitude	Remarks
Mexico-Guatemala				
1806	March 25	Jalisco		Many killed
1845	March 7	Acapulco	~ 7°	Tsunami
1845	March 15	Guatemala		
1875	February 11	Zapopan, Jalisco	7.5	
1902	April 19	Quezaltenango	8.3	Many killed
1911	June 7	Jalisco	8	45 killed, damage in Mexico City
1918	January 3	Guatemala		Several killed, destruction in Guatemala City
1943	February 22	Guerrero	7.5	Damage in Mexico City
1973	January 30	Michoacán-Colima	7.7	56 killed
1973	August 28	Puebla-Veracruz	7.1	100 kilometers deep, 600 killed
1976	February 4	Guatemala	7.6	27,000 killed
1985	September 19	Ixtapa	8.1	9000 killed
Central America				
1820	October 19	Honduras, San Pedro Sula		
1841	September 2	Central Costa Rica		
1847	July 31	Nicaragua		
1859	December 8	El Salvador		
1882	September 7	Panama		
1904	December 20	Costa Rica, Panama	8.3	
1951	May 6	El Salvador, Jucuapa	6.5	400 killed
1972	December 23	Nicaragua, Managua	6.5	About 10,000 killed
1986	October 10	El Salvador	5.4	About 1,000 killed; 200,000 homeless
Caribbean and Venezuela				
1812	March 26	Venezuela, Caracas		
1831	August 11	Barbados		
1842	May 7	North of Haiti		
1852	August 20	Cuba, Santiago		Destruction

Year	Date	Location	Magnitude	Notes
1874	September 26	Antigua		
1900	June 21	Cayman Islands	7.9	
1907	January 14	Jamaica, Kingston	6.9	1000 killed
1923	December 22	Colombia, Boyacá	8.1	Tsunami
1946	August 4	North of Santo Domingo	6.5	
1967	July 29	Venezuela, Caracas		250 killed, $100 million damage

Colombia and Ecuador, Peru-Bolivia

Year	Date	Location	Magnitude	Notes
1805	July 16	Colombia, Honda		
1838	March 30	Peru, Callao		
1859	March 22	Ecuador, Quito	8.9	
1906	January 31	North of Ecuador	8.6	
1942	August 24	Peru, Nazca	7.8	1500 killed
1946	November 10	Peru, Ancash	6.8	6000 killed
1949	August 5	Ecuador, Ambato		
1967	July 29	Colombia, Santander	7.8	40,000 killed
1970	May 31	Peru, Ancash		

Chile and Argentina

Year	Date	Location	Magnitude	Notes
1819	April 3, 4, 11	Chile, Copiapó	~ 8	Tsunami
1835	February 20	Chile, Concepción	~ 8.5	Tsunami
1861	March 21	Argentina, Mendoza		18,000 killed
1939	January 25	Chile, Chillán	8.3	30,000 killed
1944	January 15	Argentina, San Juan		5000 killed
1960	May 22	Chile, Valdivia	8.4	
1966	December 28	Chile, Taltal	7.5	
1971	July 8	Chile, La Ligua	7.5	
1977	September 23	Argentina, San Juan	7.4	
1985	March 3	Chile, Algarrobo	7.8	176 killed

°The symbol ~ means "approximately."

Abridged Modified Mercalli Intensity Scale

Note: The mean maximum acceleration and velocity values for the wave motion are for firm ground but vary greatly depending on the type of earthquake source.

Average peak velocity (centimeters per second)	Intensity value and description	Average peak acceleration (g is gravity = 980 centimeters per second squared)
	I. Not felt except by a very few under especially favorable circumstances. (I Rossi-Forel scale)	
	II. Felt only by a few persons at rest, especially on upper floors of buildings. Delicately suspended objects may swing. (I to II Rossi-Forel scale)	
	III. Felt quite noticeably indoors, especially on upper floors of buildings, but many people do not recognize it as an earthquake. Standing automobiles may rock slightly. Vibration like passing of truck. Duration estimated. (III Rossi-Forel scale)	

1–2	IV. During the day felt indoors by many, outdoors by few. At night some awakened. Dishes, windows, doors disturbed; walls make creaking sound. Sensation like heavy truck striking building. Standing automobiles rocked noticeably. (IV to V Rossi-Forel scale)	0.015g–0.02g
2–5	V. Felt by nearly everyone, many awakened. Some dishes, windows, and so on broken; cracked plaster in a few places; unstable objects overturned. Disturbances of trees, poles, and other tall objects sometimes noticed. Pendulum clocks may stop. (V to VI Rossi-Forel scale)	0.03g–0.04g
5–8	VI. Felt by all, many frightened and run outdoors. Some heavy furniture moved; a few instances of fallen plaster and damaged chimneys. Damage slight. (VI to VII Rossi-Forel scale)	0.06g–0.07g
8–12	VII. Everybody runs outdoors. Damage negligible in buildings of good design and construction; slight to moderate in well-built ordinary structures; considerable in poorly built or badly designed structures; some chimneys broken. Noticed by persons driving cars. (VIII Rossi-Forel scale)	0.10g–0.15g
20–30	VIII. Damage slight in specially designed structures; considerable in ordinary substantial buildings with partial collapse; great in poorly built structures. Panel walls thrown out of frame structures. Fall of chimneys, factory stacks, columns, monuments, walls. Heavy furniture overturned. Sand and mud ejected in small amounts. Changes in well water. Persons driving cars disturbed. (VIII+ to IX Rossi-Forel scale)	0.25g–0.30g

45–55	IX. Damage considerable in specially designed structures; well-designed frame structures thrown out of plumb; great in substantial buildings, with partial collapse. Buildings shifted off foundations. Ground cracked conspicuously. Underground pipes broken. (IX + Rossi-Forel scale)	0.50g–0.55g
More than 60	X. Some well-built wooden structures destroyed; most masonry and frame structures destroyed with foundations; ground badly cracked. Rails bent. Landslides considerable from river banks and steep slopes. Shifted sand and mud. Water splashed, slopped over banks. (X Rossi-Forel scale)	More than 0.60g
	XI. Few, if any, (masonry) structures remain standing. Bridges destroyed. Broad fissures in ground. Underground pipelines completely out of service. Earth slumps and land slips in soft ground. Rails bent greatly.	
	XII. Damage total. Waves seen on ground surface. Lines of sight and level distorted. Objects thrown into the air.	

Modified Mercalli Intensity Scale (1956 version)[*]

Masonry A, B, C, D. To avoid ambiguity of language, the quality of masonry, brick or otherwise, is specified by the following lettering.

Masonry A. Good workmanship, mortar, and design; reinforced, especially laterally, and bound together by using steel, concrete, etc.; designed to resist lateral forces.

Masonry B. Good workmanship and mortar; reinforced, but not designed in detail to resist lateral forces.

Masonry C. Ordinary workmanship and mortar; no extreme weaknesses like failing to tie in at corners, but neither reinforced nor designed against horizontal forces.

Masonry D. Weak materials, such as adobe; poor mortar; low standards of workmanship; weak horizontally.

---

[*]Original 1931 version in H. O. Wood and F. Neumann, "Modified Mercalli intensity scale of 1931," *Seismological Society of America Bulletin*, vol. 53, no. 5, 1931, pp. 979–987. For 1956 version, see Charles F. Richter, *Elementary Seismology* (San Francisco: W. H. Freeman and Company, 1958), pp. 137–138.

Intensity value	Description

I. Not felt. Marginal and long-period effects of large earthquakes.

II. Felt by persons at rest, on upper floors, or favorably placed.

III. Felt indoors. Hanging objects swing. Vibration like passing of light trucks. Duration estimated. May not be recognized as an earthquake.

IV. Hanging objects swing. Vibration like passing of heavy trucks; or sensation of a jolt like a heavy ball striking the walls. Standing cars rock. Windows, dishes, doors rattle. Glasses clink. Crockery clashes. In the upper range of IV, wooden walls and frame creak.

V. Felt outdoors; direction estimated. Sleepers awakened. Liquids disturbed, some spilled. Small unstable objects displaced or upset. Doors swing, close, open. Shutters, pictures move. Pendulum clocks stop, start, change rate.

VI. Felt by all. Many frightened and run outdoors. Persons walk unsteadily. Windows, dishes, glassware broken. Knickknacks, books, etc., off shelves. Pictures off walls. Furniture moved or overturned. Weak plaster and masonry D cracked. Small bells ring (church, school). Trees, bushes shaken visibly, or heard to rustle.

VII. Difficult to stand. Noticed by drivers. Hanging objects quiver. Furniture broken. Damage to masonry D, including cracks. Weak chimneys broken at roof line. Fall of plaster, loose bricks, stones, tiles, cornices, also unbraced parapets and architectural ornaments. Some cracks in masonry C. Waves on ponds, water turbid with mud. Small slides and caving in along sand or gravel banks. Large bells ring. Concrete irrigation ditches damaged.

VIII. Steering of cars affected. Damage to masonry C; partial collapse. Some damage to masonry B; none to masonry A. Fall of stucco and some masonry walls. Twisting, fall of chimneys, factory stacks, monuments, towers, elevated tanks. Frame houses moved on foundations if not bolted down; loose panel walls thrown out. Decayed piling broken off. Branches broken from trees. Changes in flow or temperature of springs and wells. Cracks in wet ground and on steep slopes.

IX. General panic. Masonry D destroyed; masonry C heavily damaged, sometimes with complete collapse; masonry B seriously damaged. General damage to foundations. Frame structures, if not bolted, shifted off foundations. Frames racked. Serious damage to reservoirs. Underground pipes broken. Conspicuous cracks in ground. In alluviated areas, sand and mud ejected, earthquake fountains, sand craters.

X. Most masonry and frame structures destroyed with their foundations. Some well-built wooden structures and bridges destroyed. Serious damage to dams, dikes, embankments. Large landslides. Water thrown on banks of canals, rivers, lakes, etc. Sand and mud shifted horizontally on beaches and flat land. Rails bent slightly.

XI. Rails bent greatly. Underground pipelines completely out of service.

XII. Damage nearly total. Large rock masses displaced. Lines of sight and level distorted. Objects thrown into the air.

Geologic Time Scale

Relative duration of major geologic intervals	Era	Period	Epoch	Approximate duration in millions of years	Millions of years ago	
						0
Cenozoic		Quaternary	Holocene	Approx. the last 10,000 years		
			Pleistocene	2.5	2.5	
			Pliocene	4.5	7	
Mesozoic			Miocene	19.0	26	50
			Oligocene	12.0	38	
	Cenozoic	Tertiary	Eocene	16.0	54	
			Paleocene	11.0	65	
Paleozoic						100
		Cretaceous		71	136	
						150
		Jurassic		54	190	
						200
	Mesozoic	Triassic		35	225	
						250
		Permian		55	280	
		Carboniferous				300
		Pennsylvanian		45	325	
		Mississippian		20	345	
						350
		Devonian		50	395	
						400
		Silurian		35	430	
						450
		Ordovician		70	500	500
						550
	Paleozoic	Cambrian		70	570	
Precambrian	Precambrian			4030		4600

Metric-English Conversion Table

Length

1 millimeter (mm) [0.1 centimeter]	= 0.0394 inch (in)
1 centimeter (cm) [10 mm]	= 0.3937 in
1 meter (m) [100 cm]	= 39.37 in
	= 3.28 feet (ft)
1 kilometer (km) [1000 m]	= 0.621 mile (mi)

Area

1 square centimeter (cm^2)	= 0.155 square inch (in^2)
1 square meter (m^2)	= 10.76 square feet (ft^2)
	= 1.196 square yards (yd^2)
1 hectare (ha)	= 2.4710 acres (a)
1 square kilometer (km^2)	= 0.386 square mile (mi^2)

Volume

1 cubic centimeter (cm^3)	= 0.0610 cubic inch (in^3)
1 cubic meter (m^3)	= 35.314 cubic feet (ft^3)
	= 1.31 cubic yards (yd^3)
1 cubic kilometer (km^3)	= 0.240 cubic mile (mi^3)
1 liter (l)	= 1.06 quarts (qt)
	= 0.264 gallon (gal)
1 cubic meter	= 8.11 × 10^{-4} acre feet

Mass

1 kilogram (kg) [1000 grams (g)]	= 2.20 pounds (lb)
	= 0.0011 ton (tn)
1 metric ton (MT) [1000 kg]	= 1.10 tn

Pressure

1 kilogram per square centimeter (kg/cm^2)	= 14.20 pounds per square inch (lb/in^2)
1 pascal (10 dynes/cm^2)	= 47.9 pounds per square foot (lb/ft^2)

Velocity

1 meter per second (m/s)	= 3.281 feet per second (ft/s)
1 kilometer per hour (km/h)	= 0.9113 ft/s
	= 0.621 mile per hour (mi/h)

Seismic Instrumentation of Important Large Structures

Strong-Motion Instrumentation

Instrument Characteristics   The first requirement for strong-motion instrumentation is insensitivity—the strongest possible earthquake ground motions should stay on scale. In addition, a wide dynamic range is advantageous, since valuable information can be obtained from small nondamaging earthquakes. To study the dynamic response of the engineered structure, a wide frequency-response range is also needed. Such a range requires high recording speeds that make continuous recording impracticable. An inertia trigger operated by the initial portion of the earthquake ground motion has been found to be a satisfactory solution to this problem.

In the past, most strong-motion seismographs have recorded on photographic paper (see Chapter 7, Figure 3), but now some models record discrete samples on magnetic tape cassettes.

Accelerograph Location   Adequate definition of input ground motions and structural response requires a large number of accelerographs at carefully selected points. For major projects, in highly seismic regions, detailed studies of the optimum number and location of accelerographs would be expected for the special conditions of the particular site. For minimum recommendations, however, questions of location are secondary to the prime object of ensuring that at least some information of engineering value will be obtained for all strong shaking.

Accelerograph Installation and Maintenance   It is essential that the instruments be well protected from such environmental conditions as flooding or excessive summer temperatures, and from tampering or vandalism. The accelerograph (see Chapter 6, Figure 3) can often be conveniently installed in the corner of a basement office, storage room, or gallery of a dam. If no space of this type is available near a suitable site, an insulated metal enclosure sealed against weather and interference can usually be provided. The accelerograph should be firmly bolted down to a concrete foundation, as specified by the instructions of the instrument manufacturer.

Checking, maintenance, and servicing of the accelerographs should be carried out on a regular schedule according to the instructions of the instrument manufacturer. Similarly, attention to the proper preservation of records and their transmittal for data processing must be given, so that they are not lost during or after an earthquake.

Local Seismograph Networks

Network Requirements   Sensitive seismographs to measure local earthquakes are sometimes advisable in the vicinity of projects such as large dams and nuclear reactors before major construction begins. The purposes of such instrumentation are to (1) determine the frequency of local earthquakes (if any); (2) determine the location of seismic activity and its depth; (3) determine the magnitude and some indication of focal mechanisms of the earthquakes; (4) allow prediction of the course of earthquake occurrence.

Reasonably precise location of an earthquake focus requires that the onset of P waves (and also S waves where feasible) be recorded to an accuracy of ± 0.1 second or better, at a minimum of four nearby seismographs. There must be a common time base for all seismographs, and they should ideally surround the region of earthquake activity.

For dams, it is advisable to operate at least a four-station network for a period extending some years beyond the time when maximum impounding is complete. If a sequence of earthquakes does occur, the network should be densified.

Network Location   The selection of sites for the sensitive seismographs often depends on practical considerations such as accessibility and avoidance of construction work. However, several general considerations should govern the configuration to the greatest extent practically possible. First, the sites should be uniformly spread in azimuth around the project.

The interstation distance should not be more than about 30 kilometers or less than 5 kilometers. Individual site selection should depend upon the local tectonic structures. It is best to locate the instruments on outcrops of basement rock, and they should be as remote as possible from construction activities, streams, and so on. Normally, sites should be chosen so that they do not have to be shifted throughout the life of the project. It is also helpful to make field surveys of the relative background microseismic noise at prospective sites with the use of a portable seismographic recorder before locations are finalized.

It has been found adequate to place the seismometers in shallow pits (about 1 meter deep) in the surficial rock. A generally adequate housing is a steel drum, with a watertight cover, that is set on concrete poured at the bottom of the pit.

Seismographic Characteristics   A variety of suitable components for a reliable high-gain seismographic system is now commercially available. Thus numerous systems can be designed to meet the aims previously established. The following two alternative systems—A and B—meet the minimum requirement and have been field tested. In both, the response of the overall seismographic system should be between 5 hertz and 50 hertz.

Seismographic System A   This system makes use of available portable seismometers and visual or magnetic recording units. The network stations are not connected, and they depend on separate crystal clocks at each recorder. Recording is normally on smoked paper or cassettes, and the records must be changed about every day. This can be done by a member of the maintenance staff without special training.

The portable system for each site has four parts: (1) seismometer; (2) waterproof single-packaged recording unit with batteries (size approximately $50 \times 50 \times 25$ centimeters); (3) radio receiver; (4) power source such as a solar battery charger.

Seismographic System B   This system telemeters the signals from individual seismometers of the network to a central recording room by radio or hard-wire connections. Power is needed at the individual seismometers for the amplifiers and at the recording station for the amplifiers and drum and tape recorders. This system is costlier than System A because of the cost of land lines or transmitting equipment. Its great advantage is the centralization of recording at one convenient accessible location. Maintenance personnel would rarely need to visit the seismometers in the field. Components of the telemetered system are now all commercially available.

Network Operation and Analysis Operation of either network A or B should not require instrumentation specialists or a staff seismologist. The critical requirements in all such studies of seismicity are continuity of operation and minimum system adjustments.

For either system, an operator would need to change the paper records every day at about the same hour, marking the date and location on each seismogram. Any absolutely essential changes in system characteristics would need to be logged. It may be necessary, from time to time, to readjust and calibrate the seismometers in accord with the procedures specified by the equipment manufacturers.

For telemetry system B, the discriminators, radio, clock, and recording drums can usually be located in a small room. All seismographic instrumentation should be bolted to the building structure to prevent movement and damage in case of an earthquake.

Analysis of the high-gain system often requires some seismological expertise. Special arrangements are not needed, of course, if no or very few local earthquakes are recorded. However, if the region is seismic or, at a dam, if the local seismicity increases on closure, or both, advice should be obtained on analysis from a consultant seismologist.

APPENDIX **H**

Sample Calculation of Magnitudes and Energy of an Earthquake

The following calculations are for an Alaskan earthquake recorded at Oroville, California. The energy factor (equation 4) gives us an idea of the scale of energy release that is possible for earthquakes of different magnitude. For instance, 30 earthquakes of magnitude 6 are needed to release the equivalent amount of energy in the Earth's crust that is released by just one magnitude 7 earthquake; and 900 earthquakes of magnitude 5 are needed to produce the same energy. It follows, therefore, that even if small earthquakes occur in swarms in a particular area, they do very little to reduce the reservoir of strain energy needed for a major earthquake. But tectonic energy is drained away into heat and seismic waves in a truly gigantic way by a major earthquake like that of 1906 along the San Andreas fault with a magnitude M_s of $8\frac{1}{4}$. This earthquake released about 10^{24} ergs of strain energy within 60 seconds! (Only a fraction went into ground shaking.)

It is well known that, as the threshold of earthquake size being considered in a seismic region is lowered, the number of earthquakes above that magnitude rapidly increases (see Appendix A). The rate of occurrence n of shocks above a given magnitude is again logarithmic and is measured by a parameter b (see equation 5). The smaller b is, the more numerous are the earthquakes in a given time span. When b is determined for a seismically active region, the total seismic energy released over a period can be calculated by using the energy factor.

Magnitude is also sometimes roughly estimated from the length of surface fault rupture L (in kilometers—see equation 6).

Let A be the amplitude, and T the period of a wave measured at a distance Δ from the source. One minute between gaps.

Measured values (reduced to ground motion)

$$\text{P wave, } A = 1.4 \text{ microns, } T = 12 \text{ seconds}$$
$$\text{Rayleigh wave, } A = 4.3 \text{ microns, } T = 20 \text{ seconds}$$
$$\Delta = 28°$$

Body-wave magnitude m_b $(25° < \Delta < 90°)$

$$m_b = \log A - \log T + 0.01\Delta + 5.9 \tag{1}$$
$$= 0.15 - 1.08 + 0.28 + 5.9$$
$$\approx 5.3$$

Surface-wave magnitude M_s $(25° < \Delta < 90°)$

$$M_s = \log A + 1.66 \log \Delta + 2.0 \tag{2}$$
$$= 0.63 + 2.40 + 2.0$$
$$\approx 5.0$$

Relation between moment magnitude M_w and seismic moment M_o (see Chapter 7)

$$M_w = \tfrac{2}{3} \log M_o - 10.7 \tag{3}$$

Seismic energy E

$$\log E = 11.8 + 1.5\, M_s \tag{4}$$
$$= 19.3$$
$$E = 2.0 \times 10^{19} \text{ ergs}$$

Relation between n and M_s

$$\log n = a - bM_s \tag{5}$$

Relation between M_s and L (worldwide data)

$$M_s = 6.10 + 0.70 \log L \tag{6}$$

APPENDIX I

Wave Motion

In earthquakes, the values of ground acceleration, velocity, and displacement vary a great deal, depending on the frequency of the wave motion. High-frequency waves (higher frequencies than 10 hertz) tend to have high amplitudes of accelerations but small amplitudes of displacement, compared with long-period waves, which have small accelerations and relatively large velocities and displacements. (These relations follow from equations 1 to 5.)

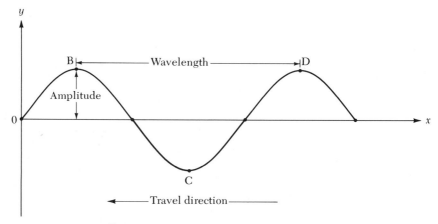

Transverse wave at a time t

For a traveling simple harmonic wave, like that shown, the ground displacement y at a given time t is a function of position x and time t:

$$y = A \sin \frac{2\pi}{\lambda} (x + vt)$$

Here A is the *amplitude* as shown and the *wave length* λ (Greek lambda) is the distance between crests B and D, and v is the *wave velocity*.

In time T, called the *period*, the wave travels a distance λ, for example, from B to D. The period T is thus the time of a complete vibration.

The velocity of travel of the wave is the wavelength divided by the period:

$$v = \frac{\lambda}{T} = f\lambda \tag{1}$$

Here f is the *frequency*, the number of vibrations per second. The angular frequency ω, in radians per second, is $\omega = 2\pi f$. (ω is the Greek letter omega.)

Thus, from (1), the sideways motion of the point O ($x = 0$) can be written:

$$\text{Ground displacement} = y = A \sin \frac{2\pi}{T} t \qquad = A \sin \omega t \tag{2}$$

$$\text{Ground velocity} \quad = \dot{y} = \frac{2\pi A}{T} \cos \frac{2\pi}{T} t \quad = \omega A \cos \omega t \tag{3}$$

$$\text{Ground acceleration} = \ddot{y} = -\frac{4\pi^2 A}{T^2} \sin \frac{2\pi}{T} t = -\omega^2 A \sin \omega t \tag{4}$$

$$= -\omega^2 y \tag{5}$$

An Earthquake Quiz

1. What mechanical idea did the Chinese scholar Chang Heng probably use in constructing the first known seismoscope? (See Chapter 6, Figure 1.)

2. What is the main difference between a seismograph and a seismoscope?

3. Why were the earliest seismographic stations in the United States established in California? Why at astronomical observatories?

4. With a ruler, measure the time interval between the phases marked P and S on the seismogram of Chapter 6, Figure 4. Then, using the values 8.0 kilometers per second for the velocity of P waves, and 4.4 kilometers per second for that of S waves, estimate the distance between the Berkeley station and the earthquake focus.

5. Measure with a ruler the largest wave amplitude shown in Chapter 6, Figure 4. If you are told that the seismograph that gave the record of earthquake waves in that figure amplifies the actual motion of the ground approximately 3000 times, and that the figure has been reproduced at the original scale, calculate the greatest amplitude (as a fraction of a millimeter) of the actual ground motion. Could you feel such a small motion?

6. By using your ruler on Chapter 7, Figure 3, determine the bracketed duration, in seconds, of the strong ground acceleration (amplitude above 0.05g) recorded on the east component at the Hollywood Storage Parking Lot in the 1971 San Fernando earthquake.

7. If the mean speed of P waves is 10 kilometers per second through the Earth, what is the approximate time for a P wave to travel from one side of the Earth to the other?

8. Why is the Earth's mantle considered to be solid?

9. Could a seismograph on a ship at sea detect an earthquake?

10. Why do seismologists object to the common usage of "tidal" wave in reference to a "tsunami"?

11. Some earthquakes in Japan are felt in Tokyo only by people at the top of a tall building. Why?

12. Why are many earthquakes not accompanied by observations of fault rupture?

13. Read Zechariah, 14:5 in the Bible. What is your interpretation of this geological event?

14. Why do you expect no great quake on the moon like that near San Francisco in 1906?

15. Based on the observed relative motion of the great tectonic plates of the Earth, what would be the direction of strike-slip faulting that you would expect to accompany large shallow earthquakes on the Motagua fault in Guatemala? The Anatolian fault in Turkey? The San Andreas fault in California? The Pyrenees?

16. Why are the sites around lakes, bays, and estuaries likely to lead to higher Modified Mercalli intensities than sites on high ground?

17. The 1964 Alaska Good Friday earthquake was rated by measuring seismograms as body-wave magnitude $m_b = 6.5$, but surface wave magnitude $M_s = 8.6$. Explain the large difference. Why does the M_s value best describe the size of this earthquake?

18. What is the point of operating sensitive seismographs around large reservoirs? What is the lowest number of seismographs you would install to locate local earthquakes?

19. Why are small shallow earthquakes often recorded during a volcanic eruption?

20. What percentage of the heat energy reaching the Earth's surface from the interior is released by earthquakes each year?

21. Is there a difference between weather prediction and earthquake prediction? In what sense are these problems different?

22. Calculate how many hours of advance warning in Japan may be possible before the arrival of a tsunami generated by an earthquake in Chile.

23. Determine the Richter magnitude (M_L) of an earthquake whose largest wave recorded by a standard seismograph is 10 millimeters at a distance of 100 kilometers from the epicenter.

24. What is the energy in ergs of this earthquake?

25. Why are at least three seismographic stations required to locate earthquake epicenters on the basis of P-wave arrival times?

26. Show from the left-hand scale in the box on page 113 in Chapter 7 that a handy approximation to remember between the S-minus-P-wave travel times and distance d kilometers to the earthquake focus is $S - P \simeq d/8$ seconds (for short distances).

27. From the S-minus-P interval on the seismograms of Chapter 7, Figure 3, estimate how far the earthquake source is from the strong-motion instrument.

28. At the present rate of slip (say 3 centimeters per year) on the San Andreas fault, how long will it be before Los Angeles is a suburb of San Francisco? Will it matter?

29. A large dam impounds an extensive lake about 200 meters deep. What is the extra pressure (in bars, that is, 10^6 dynes per square centimeter) placed on the Earth's crust by the water load? How does this quantity compare with the stress released along a rupturing shallow fault (5 to 50 bars, approximately)? Does this result necessarily imply that reservoir loads can produce earthquakes?

30. It has often been observed that some farm animals become disturbed just before a substantial earthquake in the area. Can you make some suggestions that might explain this?

31. Many earthquakes are accompanied by audible noises. Can you explain them in terms of the P waves of seismology?

32. After the great India (Assam) earthquake of June 12, 1897, farmers found piles of sand in their fields that hindered civilization. Explain this circumstance.

33. The earthquake harvester: In the Kwanto (Japan) earthquake of 1923, potatoes emerged from soft farm ground. Why?

34. Fish are often reported stunned or killed by strong earthquakes originating from under the sea. Explain.

35. Can you explain why the flow of natural springs is often affected by large earthquakes? Why would some cease to flow and others have an increased flow?

36. Compute the energy available to go into seismic waves when the great rock avalanche fell down the face of Mt. Huascarán in the Peru earthquake of May 31, 1970. (Assume 50 million cubic meters of rock fell 1 kilometer.) What is the equivalent earthquake magnitude?

37. You are lying in bed when you notice a light fixture, 1 meter long, hanging from the ceiling start to swing. Having read this book, you make some measurements. You count swings and find that 10 occur in 20 seconds. The free end of the fixture swings through 1 centimeter. You then calculate that an earthquake of a certain magnitude has occurred, centered a certain distance away. What is the rough magnitude and distance?

38. The jelly earthquake machine: Make a model of an elastic crust of the Earth by pouring a stiff jelly mixture into a wide shallow square or rectangular pan. Make a vertical cut down the center of the jelly with a sharp knife. Then slide, by pulling horizontally in opposite directions, opposite sides of the jelly, parallel to the cut. Describe what happens when the sides of the cut slip.

39. How long does it take a stone to fall 60 meters? Now estimate how long it will take rubble to fall from the top of a high building in an earthquake.

40. In an earthquake, a fault ruptures through your property. Would you gain or lose land in strike-slip faulting? Normal faulting? Thrust faulting? Discuss the legal implications for such property in a built-up area.

41. You have just taken off in an airplane. Will you know if a great earthquake then shakes the airport?

42. Why did Japanese peasants associate catfish with the cause of earthquakes?

43. In the Mexico earthquake of September 19, 1985, most collapsed buildings in Mexico City were 10- to 12-story concrete-frame apartments. Why would such buildings be more likely to collapse in this earthquake than shorter buildings?

44. The State Office of Emergency Preparedness has just issued a warning that there is a 50 percent chance of a damaging earthquake occurring in your area next week. What would be your program of preparedness?

45. Suppose that five damaging earthquakes have occurred in your area in the last 100 years. During that time about 500 earthquakes (most small) have been recorded by the local seismographic station. What are the simple odds that the next earthquake will be damaging?

46. The dice earthquake game: You and your opponent should take turns in rolling two dice. The sum of the numbers in any throw will lie between 2 and 12. Suppose these numbers refer to intensities (II to XII) on the Modified Mercalli scale. An intensity of X or above scores 0; a lower intensity scores 10. The player to accumulate a score of 100 wins. Do large intensities always follow small ones?

47. For the mathematically minded, what is the probability in the game above of getting an intensity of X or XI in one throw of the two dice?

48. The biggest earthquakes, such as the 1960 Chile earthquake, shake the whole Earth, like a hammer ringing a bell. The deepest free vibrations, or tones, of the Earth are 53 minutes a period. How long would a simple pendulum be to have such a period?

49. Gravity on the moon is only one-sixth of that on Earth. Explain why, if quakes of equal magnitude occurred on the moon and the Earth, the seismic hazard on the lunar surface would be greater than on Earth.

50. The figure below shows waves due to kangaroos jumping near a seismograph at Woomera, southern Australia. The jumps are recorded as a series of sharp peaks. Measure the average frequency at which the hops occur. Explain the increase and decrease of amplitude and the duration of the kangaroo signal. [Seismogram obtained by I. C. F. Stewart and P. J. Setchell, *Search* 5, (1974): 107.]

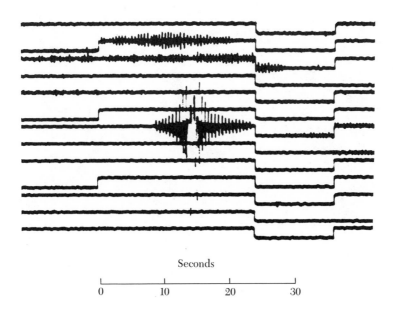

Seconds

0	10	20	30

51. In 1982 a small aircraft collided with Soufrière volcano on St. Vincent, West Indies, tragically killing all aboard. A nearby seismograph recorded the impact with seismic magnitude $m_b = 1.0$. For airspeed 250 kilometers/hour and plane weight 2650 kilograms, determine the kinetic energy lost on impact and the maximum coupling efficiency for seismic energy (see Appendix H).

Answers are on the facing page.

Answers to Quiz

1. An inverted pendulum.
2. Seismoscopes register no time marks.
3. California is a seismic region. Astronomers kept accurate time.
4. 200 kilometers.
5. 0.01 millimeter. No.
6. About 6 seconds.
7. 21 minutes.
8. S waves pass through.
9. Yes, from the P wave.
10. There is no connection with the sun or moon.
11. Long-period seismic waves are amplified by building response there.
12. Many faults are deep underground or submarine.
13. Dip-slip faulting with strike EW.
14. There is no plate-tectonic activity.
15. Left-lateral. Right-lateral. Right-lateral. Left-lateral.
16. Soil fracture including liquefaction.
17. Surface waves correspond better to fault rupture length.
18. For the detection of increased seismicity. Three.
19. Movements of liquid magma affect rock strength.
20. Less than 0.001 percent.
21. Yes. Weather observations occur within the atmosphere, and faster variations occur in the atmosphere.

22. 22 hours.
23. Four.
24. 10^{17} ergs.
25. One is required for each of the three unknowns (latitude, longitude, origin time).
27. About 15 kilometers.
28. 20 million years.
29. 20 bars. Similar. No.
30. Perhaps small foreshocks.
31. High-frequency P waves refracted into the air.
32. Liquefaction of sandy soils.
34. Shock of intense P wave.
36. 5×10^{21} ergs. About 6.
37. Greater than 7, over 20 kilometers away.
39. 3.5 seconds.
40. No change; gain; lose.
41. Probably not. Seismic air waves are too small.
43. Corner columns unconnected on two sides.
45. 1/100.
47. 5/36.
48. About 2300 kilometers.
49. Ground accelerations would much exceed lunar gravity.
50. 2 hops per second.
51. 6×10^{13} ergs, 10^{-1}.

Glossary

accelerometer   A seismograph for measuring ground acceleration as a function of time.

active fault   A fault along which slip has occurred in historical (or Holocene) time or earthquake foci are located.

aftershocks   Smaller earthquakes following the largest earthquake of a series concentrated in a restricted crustal volume.

amplitude (wave)   The maximum height of a wave crest or depth of a trough.

aseismic region   One that is almost free of earthquakes.

asperities (fault)   Roughness on the fault surface subject to slip.

asthenosphere   The layer below the lithosphere that is marked by low seismic-wave velocities and high seismic-wave attenuation. It is a soft layer, probably partially molten.

barrier (fault)   An area of fault surface resistant to slip because of geometrical or structural changes.

Benioff zone   A narrow zone, defined by earthquake foci, that is tens of kilometers thick dipping from the surface under the Earth's crust.

capable fault   A fault along which it is mechanically feasible for sudden slip to occur.

core (of Earth)   The central part of the Earth below a depth of 2900 kilometers. It is thought to be composed mainly of iron and silicates and to be molten on the outside with a solid central part.

creep (slow fault slip)   Slow slip occurring along a fault, without producing earthquakes.

crust (of Earth) The outermost rocky shell.

density The mass per unit volume of a substance, commonly expressed in grams per cubic centimeter.

dilitancy (of rocks) The increase in the volume of rocks due to elastic and nonelastic changes.

dip The angle by which a rock layer or fault plane deviates from the horizontal. The angle is measured in a plane perpendicular to the strike.

dip-slip fault A fault in which the relative displacement is along the direction of dip of the fault plane; the offset is either normal or reverse.

dispersion (wave) The spreading out of a wave train due to each wave length traveling with its own velocity.

duration (of strong shaking) The (bracketed) duration is the time interval between the first and last peaks of strong ground motion above a specified amplitude.

earthquake The vibrations of the Earth caused by the passage of seismic waves radiating from some source of elastic energy.

elastic rebound theory The theory of earthquake generation proposing that faults remain locked while strain energy slowly accumulates in the surrounding rock and then suddenly slip, releasing this energy.

epicenter The point on the Earth's surface directly above the focus (or hypocenter) of an earthquake.

fault A fracture or zone of fractures in rock along which the two sides have been displaced relative to each other parallel to the fracture. The total fault offset may range from centimeters to kilometers.

fault plane The plane that most closely coincides with the rupture surface of a fault.

first motion On a seismogram, the direction of motion at the beginning of the arrival of a P wave. Conventionally, upward motion indicates a compression of the ground; downward motion, a dilatation.

focal depth (of earthquakes) The depth of the focus below the surface of the Earth.

focus (hypocenter) The place at which rupture commences.

foreshocks Smaller earthquakes preceding the largest earthquake of a series concentrated in a restricted crustal volume.

geodimeter A surveying instrument to measure the distance between two points on the Earth's surface.

gouge Crushed, sheared, and powdered rock altered to clay.

graben A crustal block of rock, generally long and narrow, that has dropped down along boundary faults relative to the adjacent rocks.

hertz The unit of frequency equal to 1 cycle per second, or 2π radians per second.

intensity (of earthquakes) A measure of ground shaking obtained from the damage done to structures built by humans, changes in the Earth's surface, and felt reports.

isoseismal Contour lines drawn to separate one level of seismic intensity from another.

lava   Magma or molten rock that has reached the surface.

left-lateral fault   A strike-slip fault on which the displacement of the far block is to the left when viewed from either side.

liquefaction (of soil)   Process of soil and sand behaving like a dense fluid rather than a wet solid mass during an earthquake.

lithosphere   The outer, rigid shell of the Earth above the asthenosphere. It contains the crust, continents, and plates.

Love waves   Seismic surface waves with only horizontal shear motion transverse to the direction of propagation.

magma   Molten rock material that forms igneous rocks upon cooling.

magnitude (of earthquakes)   A measure of earthquake size, determined by taking the common logarithm (base 10) of the largest ground motion recorded during the arrival of a seismic wave type and applying a standard correction for distance to the epicenter. Three common types of magnitude are Richter (or local) (M_L), P body wave (m_b), and surface wave (M_s).

mantle (of Earth)   The main bulk of the Earth, between the crust and core, ranging from depths of about 40 to 3470 kilometers. It is composed of dense silicate rocks and divided into a number of concentric shells.

mare   A dark, low-lying lunar plain, filled to an undetermined depth with volcanic rocks. (Plural: maria.)

meizoseismal region   The area of strong shaking and significant damage in an earthquake.

microseism   Weak, almost continuous background seismic waves or Earth "noise" that can be detected only by seismographs; often caused by surf, ocean waves, wind, or human activity.

Mohorovičić discontinuity (M-discontinuity)   The boundary between crust and mantle, marked by a rapid increase in seismic P-wave velocity to more than 8 kilometers per second. Depth: 5 kilometers (under oceans) to 45 kilometers (under mountains).

moment (of earthquakes)   The rigidity of the rock times the area of faulting times the amount of slip. A measure of earthquake size related to the leverage of the forces (couples) across the area of the fault slip.

normal fault   A dip-slip fault in which the rock above the fault plane has moved downward relative to the rock below.

oblique-slip fault   A fault that combines some strike-slip motion with some dip-slip motion.

period (wave)   The time interval between successive crests in a sinusoidal wave train; the period is the inverse of the frequency of a cyclic event.

plate (tectonic)   A large, relatively rigid segment of the Earth's lithosphere that moves in relation to other plates over the deeper interior. Plates meet in convergence zones and separate at divergence zones.

plate tectonics   The theory of plate movement and interaction; the attempt to explain earthquakes, volcanoes, and mountain building as consequences of large horizontal surface motions.

prediction (of earthquakes)   The forecasting in time, place, and magnitude of an earthquake; the forecasting of strong ground motions.

P wave The primary or fastest wave traveling away from a seismic event through the rock and consisting of a train of compressions and dilatations of the material.

Rayleigh waves Seismic surface waves with ground motion only in a vertical plane containing the direction of propagation of the waves.

refraction (wave) The departure of a transmitted wave from its original direction of travel at an interface with a material of different wave velocity.

ridge (midoceanic) A major linear elevated landform of the ocean floor, many hundreds of kilometers in extent. It resembles a mountain range with a central rift valley.

right-lateral fault A strike-slip fault on which the displacement of the far block is to the right when viewed from either side.

rigidity The ratio of the shearing stress to the amount of angular rotation it produces in a rock sample.

risk (seismic) The relative risk is the comparative earthquake hazard from one site to another. The probabilistic risk is the odds of earthquake occurrence within a given time interval and region.

sag (fault) A narrow geological depression found in strike-slip fault zones. Those that contain water are called sag ponds.

scarp (fault) A cliff or steep slope formed by displacement of the ground surface.

sea-floor spreading The process by which adjacent plates along midoceanic ridges move apart to make room for new sea-floor crust. This process may continue at 0.5 to 10 centimeters per year through many geologic periods.

seiche Oscillations (standing waves) of the water in a bay or lake.

seismic discontinuity A surface or thin layer within the Earth across which P-wave and/or S-wave velocities change rapidly.

seismic moment See **moment (of earthquakes)**.

seismic wave An elastic wave in the Earth usually generated by an earthquake source or explosion.

seismicity The occurrence of earthquakes in space and time.

seismograph An instrument for recording as a function of time the motions of the Earth's surface that are caused by seismic waves.

seismology The study of earthquakes, seismic sources, and wave propagation through the Earth.

seismometer The sensor part of the seismograph, usually a suspended pendulum.

seismoscope A simple seismograph recording on a plate without time marks.

slip (fault) The relative motion of one face of a fault relative to the other.

strain (elastic) The geometrical deformation or change in shape of a body. The change in an angle, length, area, or volume divided by the original value.

stress (elastic) A measure of the forces acting on a body in units of force per unit area.

stress (drop) The sudden reduction of stress across the fault plane during rupture.

strike-slip fault A fault whose relative displacement is purely horizontal.

strong ground motion   The shaking of the ground near an earthquake source made up of large-amplitude seismic waves of various types.

subduction zone   A dipping ocean plate descending into the Earth away from an ocean trench. It is usually the locus of intermediate and deep earthquakes defining the Benioff zone.

surface waves (of earthquakes)   Seismic waves that follow the Earth's surface only, with a speed less than that of S waves. There are two types of surface waves—Rayleigh waves and Love waves.

swarms (of earthquakes)   A series of earthquakes in the same locality, no one earthquake being of outstanding size.

S wave   The secondary seismic wave, traveling more slowly than the P wave and consisting of elastic vibrations transverse to the direction of travel. It cannot propagate in a liquid.

tectonic earthquakes   Earthquakes resulting from sudden release of energy stored by major deformation of the Earth.

tectonics   Large-scale deformation of the outer part of the Earth resulting from forces in the Earth.

thrust fault   A dip-slip fault in which the upper rocks above the fault plane move up and over the lower rocks, so that older strata are placed over younger.

transform fault   A strike-slip fault connecting the ends of an offset in a mid-oceanic ridge, an island arc, or an arc-ridge chain. Pairs of plates slide past each other along transform faults.

travel-time curve   A graph of travel time versus distance for the arrival of seismic waves from distant events. Each type of seismic wave has its own curve.

tsunami   A long ocean wave usually caused by sea-floor movements in an earthquake.

volcano   An opening in the crust that has allowed magma to reach the surface.

volcanic earthquakes   Earthquakes associated with volcanic activity.

wavelength   The distance between two successive crests or troughs of a wave.

Bibliography

Titles preceded by an asterisk are recommended elementary discussions on earthquakes, and most parts are suitable for the general reader and first-year college students.

Adams, W. M., ed. *Tsunamis in the Pacific Ocean*. Honolulu: East-West Center Press, 1970.

Anderson, C. J., "Animals, Earthquakes, and Eruptions." *Field Museum of Natural History Bulletin*. Chicago: vol. 44, no. 5, 1973, pp. 9–11.

°Anon. "The Amateur Scientist." *Scientific American*. January 1963.

Båth, M. *Introduction to Seismology*. Basel, Switz.: Birkhäuser Verlag, 1979.

°Bolt, B. A. *Inside the Earth*. New York: W. H. Freeman and Company, 1982.

°Bolt, B. A. *Nuclear Explosions and Earthquakes: The Parted Veil*. San Francisco: W. H. Freeman and Company, 1976.

°Bolt, B. A., W. L. Horn, G. A. Macdonald, and R. F. Scott. *Geological Hazards*. Berlin: Springer-Verlag, 1975.

Bullard, F. M. *Volcanoes in History, in Theory, in Eruption*. Austin: University of Texas Press, 1962.

Cox, A., ed. *Plate Tectonics and Geomagnetic Reversals*. San Francisco: W. H. Freeman and Company, 1972.

°Davison, C. *The Founders of Seismology*. Cambridge, Eng.: Cambridge University Press, 1927.

°Eiby, G. A. *Earthquakes*. Auckland, N.Z.: Heineman, 1980.

Freeman, J. R. *Earthquake Damage and Earthquake Insurance*. New York: McGraw-Hill, 1932.

Gere, J. M., and H. C. Shah. *Terra Non Firma.* New York: W. H. Freeman and Company, 1984.

Gutenberg, B., and C. F. Richter. *Seismicity of the Earth and Associated Phenomena.* Princeton, N.J.: Princeton University Press, 1954.

Hass, J. E., and D. S. Mileti. *Socioeconomic Impact of Earthquake Prediction on Government, Business and Community.* Boulder: Institute of Behavioral Sciences, University of Colorado, 1976.

°Herbert-Gustar, A. L., and P. A. Mott. *John Milne: Father of Modern Seismology.* Tenterden, Eng.: Paul Norburg Pub. Ltd., 1980.

°Iacopi, R. *Earthquake Country.* San Francisco: Lane Book Company, 1964.

Jeffreys, H. *Earthquakes and Mountains,* 2nd ed. London: Methuen, 1950.

Karnik, V. *Seismicity of the European Area,* 2 vols. Dordrecht, Holland: Reidel, 1969.

Lawson, A. C. *The California Earthquake of April 18, 1906. Report of the State Earthquake Investigation Commission.* Washington, D.C.: Carnegie Institution, 1908.

°Oakeshott, G. B. *Volcanoes and Earthquakes.* New York: McGraw-Hill, 1976.

Panel on Earthquake Prediction of the Committee of Seismology. *Predicting Earthquakes.* Washington, D.C.: National Academy of Sciences, 1976.

Press, F., and R. Siever. *Earth,* 4th ed. New York: W. H. Freeman and Company, 1986.

Richter, C. F. *Elementary Seismology.* San Francisco: W. H. Freeman and Company, 1958.

Rikitake, T. *Earthquake Prediction.* Amsterdam: Elsevier, 1976.

Rothé, J. P. *The Seismicity of the Earth,* 1953–1965. Paris: UNESCO, 1969.

Steinbrugge, K. V. *Earthquakes, Volcanoes, and Tsunamis.* New York: Scandia America Group, 1982.

Vitaliano, D. B. *Legends of the Earth.* Bloomington: Indiana University Press, 1973.

°Walker, B. *Earthquake.* Alexandria, Va.: Time-Life Books, 1982.

Wiegel, R. C., ed. *Earthquake Engineering.* Englewood Cliffs, N.J.: Prentice-Hall, 1970.

Yanev, P. *Peace of Mind in Earthquake Country.* San Francisco: Chronicle Books, 1974.

In addition, valuable sources of current information on earthquakes, available to the public and to schools by subscription, are the following:

Earthquakes and Volcanoes (bimonthly). U.S. Geological Survey, U.S. Government Printing Office, Washington, DC 20402.

California Geology (monthly). California Division of Mines and Geology, Sacramento, CA 95812.

Earthquake Sounds. A tape cassette containing sounds recorded in various earthquakes is available with catalog (by K. V. Steinbrugge) for $13 from the Seismological Society of America, 6431 Fairmount Avenue, Suite 7, El Cerrito, CA 94530.

Earthquake Slides. Photographs of earthquake effects, copies of seismograms, and seismicity maps can be obtained from the National Geophysical and Solar Terrestrial Data Center, Code D62, NOAA/EDS, Boulder, CO 80302.

Classroom and community *Group Material* and *Kits* on earthquake science and preparedness (including learning games) can be purchased from the California Earthquake Education Program, Lawrence Hall of Science, University of California, Berkeley, CA 94720.

A valuable field guide for studying earthquakes, *Learning from Earthquakes*, is available for $5 from the Earthquake Engineering Research Institute, 6431 Fairmount Avenue, Suite 7, El Cerrito, CA 94530.

Index

7/94 ³²

11/94 ³³